T0038774

GRAVEYARD
OF THE
PACIFIC

Also by Randall Sullivan

The Devil's Best Trick

Dead Wrong

The Curse of Oak Island

Untouchable

The Miracle Detective

LAbyrinth

The Price of Experience

GRAVEYARD
OF THE
PACIFIC

Shipwreck and Survival on
America's Deadliest Waterway

RANDALL SULLIVAN

Grove Press
New York

Copyright © 2023 by Randall Sullivan
Maps © Martin Lubikowski, ML Design, London

All rights reserved. No part of this book may be reproduced in any form or by any electronic or mechanical means, including information storage and retrieval systems, without permission in writing from the publisher, except by a reviewer, who may quote brief passages in a review. Scanning, uploading, and electronic distribution of this book or the facilitation of such without the permission of the publisher is prohibited. Please purchase only authorized electronic editions, and do not participate in or encourage electronic piracy of copyrighted materials. Your support of the author's rights is appreciated. Any member of educational institutions wishing to photocopy part or all of the work for classroom use, or anthology, should send inquiries to Grove Atlantic, 154 West 14th Street, New York, NY 10011 or permissions@groveatlantic.com.

Any use of this publication to train generative artificial intelligence ("AI") technologies is expressly prohibited. The author and publisher reserve all rights to license uses of this work for generative AI training and development of machine learning language models.

Photo credits are as follows: Photo 2.1: Naval History and Heritage Command; Photos 2.2, 4.2, 9.1: Wikimedia Commons; Photo 3.1: Greg Vaughn / Alamy Stock Photo; Photo 3.2: Wikimedia Commons via Clatsop County Historical Society; Photo 4.1: PD-US; Photos 5.1, 6.1, 6.2, 6.3, 14.1: Courtesy of author; Photo 5.2: Courtesy of US Coast Guard Cape Disappointment; Photo 7.1: Courtesy of Nick Chipchase; Photos 8.1, 8.2: Washington State Digital Archives; Photo 9.2: Xander Fulton via Flickr; Photo 10.1: Photo Kiser Photo Co. photographs, 1901-1999; bulk: 1901-1927; Org. Lot 140; OrHi 56563, Photo 10.2: Flickr © 2011 Kay Gaensler; Photos 7.2, 11.1, 11.2, 12.2: Columbia River Maritime Museum; Photo 12.1: Columbia River Maritime Museum / Lawrence Barber; Photos 13.1, 13.2, 13.3, 13.4: Port of Portland YouTube @portofportland; Photos 15.1, 15.2, 16.1, 16.2: Courtesy of the US Coast Guard Auxiliary; Photos 13.5, 14.2: Columbia River Bar Pilots Association.

Printed in Canada

This book was set in 11-pt. Janson Text LT
by Alpha Design & Composition of Pittsfield, NH.

First Grove Atlantic hardcover edition: June 2023
First Grove Atlantic paperback edition: June 2024

Library of Congress Cataloging-in-Publication data is available for this title.

ISBN 978-08021-6337-0
eISBN 978-08021-6241-0

Grove Press
an imprint of Grove Atlantic
154 West 14th Street
New York, NY 10011

groveatlantic.com

24 25 26 27 28   10 9 8 7 6 5 4 3 2 1

For Delores,
who calls me back to shore like no other.

Imagine an enormous row of waves breaking for a distance
of three leagues from Cape Disappointment to Point Adams,
and forming kind of a sandy crescent about 1500 meters long
at the river's mouth. The sea water, whipped in by the wind
towards the river mouth, encountered the river water on this
enormous sand bar, producing frightful impact; the noise is so
loud that you can hear it several leagues away, and the
mountainous waves—resulting from the meeting of two
opposing currents—reach a height of sixty feet . . .
Expert English, American, and other navigators have asserted
that there is no worse sea lane than this in the known world . . .
Its currents, its rip tides, its storms, its sudden wind changes
make it exceptionally dangerous, and the enormous bar docs
nothing to lessen the danger, especially in bad weather.

Louis S. Rossi,
Six Years on the West Coast of America, 1856–1862

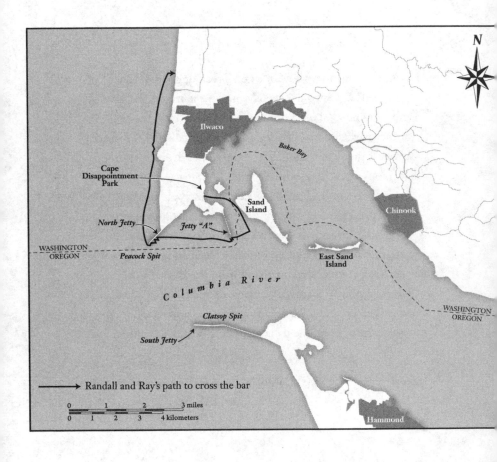

N

Ilwaco

Baker Bay

Cape
Disappointment
Park

Sand
Island

Chinook

North Jetty

Jetty "A"

WASHINGTON
OREGON

Peacock Spit

East Sand
Island

Columbia   River

WASHINGTON
OREGON

Clatsop Spit

South Jetty

→ Randall and Ray's path to cross the bar

0   1   2   3 miles

0   1   2   3   4 kilometers

Hammond

THE GREAT RIVER OF THE WEST was born from violence, from fire, and from ice. Fire came first. More than 250 million years ago, when most of the landmass of Earth was contained within the supercontinent Pangea, superheated liquefied rock, magma, burned a three-pronged rift through the crust and began the tectonic separation of North America, Europe, and Africa. As the new continents drifted apart, somewhere between one hundred million and ninety million years ago, the movement of plates floating atop a fiery mantle pushed long chains of active volcanoes hard against the upper left edge of North America, a scorching fusion that created what is now the Pacific Northwest.

The future basin of the Great River was surrounded then by the continuously bubbling, spewing, spreading eruptions of the young mountains that shaped the original configuration of a track flowing out of what is now Canada toward the Pacific Ocean. It was the molten lava that pulled the moisture out of the Earth's interior and left water on the planet's surface as it cooled. An ancestral version of the river was soon descending from a long, sunken fault line that would become the Rocky Mountain Trench.

The Rockies themselves rose as massive upwelling explosions between eighty and fifty-five million years ago, and off their western flanks sent huge flaming flows of basalt lava south to push out an inland sea and shape the path of the still-forming Great River beneath it. The Cascade Mountains are much younger than the Rockies—they did not uplift out of the Earth's mantle until five to four million years ago—but they were also enormous fulminations that further seared and shifted the region's topography, helping to define the outline of an immense waterway.

Then, about thirty-three thousand years ago, North America's volcanic fires were overtaken by a rapid expansion of ice spreading south, caused, scientists believe, by a shift in the Earth's orbit around the sun. Five thousand years later, much of North America was under two enormous ice sheets. The one to the west, the Cordilleran, covered at its maximum nearly two million square miles of land, stretching from Alaska to Montana, and may have reached as far south as the northeast corner of Oregon.

That ice is what put the finishing touches on the formation of the Great River. The gouging of glaciers moving south and west did a good bit of the work, but it was the melting of the ice that had the greater effect. Around nineteen thousand years ago, when the glaciers began to once again retreat, a gigantic frozen wall, an ice dam, embanked an enormous body of fresh water that geologists call Glacial Lake Missoula. The gargantuan pond was two thousand feet deep then and about the size of today's Lake Ontario. On at least forty occasions between nineteen and thirteen thousand years ago, the ice dam that held back Lake Missoula failed. The resulting floods were epic on a scale that defies human imagination. Each one unleashed more water than was in all of the Earth's rivers combined, scouring its way through mountain ranges to inundate an area of sixteen thousand square miles to a depth of up to several hundred feet. In the center of the flood path was what would become the bed of the Great River. When the waters receded, the ultimate course of that river, and of its connection to a vast system of tributaries, was left behind.

Where the river began then was where it does now, spilling out of the remnant of a smaller glacial lake that had been swept up into the Lake Missoula floods. Situated today in southwestern Canada, the lake bears the name of the river it has spawned, Columbia.

Given the underlying law of rivers—water runs downhill—it's surprising that the headwaters of the Columbia River are at a modest elevation of 2,690 feet. The Columbia's long descent to the ocean, though, is not only expanded but also hastened by the rivers, creeks, and streams pouring down into it from the mountains on both sides.

Curiously—one is tempted to say, perversely—a river that for most of its more than twelve-hundred-mile length flows south and west begins by heading north for 218 miles in a detour around the Selkirk Mountains, taking in, among other lesser tributaries, the icy Spillimacheen River that plunges down from the eastern edge of Glacier National Park, dropping nearly six thousand feet in elevation in fifty miles before pouring out of the rocks like a long waterfall into the Columbia. Then, at what has become known as the Big Bend, just above the northern reach of the Selkirk Range, the river makes a dramatic reversal of course, turning sharply almost due south as it drops through Canyon Hot Springs.

Soon after, sixty miles above what is now the United States border, and still headed south, the Columbia is joined by its first truly major tributary, the Kootenay River, 485 miles long and draining an area of more than 50,000 square miles, dropping 6,600 feet in elevation from its headwaters on the northeast side of the Beaverfoot Range before it merges with the greater river. Flowing through and alongside steep mountains, the Kootenay collects the waters of its own sizeable tributaries, including the 128-mile-long Duncan, before emptying them into the flow of the steadily swelling Columbia.

A thousand years ago, two large tribes lived in this area, on each side of what they called, in different tongues, Big River. To the west were the Sinixt, the Lake People, inhabitants of the region for ten thousand years, whose dwellings during the winter months were half-buried houses. East of the Columbia, the Kootenai nation used an "isolate language"—one that had no relation whatsoever to those spoken by neighboring tribes; some scholars contend that their ancestors migrated from what is today the Michigan side of Lake Superior. The Kootenai traveled the rivers in canoes as original as their language, made of dug-out cedar logs with pine bark on the bottom and birch bark at the gunwales, remarkable mainly for the way both ends were bent sharply inward, the same on one end as on the other, so that when spinning in rapids there was no definite front or back.

South of what is now the border between Canada and the United States, the Columbia is joined by the Pend Oreille and the Spokane, rivers that between them drain nearly 34,000 square miles stretching across Montana, Idaho, and Washington. The Big River continues west until its confluence with the 115-mile-long Okanogan River, then turns south again on a stark but achingly beautiful granite plateau where rattlesnakes live among sagebrush, prickly pear cactus, and tumbleweed.

Passing through the arid but fertile plain of central Washington State, the Columbia absorbs yet another large tributary, the 214-mile-long Yakima River, one more part of the Big River's system that bears the name of the people who lived there before the arrival of Europeans.

Nearly forty miles south of the Yakima, the Columbia's largest tributary, the Snake, a great river in its own right, adds the waters it has collected from six US states and a drainage area of more than one hundred thousand square miles. The Snake is smooth and wide where it enters the Columbia in today's southeastern Washington, but for most of the 1,078 miles behind it the river is as dramatic as any on the continent. Beginning at the confluence of three tiny streams in what is now the Wyoming section of Yellowstone National Park, flowing west and south into Jackson Hole, through the most spectacularly lovely mountain range in America, the Tetons, the Snake crosses plains and deserts as it turns up, then down, then up again across the entire width of Idaho before entering what is possibly the most impassable section of river on the planet, Hells Canyon, a 7,993-foot gorge (North America's deepest) forming what is today the eastern border of Oregon, which separates it from Idaho and Washington.

The people most associated with the Snake River are the Nez Perce. Powerful in war and trade, the Nez Perce nation lived in seventy separate villages, inhabited a territory of seventeen million acres, and networked with other tribes all the way from the Pacific shores of present-day Oregon and Washington to the high plains of Montana to the Great Basin part of Nevada.

Nearly a mile wide by now, the Columbia moves more slowly west through the lava plateau on both sides of it, taking in, among other rivers, the 252-mile Deschutes and the 284-mile John Day. The Great River narrows and accelerates as it enters the gloriously lovely Columbia Gorge, a four-thousand-foot deep, eighty-mile-long canyon with what is now Oregon on the south shore and Washington on the north. As the gorge deepens, the river's run passes from grasslands marked by widely spaced lodgepole and ponderosa pines into a thick rainforest of firs and maples that tower on the cliff face above. The deepest cut of the gorge is a wind tunnel that propagates howling snow and ice storms during winter months. Waterfalls abound on both sides of the river in the gorge, and one of them, Celilo, was not only a prime fish-catching spot but the main trading station between the upriver tribes that spoke the Sehaptian tongue and the peoples downriver that spoke the Chinookan language.

Passing through the gorge, the river is headed to where its truly great wealth lies. The Columbia's size is of course part of what makes it a great river. Only the Missouri/Mississippi system exceeds it in annual runoff, and there are years when the Columbia's flow is greater. Both of America's major river systems work off the "tilt" of the Continental Divide, one running toward the Pacific Ocean off the divide's western flank, the other running off the eastern flank into the Gulf of Mexico. The Columbia is unique among all rivers of the world, though, in the combination of its close proximity to the ocean and the tall mountain ranges that feed it all along the way there. Fifty miles west of the Columbia Gorge, the Big River's second-largest tributary, the Willamette, each spring carries the snowmelt from the Cascade Range north through a valley where volcanoes and glacial floods deposited some of the richest soil on the planet, then pours it into the Columbia, also fed largely by snowmelt from the mountain ranges it has passed through and alongside. Thirty-two other tributaries feed the Big River with rainwater in the ninety miles between the Willamette and the Pacific Ocean, and by late May and early June the flow of the lower Columbia becomes truly stupendous, carrying up to 1.2 million cubic feet of water per second at its mouth, nearly five times its average discharge. Two hundred years ago, all of that free-flowing cold water in late spring provided the perfect spawning grounds for anadromous fish, those that live in the ocean but lay their eggs in fresh water.

Before fourteen dams were built on the river, the Columbia's salmon runs exceeded any on Earth. Four million of the big fish would spawn in the river each spring. What became known as Chinook salmon grew to weigh more than one hundred pounds in those days, and the Columbia was so thick with them that in the nineteenth century more than one man would report being tempted to try to walk across the river on their backs. Not only delicious but immensely rich in protein and omega-3 fatty acids, they were a primary food source for the peoples who lived along the Columbia for hundreds of miles to the north and east. But on the lower Columbia the salmon runs were far beyond abundant, and they were a good part of what made the tribal villages there the richest, in nearly every material sense, on the planet. The plentitude of food they enjoyed was unimaginable to nearly everyone else on Earth. Apart from the staggering salmon runs, the Columbia was filled with uncountable sturgeon, steelhead, and shad. The evergreen forests alongside teemed with deer, bear, and elk. Blackberries, huckleberries, and salmonberries were profuse in late summer. The result of such an extravagant supply of sustenance was a settled people who lived not by the egalitarian principles of nomadic inland tribes like the Shoshone, Sioux, and Blackfoot, but who were nearly as hierarchical as Europeans.

Chiefs of Northwest Pacific Coast tribes dwelled in fur-upholstered cedar longhouses, elaborately carved, that could accommodate as many as seven hundred people. Tribal headmen regularly staged "potlatch" ceremonies, essentially giveaway competitions that ended only when one chief had no more lavish gifts to bestow upon another, and so surrendered his prestige. Some chiefs went so far as to destroy what they had been given, so as to demonstrate how little value they placed on such trifles. Common tribal members lived far better than the average citizen in London or Paris, and in each village most of the hard labor was done by slaves captured in battle.

The Chinookan tribe at the mouth of the Columbia, the Clatsop, enjoyed bounties beyond even those of the wealthy tribes upriver. Where it entered the ocean, the Big River's bays and estuaries, along with the ocean beaches just beyond, provided endless crabs, mussels, and clams. Halibut were easily caught right outside the river's mouth, while seals and whales could be taken within sight of land.

For thousands of years the Clatsop lived with a security that only island peoples knew so well. To the east and north were other Chinookan tribes that only infrequently contested the Clatsop's territory. To the south, the Salish and Klamath nations were trading partners more than rivals. And the Clatsop certainly had nothing to fear from the west, where the mouth of what they called *Wimahl* (again "Big River") drove its way into the ocean.

The Clatsop couldn't know there was nothing equal to this encounter of current and tide on the continent—or on the entire planet, for that matter—only that there was nothing like it in the world where they lived. The collision of these two immense forces, the Pacific Ocean and the largest river of the Western Hemisphere that drains into it, created a spectacle that was stupendous even to a people that had been living next to it for a thousand years. On many days, the line of breakers where the river met the ocean stretched five miles across, and the roar was thunderous. During winter storms, the waves at the outside of the river's mouth would reach the height of ten men. The Clatsop on occasion dared to cross out into the ocean from the river in immense, sixty-five-foot-long canoes that could carry more than fifty paddlers. This they did only when conditions were perfect, however, and only they knew when perfect conditions existed. The notion of some other tribe coming in off the ocean into the river through the maelstrom that would almost certainly greet them was unthinkable.

Until it happened.

The Clatsop passed down the story like this: An old woman living in the village closest to where the river entered the ocean, Ne-ahk-stow, was walking along the beach toward the giant sand spit at the end of the southern shore when she saw something strange and frightening approaching out of the sea. At first she thought it might be some kind of unknown whale, the story went, then saw that there were two trees growing out of it. The outside of the strange thing was covered with shiny metal, and ropes were tied all over the trees. As it came closer, the old woman saw that a creature that looked like a bear but had a human face, only one with hair covering most of it, was standing between the two trees. She hurried home in great fear and told the other villagers what she had seen. The warriors sprinted up the beach in the direction the old woman pointed, armed with bows and arrows, and found that the strange thing with trees growing out of it had come ashore. Now there were two of the bear-men standing between the trees. The warriors watched from the forest at the edge of the beach as the two bear-men carried a kettle ashore, lit a fire under it, and threw dried corn inside. The crackling, startling result so intrigued the warriors that they came out of the trees. The bear-men offered them some of the popped corn, then signaled that they themselves needed water. The village chief sent men to get them water while he studied the strange thing, which he decided was an enormous canoe that for some reason had two trees driven into it. The chief then inspected the hairy-faced creatures and, after examining their hands, decided that they were in fact men. While the bear-men slaked their thirst, a young warrior climbed up the side of the great canoe and looked down onto its deck, where he saw not only many boxes and strings of buttons nearly as long as the beach, but also, most excitingly, an abundance of metals: iron, copper, and brass. To take that metal, and to hold the bear-men captive, the chief ordered that the great canoe be burned.

Word of this event spread, and soon tribes from all over the region sent warriors to take a look at the "Thlehonnipts," as they were called, "those who drifted ashore." Groups of Quinaults, of Chehalis, of Willapas, of Cowlitz, even of the far-off Klickitat arrived, and all laid claim to the Thlehonnipts. It nearly came to war, until the Clatsop chief agreed to surrender one of the two Spanish sailors, but he insisted upon keeping the Thlehonnipt he most prized, the one who had shown he knew how to make knives and hatchets from pieces of iron. Konapee, or "Iron-Maker," the Clatsop had named him.

Konapee became a highly valued member of the tribe and lived with them for the rest of his life. The Clatsop did not expect that other such men would be drifting ashore, and none did for many years. Then, though, they began to arrive one after the other. The forbidding barrier of breakers and shoals at the mouth of the river had frightened some away, and many who did try to pass through disappeared beneath the waves. But enough of the Thlehonnipts made it across to encourage others, and within a span of less than fifty years a Clatsop way of life that had gone on for century after century vanished forever.

No future apologies or reparations were going to change what had happened. The best that could be hoped for was that those who drifted ashore would have stories worth hearing.

GRAVEYARD
OF THE
PACIFIC

CHAPTER ONE

Friday, July 16, 2021

AS WE LIFTED OUR BOATS off the trailer, the sky was low and gray all the way to the horizon, with only a faint spot of lightening in the south to suggest that the sun was there at all. The air was filled with drizzle and mist, precipitation and evaporation, falling and rising. Lowering my end of the main hull onto a damp patch of mossy grass, I felt a slightly claustrophobic sensation of not just the weather closing in around me but the whole world with it. The scene was so far from what I'd imagined, from the picture in my mind of luminous blue overhead and vivid white caps marking our distant goal, that for the first time I felt doubt slipping in through the cracks in my resolve, and wondered about continuing forward.

FOR MONTHS NOW, MY FRIEND Ray Thomas and I had been talking about the RIGHT DAY to cross the Columbia River Bar. The words had been in quotation marks the first few times we'd used them, but grew into all caps as the concept loomed larger and larger in our thoughts. The venture we had in mind would only make sense, we kept reminding each other, if we found the Right Day.

When I'd first spoken to Ray about "the right day" back in April, I'd been quoting Bruce Jones, who, along with occupying the office of mayor of Astoria, Oregon, served as deputy director of the Columbia River Maritime Museum. In the email in which he introduced himself and suggested we meet at the museum, Mayor Jones had attached a photograph of the astounding turbulence a person might encounter at the place where one of the world's largest, most powerful, and fastest-moving watercourses spills into the Pacific Ocean. Actually, this intersection of river and sea is more of a slam than a spill—"like two giant hammers pounding into each other," as the head of the Columbia River Bar Pilots Association described it to the *New York Times* back in 1988.

I studied the image Jones had sent—lashing towers of white water swamping the massive wall of mounded stones that formed the Columbia Bar's North Jetty—and felt a contraction run through me from throat to sphincter. He had taken the photograph in "my previous life," Jones explained in his email, while flying the Bar Pilots Association's Seahawk helicopter, his primary job to drop pilots on inbound ships five miles outside the entrance to the bar.

The photograph, taken during a November squall, "doesn't do justice to the violence of the seas and wind" he saw that day, Jones had written. Those words would have seemed even more ominous if I'd known when I read them what an understated man Bruce Jones is. There was one word in his brief email that gave me comfort, though, and it was "November." While I realized it was impossible to ever be entirely certain about the weather on the Columbia Bar, because conditions were known to deteriorate dramatically in a span of minutes during any season of the year, I knew Ray and I weren't going to be attempting any crossing of the bar in either water or air as cold as November's.

Based on his email, and in particular on the photograph he'd attached, I had expected Jones to be somewhere between aghast and dismissive when I told him at the beginning of our meeting in the museum's conference room that, as part of a book I was researching, my friend and I wanted to cross the Columbia Bar in what was essentially a sail kayak, a Hobie Adventure Island trimaran. Instead of scorning the idea, though, Jones sat silent for a few moments, considering, then told me it was "doable" if we chose the right day.

A little later, Jones asked if my friend was my age. He was, I answered. Jones knew from an article about me that had been published recently on the front page of the *Daily Astorian* that I would turn seventy on my next birthday, in December. Ray would turn seventy himself four days after I did. Jones saw, I think, that I was in good shape for a man my age. Ray was even more fit, if less strong. Jones made no comment about the advisability of senior citizens, no matter how fit or strong, challenging the Columbia Bar in a nonmotorized light craft, and I appreciated that.

Bruce was a sturdy but not imposing man with gentle eyes and a bookish manner. I would have more likely made him for a professor at a small private college who hit the gym several times a week than for a helicopter pilot who'd made a career of flying in terrifying conditions. Even after our meeting at the museum, I wouldn't learn for another week what a truly formidable fellow he was, a man whose accomplishments included commanding all and performing many of the air rescues in New Orleans during Hurricane Katrina. I should have seen him more clearly, I think now. And also, I should have shown more gratitude when he offered me the museum's resources, including its library, which, although operated by volunteers, houses by far the best-documented history that exists of the Columbia River in general and of the bar in particular.

At the end of our meeting, Jones permitted me to roam freely through the museum, where the most arresting display was a large illuminated map of the bar highlighting two hundred of the more than two thousand shipwrecks that have happened there during the past couple of centuries. An estimated twelve hundred people, nearly all men, have died in those wrecks, though this estimate is rough, given that some of the oldest records state simply that "the entire crew" was lost. THE GRAVEYARD OF THE PACIFIC, read the heading on the display; it was the sobriquet seamen had bestowed on the Columbia Bar more than a century earlier.

I had known since I was a boy that the Columbia River Bar was generally regarded as the most dangerous entrance to a commercial waterway on the planet. It has been described many times as the world's most dangerous bar to cross, period. One of those who said this was my father, who was a merchant marine when I was born and had by age twenty-five traveled to virtually every corner of the earth. The single most frightening experience he ever had aboard a ship, my father said, came the first time he entered the Columbia River Bar. The freighter he was aboard was about to run aground on a hidden sandbar that had appeared suddenly out of the fog off the port side of the bow, he recalled. Only a brilliant maneuver by the captain that bounced the ship off a smaller sandbar on the starboard side and spun it slightly had saved him and the others aboard, he said. My father was a man who almost never showed fear, or any other emotion that betrayed vulnerability, but I could hear the resonance of panic in his voice then, describing an experience he'd had twenty years earlier.

NO ONE OUTSIDE THE BAR PILOTS' association knew the perils of the Columbia River Bar better than Tom Molloy, the commanding officer at the United States Coast Guard's National Motor Lifeboat Rescue School. The Coast Guard's main high seas rescue academy was located at Cape Disappointment, on the Washington State side of the Columbia's mouth, because, as Chief Warrant Officer 3 Molloy told me, "we figure that the best place to learn this stuff is in the most challenging environment in the country."

I liked Molloy a lot within a few minutes of meeting him. The same word that had come into my mind while talking with Bruce Jones occurred to me while getting to know Tom: "solid." Only in Molloy's case this word had a more distinctly physical aspect. Molloy was not a tall man—five nine, I'd reckon—but with a pair of shoulders on him that easily would have filled out a size 48 suit jacket. He had been built up, I would learn, from a life spent largely on the water. Having grown up as a surfer on the Atlantic coast of Florida, Molloy had joined the Coast Guard mainly as a way to stay close to the sea. Even now he kept a private surf spot in a cove hidden by a spill of rocks on the west side of the rescue school and the adjacent Coast Guard base. "I go out whenever I get the opportunity," he told me with a grin that made me love him. Molloy was in his early forties, but there was something of the sunburnt boy about him, perpetually at play in the fields of the Lord. Yet he must take his duties seriously, I thought, or otherwise he wouldn't occupy the position that he did.

I knew that was true when I observed the respect Molloy commanded from the young men and women he was training, evident in their admiring eyes as they saluted him passing them while showing me around the rescue school. Along with a rank that made him one of the more versatile members of the US Armed Forces, Molloy had been awarded what is probably the most coveted title in the Coast Guard, the "Surfman Badge," conferred only upon coxswains who have qualified to operate boats in the "heavy surf" that is encountered regularly on the Columbia Bar. The surfman's motto was: "The book says you've got to go out, but it doesn't say a word about coming back."

Molloy had bright eyes and a broad, open face. Perhaps the most telling thing I learned about him during the time I spent with Tom was that the tattoo on the third finger of his left hand was a replacement for the wedding ring he'd lost during a Coast Guard operation. He'd had the image of that ring inked onto his finger, made it literally part of his flesh, not simply as a form of apology to his wife but in order to demonstrate to her that his commitment was absolute.

I was pretty sure that Tom Molloy was what my friend Ray would have described as "one tough boy," but there was nothing cocky or pugnacious about him. The man had the same sort of quiet confidence that I had recognized in his friend Bruce Jones, and there was something uplifting about meeting the two of them back-to-back, a confirmation of what I wanted to believe about the quality of the men who held sway on the Columbia Bar. My father, whom I grew up hearing described by the longshoremen working under him as the toughest man on the West Coast waterfront, might have had that same quality, I felt, if he hadn't been so tortured inside and so prone to meanness.

My confidence was buoyed when Molloy agreed with Bruce Jones that crossing the bar in a trimaran could be done. And just like Jones, he said it was all about choosing the right day. Actually, "the right day at the right time of day" was what Tom said. I recalled that Bruce Jones had told me that finding a day in the second half of July or the first half of August was advisable, because both the air and the water would be warmer than at other times of the year. Molloy again agreed, but added, "Even in August the weather on the bar can turn nasty in no time. Boats go down and people drown out there in the summertime, too."

There were three awesome forces to contend with on the bar, Molloy reminded me: tide, current, and wind. All had to be accounted for in any calculation of the risk involved in being out there.

I had understood even before my meeting with Bruce Jones that Ray and I did not want to be out on the bar in an outgoing tide, because the greatest danger to us, in a nonmotorized craft, was being capsized and swept out to sea. Jones's colleague Jeff Smith, the museum's curator, had suggested setting out on a slack tide, in the interval between the ebb and flood tides. Molloy disagreed slightly: he believed it would be best for us to launch about an hour before low tide. "That last bit of ebb tide will help push you out into the river, you can get going during slack tide, then use the flood tide to hold you in until you get back on land," Molloy said. We wanted to be sure we had as many hours of rising tide as possible to work with, he explained, "because you never know what kind of complications might come up. Believe me, if your boat capsizes you want to be in the water with the tide coming in. Much better chance of making it to shore, or being located and rescued should the need arise."

RAY AND I HAD MANAGED to get together for three practice sessions in the trimaran, each several hours long. Our first was on the

Willamette River, which is the arterial center of Portland, Oregon. Ray kept seven boats of various sizes—the largest being a Kenner Suwanee houseboat equipped with a working woodstove we'd enjoyed on a fair few winter evenings—at Portland's gem of a downtown marina, Riverplace.

Ray had gotten rich about a dozen years earlier, when he'd finally collected his share of attorney fees from a lawsuit against the cigarette manufacturer Philip Morris that went all the way to the United States Supreme Court. I'd remarked several times that Ray was the only person I'd ever known who seemed to have been made happier by becoming wealthy, but I wasn't sure I meant it. He did seem to be having more fun, though, and definitely owned more expensive toys to have fun with. Crossing the bar on his Honda jet skis would have been many times easier than in the trimaran, Ray had pointed out, but I didn't want it to be easy, and he understood that.

When I'd first proposed this undertaking, I could see Ray calculating not only the factors of risk and reward but also just how much he trusted me. I'd explained to him that part of what the book I wanted to write would be about was the effects on us both of having grown up amid so much violence, a great deal of it inflicted on us by our fathers. I felt it had a lot to do with why we'd each been driven to do difficult and dangerous things, as a way of demonstrating our ability to cope with and even master those difficulties and dangers.

Ray's enthusiasm appeared to waver. He was wary of any encapsulation of him I might attempt. "I'm not ever trying to prove anything to anyone," he told me.

The right thing to do as his friend, I decided, was accept this. "Me neither," I told Ray. "Except maybe to myself."

"Not even to myself," Ray said. "I do what I do because I want to, period."

If you say so, Ray, I thought this time, but just nodded.

By the time we first sat down together in the trimaran, me in the front position, him in the rear, on a glimmering May afternoon, I had accepted that Ray felt a need to test me. I understood already that his trimaran was a unique vessel. A two-seat kayak, nineteen feet long by just a little more than two feet wide, was the centerpiece, but Hobie had equipped the boat with assorted special features, including a pair of collapsible outriggers (called by their Polynesian name, "amas") that provided an extraordinary enhancement of stability on the water, even though each was only about six inches wide. In addition to paddles that were generally used only in shallow water or tight spaces, the trimaran provided two superior methods of moving across the water's surface: a removable single mast and sail was one; the other was Hobie's marvelous Mirage Drive system—two "kick-up fins" attached to pedals that can nearly double the boat's speed even when the sail is full. What Ray wanted me to prove was that I could pedal in the trimaran for up to three hours at a stretch. The Mirage Drive might be our main form of propulsion out on the Columbia Bar, depending upon the wind, and especially given that we would be pushing against a flood tide for most of the trip.

Still, I felt Ray had reminded me one time too many that for more than twenty years he'd been leading a weekly bicycle ride into the steep hills above Northwest Portland in which the other participants were lawyers less than half his age. My only bike was a beach cruiser that I rode eight or nine times every summer. I needed to demonstrate that I could "keep up," Ray said, for him to feel confident going forward.

In addition to testing me, Ray also wanted me to understand that he was our captain. It was his boat, one he'd sailed off both the East and West Coasts of the country (and on the Mississippi River as well), in a variety of challenging conditions. But the way he barked orders once we were out on the water began to bring back some unpleasant memories from my childhood, and finally I told him to dial it down. "You rebel against every form of authority," Ray said. "That concerns me."

I was able to laugh and keep on pedaling.

The Willamette is a major river, the largest "in" the state, given that the Snake and Columbia run along Oregon's eastern and northern borders. Sailing the Willamette, though, was like boating on a small lake compared to how it would be on the Columbia Bar. When we returned to the boat launch at Willamette Park after a pleasant if exhausting excursion, Ray was cheery, telling our six-foot-nine-inch training advisor, Kenny Smith, who lived with his girlfriend, Candy, aboard the biggest boat on the Willamette, a sixty-eight-footer he'd bought from a professional hockey player and hauled down from Canada, that I had "performed excellently" and really surprised him by pedaling steadily for two and a half hours.

Positions, both literal and figurative, began to shift between Ray and me during our two practice sessions in the trimaran on the Columbia. We set off on the first of these from the boat launch in Hammond, a community spread along the westernmost reaches of Youngs Bay, a huge spread of choppy water created by the flow of the Youngs River into the Columbia close to the bigger river's mouth. Hammond had been through several iterations. For centuries it was the village the Clatsop tribe called Ne-ahk-stow. Then, in 1899 it became New Astoria, a name I found pretty amusing when I first heard it. Astoria—"old Astoria," so to speak—was less than six miles to the east. The "New" part made some sense, I supposed, given that Astoria itself is the oldest enduring American settlement west of the Rocky Mountains. Beginning with the winter of 1805–1806, when the Lewis and Clark Expedition waited in vain for a ship at a tiny log structure they called Fort Clatsop, just southwest of where the city stands today, Astoria has been one of the most storied towns in the entire United States. During the nineteenth century alone, Astoria transitioned from frontier trading outpost to crucial military installation to wide-open seaport, where tall ships crowded into its harbor while disembarked sailors swarmed the dozens of saloons, brothels, and card parlors ashore.

Hammond's history is considerably more modest, even though its access to the mouth of the Columbia River had positioned it to be "the greatest harbor on the Pacific coast north of San Francisco," according to an *Oregonian* article published in July of 1895. The name Hammond was given to the former New Astoria in 1903 by a man who promised to build a gigantic sawmill on the two thousand feet of waterfront he had purchased there. Instead, Andrew B. Hammond built his mill at Tongue Point, on the peninsula north of Astoria, and the town that bore his name languished. By 1991, Hammond had been absorbed into the town of Warrenton, but the community still identified as a distinct entity, and as good a place for a fisherman to live as existed on the West Coast.

Hammond's most notable feature, for Ray and me, was its marina, which allowed one to put in off a launch that offered a remarkably close view of the Columbia River tumbling past in all its immense and astonishing power. The Hammond Boat Basin was not only literally the last place on the Oregon side where one could board a vessel before

11

approaching the Columbia Bar, but the little marina's channel was so short that even our trimaran passed out of it into the river after only a couple minutes of paddling and pedaling on the afternoon of May 21.

We knew already that the wind that day was steady at about twenty-two miles per hour, too intense for a bar crossing in a kayak, but neither of us was prepared for what that felt like on a span of the river where the Columbia's mouth was only a little more than a mile to the west. The wind waves were three and four feet, not coming in sets at intervals of seven to nine seconds like on the ocean, but in an incessant and erratic chop that struck our boat from changing directions as current and tide thrashed against one another. I was in the front position again, and up there I felt more like a buckaroo than a sailor, being tossed not only from side to side but also fore and aft as we passed abruptly over peak and into trough and then onto peak again, and so forth, our heads soaked, gasping in awe. Our sail was full, and we were both pedaling, going at what was probably the trimaran's max velocity, about seven miles per hour.

After a few moments of being shaken, I felt exhilaration rise in me, and I was grinning crazily, marveling at how well the Hobie absorbed the pounding it was taking, continuously oscillating back to equilibrium, no matter how tilted it was by the waves. We had headed out of the boat basin straight for the buoy that floated in the middle of the river, intent on crossing to the Washington side, a distance of nearly four miles. We got only as far as about a hundred yards from the buoy, though, when Ray, who had the rudder, turned us back to shore.

The wind and our front-to-back positions made explanation difficult, but when I turned to look at Ray, I was pretty certain I saw fear in his eyes. This was perfectly understandable under the circumstances, I knew, but I was disappointed that we hadn't continued across the river. And I was surprised. I knew Ray as a risk-taker. He had long been unpopular among the wives of various friends and associates, mainly because they believed he was determined to put not only himself but also their husbands into life-threatening situations. It was a reputation that discomfited him even as he cultivated it.

Yet Ray had been circumspect from the first about the idea— my idea—of us crossing the bar in his trimaran, warning me more than once that it would have to be approached in stages that started with building trust that we could work as a team on the water, and then together studying the Columbia Bar in depth and at length before venturing onto it. That was fine. I was already committed to doing the research in order to write this book, and it seemed like an excellent idea for Ray and me to practice in the trimaran for some number of times before taking on the bar. To my growing concern, and even annoyance in a couple of cases, though, Ray had begun to remark that he wasn't sure about this whole project, that he doubted I understood how dangerous it was, and that it didn't mean nearly as much to him as it did to me.

That morning of our first practice session on the Columbia, Ray had equivocated again, informing me, "Grace told me this morning she doesn't want to be planning my funeral in the near future." Grace was Ray's third ex-wife. They'd been divorced for more than twenty years but still traveled together. There had been a period of a few years when Ray had tried to convince himself, and me, among others, that he was capable of sustaining relationships with several women at once, all out in the open, on the up-and-up with each of them. I'd enjoyed more than a little acerbic humor at his expense as, one by one, they dumped his ass for such a delusional presumption. But he'd been in love with Grace all along. They were so cozy these days that they'd recently bought a house together. It was one of a number of houses owned by Grace, but Ray's only real residence, other than the small apartment he maintained in the office building that housed his law practice.

Among our sorrowful bonds was that my life was at least as messy as Ray's. I had three ex-wives also and was now married to my "fourth and final wife," as I regularly described her. Like Ray's relationship with Grace, this one was going to last, I knew, both because I loved Delores dearly and because I had run out of time and excuses. On our honeymoon in Ireland, my new wife took to telling the women she met in pubs that she had waited eighteen years to marry me. That was true, except for the eighteen months we spent apart when she got fed up with me and moved to North Carolina. The women in Ireland responded to whatever it was Delores told them about this with a depth of emotion that flabbergasted us both. Whole tables wept with joy. Irish women of all ages actually stood to cheer and applaud this tale of triumphant endurance, which in private Delores offered up to me as proof that she always got what she wanted, in the end.

Delores was no less apprehensive about the bar crossing than Grace, and had attempted to talk me out of it half a dozen times. She collected warnings from various neighbors in the small beach community where we lived, about fifteen miles south of Astoria, who wondered whether I had a death wish or was merely an idiot. When I told her there was no point, that I was determined to do this, that I *needed* to do it, Delores relented and began to offer, if not approval, at least implicit support. But I was pretty sure she thought I was childishly reckless, heedlessly selfish, and fundamentally incorrigible. And Ray told me that Grace thought all of that about him.

As Ray and I pedaled downriver and toward shore after retreating from the tempest mid-river, most of what we shouted to each other was lost in the wind. Part of our difficulty was that I sat with my back to him, but the larger problem was that we both had suffered major hearing loss in our left ears when we were young. Ray's damage had been inflicted at the age of fourteen, when his father fired off five rounds from a Walther P38 in the study of the Laurium, Michigan, mansion he was restoring, with the barrel right next to his son's head. I had been ten when one of my earliest attempts at defiance resulted in my father's chasing me into the next room and whacking me with a swinging right that landed open-handed but, with all his consider-able power behind it, knocked me briefly unconscious and ruptured my eardrum.

Eventually, Ray and I found a sheltered spot close to shore beside some rotted pilings that we guessed had once been a fish trap. I turned in my seat and told him how impressed I'd been by the Hobie, that I thought both it and we had been doing well, and was confident we could have made it across the river.

Ray wasn't having it. He knew this boat, Ray said—I couldn't argue with that—and recognized it had reached "at least seventy-five percent of capacity" as we made our approach to the buoy. "You never want to get to eighty percent of capacity," Ray said, "because eighty percent can turn to ninety percent in a minute and ninety percent can turn to a hundred percent in a second." Yes, that was definitely fear I'd seen in Ray's eyes.

The nature of a trimaran is that, once flipped, the boat can only be clung to or abandoned; it is going to stay upside down until it is dragged ashore and turned over. That is why some serious sailors insist upon monohulls, because even though the single-hulled kayak is much more likely to turn over and dump you in the water, chances are good that the monohull can be righted and reboarded. That day would put me forever on the trimaran side of this debate. The amas, narrow as they were, provided the Hobie with phenomenal buoyancy. Several times in our aborted attempt to cross the Columbia that afternoon, the trimaran had been tipped well past forty-five degrees by the waves, but the ease with which it settled and floated over the next breaker was tremendously reassuring. There had been a couple of moments when I thought the braces ("akas") of the portside ama were going to snap, but the design allowed for just enough give to prevent that.

Still, it was Ray's boat and he was calling the shots. We pedaled with on-and-off aid from the wind along the Columbia's southern shore, pushing against a current that slowed us to one or two miles per hour. We were right next to an industrial area of fish-packing plants and boat-storage facilities. The uninspiring scenery and our sluggish pace enervated me, and I simply listened and nodded as Ray set the parameters of the conditions that would make a bar crossing feasible: a wind no stiffer than twelve miles per hour and an ocean swell of less than four feet at intervals of seven seconds or more being the two main ones.

I was distracted from this conversation by the fascinating realization that, all of a sudden, I had become the one of us who was insisting on pushing the bet, urging Ray to join me in a gamble that had a potentially lethal downside with an argument that the probability was success, while Ray, that longtime menace to domestic tranquility, was the one compelled to remind me that, as he put it in a text message, "what we both really want is to die in our beds forty years from now." Forty years was asking a lot, but the point was taken. Ray had become the voice of caution. I wondered if perhaps he was more willing than I was to accept that we were older and weaker.

The stated aim of our next session on the Columbia was to travel west, upriver, close to shore, then creep along the bar's South Jetty as far as we felt safe doing so. Since 1917, the Columbia Bar has been flanked by the two enormous rock walls that project out at angles, from Point Adams on the south side and from Cape Disappointment on the north. "The Jaws," these opposite-facing jetties that mark the entrance to the bar are commonly called, short for the Jaws of Death.

The forecast was again for high winds, but Ray had already towed his boat from Portland to the house in Cannon Beach he and Grace had bought together, so I was able to convince him we should get out on the river and see how it felt. "If it's too much, we can pack it in whenever you say," I assured him.

I realize now that Ray was mainly trying to please me by agreeing, but such magnanimity extended only so far. When we climbed out of his big blue van above the ramp at the Hammond Boat Basin, Ray pointed at what we could see of the river, and it looked daunting, I had to admit. The waves were even higher than they had been three weeks earlier, and the current, accelerated by an ebb tide, would make returning upriver a possibly losing battle. Nevertheless, I did my best to convince Ray we should at least launch and "see what it feels like out there." I was becoming concerned about how slow our progress toward a bar crossing seemed to have become. It was June 16. July was just around the corner. I felt the time had come to start pushing.

But Ray simply shook his head. "You told me that if I said it was too much, you'd accept that," he said. "And I say it's too much."

He would be borne out only a couple of hours later, when the Coast Guard closed the bar to small craft. Ray was excellent about refraining from I-told-you-so, and he suggested that we put in about ten miles east, at the channel that fed the John Day River* into the Columbia. I took the rear position this time and had the rudder most of the trip, taking us once again west along the river's south shore.

The wind was light here and the sun was bright. We were warm to the point of discomfort, even without the drysuits we had worn on our previous Columbia excursion, and appreciated the splashes of water that soaked our T-shirts and cooled us off.

"This is the way I like it," Ray, who was sipping beer from a can, called to me over his shoulder.

When I didn't reply, Ray shot me another over-the-shoulder look. "Being on the river doesn't have to be a challenge," he said.

Again, I said nothing. Ray turned his head slightly but didn't look back this time. "At this stage of our lives, taking it easy makes more and more sense to me."

"I still want to cross the bar, Ray," I told him.

"I know," he said. "But I'm not sure I do."

I studied his sinewy back. Ray was by nature an ectomorph, six two, with wrists and ankles that had always looked delicate to me. Even at almost seventy, though, his upper body was girdled with ropy muscles, the result of a decades-long commitment to intense daily exercise. This took multiple forms, from running to rowing to bicycling to chopping wood for the fireplace at the astounding farmhouse on Grace's nursery. Ray treated the various injuries he

* There are two John Day Rivers in Oregon, one in the east and one in the west, both named for the same legendary hunter.

suffered much as professional athletes do, as temporary impediments to playing at full speed that he rehabilitated with impressive discipline.

He had lost most of his dark brown hair on top during the decades I'd known him, and this, combined with his lack of a high brow, seemed to have foreshortened his square, handsome face. Ray's most arresting features, by far, were his shockingly pale blue eyes, almost albino-like in their bleached uniformity, broken only by a black pellet of pupil in the center. Holding his intense and unblinking gaze was always at least vaguely unsettling; the thought had occurred to me that this was someone for whom hysteria had become a set point, a state he had relaxed into years earlier. That perception wasn't quite right, or at least not complete, I knew. Ray was highly intelligent and supremely rational. The most impressive thing about him was his unflagging commitment to doing and being good, despite a deep instinct to do and be bad. He was generous and brave and deeply conscientious, all as a considered choice.

At his sixty-fifth birthday party, Ray's partner in the Philip Morris case, Bill Gaylord, told the story of how Ray had saved his life. They were at a resort on Waikiki Beach with their families, celebrating a huge award they had just collected in the first big case they tried together, Bill recalled. After a couple of happy-hour mai tais, Ray persuaded Bill to go for a swim, leading him out toward where the surfers were lined up. This was late in the day, and they were a bit too inebriated to consider in advance how early and quickly it gets dark in Hawaii. When the two of them reached the lineup, the surfers were all gone. Bill turned back toward the beach, he remembered, but found himself suddenly in a riptide that he couldn't swim against. "I was in ten feet of water, looking down, and seeing that I was moving backward, not forward," Bill would tell me in a Cannon Beach pub five years after the birthday party. He had exhausted himself completely, Bill recalled, and was barely afloat, panicked but at the same time resigned to drowning, when Ray appeared. "Grab my legs," he said, then towed Bill out of the riptide and back to the beach, swimming with only his upper body. "When I say he saved my life, I mean he *literally* saved my life," Bill told me.

This was one of my favorite Ray stories, in part because it involved him making superb use of a lifetime of training, but also because it captured the inherent contradiction in his character, a rash tendency to push people beyond their limits combined with the decency and courage to rescue them from the peril he had placed them in.

I was of the opinion that the incident with Bill in Hawaii had been the catalyst for an inner about-face Ray had described to me the previous January, a change of mind that he had commemorated with a New Year's resolution to stop inflicting his impulse to conquer hazards on the people he cared about.

In our situation, though, Ray seemed inclined to stop letting a person he cared about inflict my impulse to conquer hazards on him. Only once had he pushed me to tell him what it was all about, what *really* made me insist that we must cross the Columbia Bar in a kayak when we were almost seventy. The best I could do was "Because we still can, but only for a little while longer." There was truth in that, and a connection, it occurred to me shortly after the words were out of my mouth, to the way crumbling denial and a procrastinator's realization that time is short had ramped up my libido in recent years.

In my answer to Ray, I had also implied that a deeper impulse was driving me, the wish for some unpronounceable rite of passage that could only happen in the late stage of life.

I wouldn't have dared speak out loud that in moments I had imagined our project as a salvage operation, one involving the recovery of something lost in childhood and reconciliation with the ghosts of our fathers.

Whatever I chose to say or not say, Ray wanted me to understand one thing clearly: "Giving you something to write about is not worth me dying for."

CHAPTER TWO

THE TENSION BETWEEN RAY AND ME came to a head of sorts on July 7, when I sent him a text that read, "I am becoming concerned that the summer may get away from us before we can complete our adventure."

When he came back with "I am less ambitious toward completion of this quest and challenge than you," I fumed silently, offering no reply, my method of letting him know I was not happy with him.

I knew Ray would get that, and was pleased when he followed up with a text two days later that he was "thinking about the trip now." He caught me by surprise, though, with his suggestion in the next sentence that "we need a second boat for safety."

Kenny Smith had volunteered to join us, Ray informed me. I understood this was a big boost to the endeavor. Kenny was a water dog of the first degree, one who could handle virtually every kind of craft, from motor yachts to sailboats to sea kayaks and canoes, with ease. He and Candy had lived full-time for more than a decade on the Willamette aboard their big boat, *Plum Krazy* (the accent color was purple), traveling to and from shore and around the stretch of the river that ran between Willamette Falls to the south and Swan Island to the north in an assortment of vessels that were tied to their boat: a skiff, a water bike, a paddle board, and so on.

As a teenager, Kenny had driven his father's large motorboat* across the Columbia Bar any number of times, and he knew the river's mouth well. On top of all that, he was the most versatile gearhead I had ever met, a retired electrical engineer who held several microprocessor patents, and a fellow whose fascination with, and mastery of, mathematics, mechanics, meteorology, and every conceivable aspect of the applied sciences exceeded mine by far. When Ray wrote that Kenny was researching bar forecasts for the next week, I knew that we had been relieved of all responsibility for selecting the Right Day.

Still, I struggled with the news that Kenny would be joining us, mainly because I had envisioned the bar crossing as a joint effort by Ray and me, the two of us connected by a quarter century of friendship that from the beginning had involved a shared sense of childhood trauma. Kenny, on the other hand, had grown up in a household that sounded surreal in its wholesomeness. His father had been a chemical engineer who produced three sons that were engineers also, Kenny told me, while his mother had raised four children while buying and running an assortment of small businesses that were intended mainly to keep him and the other kids employed during the summers.

"Remarkably reasonable people," he described his parents.

---

* For the record, both Ray and I had crossed the Columbia Bar previously in boats with powerful motors. In my case, I had made two trips out and in aboard charter fishing boats.

He couldn't remember any scenes, any fights, any real family disputes at all growing up, Kenny said. "My mom and dad were a classic case of nice people. I don't know how else to put it. They got along with each other and with all of us, all the time."

I had difficulty believing this could be possible, but Ray, who had known Kenny longer and better, told me it was true. "This is how people raised in healthy families are," Ray, arching an eyebrow, had pointed out to me on a number of occasions when Kenny did something strange like cheerfully admit a mistake and move on.

Even when I asked him about his basketball career, Kenny described its ups and downs with perfect equanimity. Being the tallest boy at his high school in Hillsboro, Oregon, Kenny was expected to play, but he had never done so out of any sense of obligation. "I enjoyed basketball, and my parents encouraged me to enjoy it," he said. "But I never felt any pressure." Playing in high school at six seven and 165 pounds—"Concentration Camp Kenny," he called himself—he had accepted early on that he was good, but not great. "Competing against the big college guys, I knew they were better than me," he said, without a trace of rancor or regret in his voice. He got a two-year scholarship to play junior college ball—"which was way more than I expected," Kenny said—growing another two inches in the process, then transferred to Oregon State University, from which his father and engineer brothers had graduated also, before moving on into a career he had thoroughly enjoyed.

I secretly suspected Kenny had not been more successful as a basketball player because he lacked a relative ferocity. "If I'd been six nine," I told him once, "I'd have hurt people." He laughed. "I was competitive," he said, "but not really aggressive in that way. I wasn't violent out there."

Okay, I thought, *where does this guy fit in with Ray and me?*

A satisfying answer to that question presented itself almost immediately. Studying an assortment of weather charts, wave and wind forecasts, high- and low-pressure systems, etcetera, Kenny concluded that the coming Friday was as right a day as we were likely to find for crossing the Columbia Bar.

There was a vacant spot of sorts between a high-pressure ridge sitting over the Willamette Valley and a low-pressure front moving in off the ocean, Kenny explained to me, tracing with his long fingers the isobars ("iso" for constant and "bar" for barometric pressure) on a chart I could never have read independently. Wave and wind forecasts were quite reliable inside of a week, Kenny added, and what the charts predicted for Friday, July 16, was an ocean swell of less than three feet with the waves coming at seven- to eight-second intervals, and wind speed holding steady at ten to twelve miles per hour, just enough to fill our sails without overwhelming them. "It's really just perfect," Kenny said.

I confirmed this in an email exchange with Tom Molloy, who wrote back that "Friday does look good." Tom then added a piece of news that gave me slight pause, this being that the Coast Guard station and school at Cape Disappointment would be holding their annual "morale barbecue" that day, meaning only a skeleton crew would be manning the station itself. Tom didn't say so, but I imagined that if we got into trouble, help might be a little slower in arriving.

Kenny said he wasn't worried about it. "There still won't be a safer day to do this," he said.

What I wasn't prepared for was that the ideal day to cross the bar would be such a dreary one. The weather was leaden and damp in Astoria, where the three of us met for breakfast before beginning what we knew would be a long stretch on the water. It had been a strange July at the Oregon coast already. This was my fourth summer living at the beach full-time but my first since selling my house in Portland. The three previous Julys had been sunny day after day, but this fourth one was something else.

June 2021 had ended with record heat all across the Pacific Northwest. The temperature reached 116 in Portland on June 29, nine degrees higher than any temperature ever recorded in the city previously. The thermometer at our beach house hit 100 that day, an unheard-of number on the northern Oregon coast. The reality of global warming struck home at a depth it never had before.

By July, though, a thick marine layer had settled in along the Coast, resulting in early-morning drizzle and days that stayed overcast until the sun finally burned through at three or four p.m. This, combined with the continuing high temperatures inland, had resulted in the strong onshore winds Ray and I had encountered on the Columbia in May and June.

The meteorology of it was fairly simple: When the land in Portland and the rest of the Willamette Valley warmed to eighty degrees or more, the air above it began to rise skyward, drawing in cool air off the ocean, producing brisk sea breezes almost every afternoon. The wind at the coast was nearly always coming from the northwest, as Kenny explained to me over breakfast, because of the Coriolis effect, whereby any mass in motion (including planet Earth) is influenced by a force acting perpendicular to the direction of the motion and to the axis of rotation. Kenny, who could have been an excellent teacher, offered an analogy simple enough for me to understand: "Say we're sitting on a merry-go-round on opposite sides and I throw a rock at you. From my perspective, the rock will look like it bends off to the right." It all had to do with the conservation of angular momentum, Kenny explained: any freely moving object will bend to the right in the Northern Hemisphere and to the left in the Southern Hemisphere; only at the Equator is there no Coriolis effect.

It was by factoring in the Coriolis effect that meteorologists were able to predict synoptic wind, the global breeze pattern that is independent of local conditions. With that forecast in hand, it was possible to see with considerable certainty the movement of pressure systems, and that was how he had been able to say with confidence that there would be an extraordinarily low pressure gradient on Friday, July 16, Kenny concluded.

It sounded good to me, and I even understood a lot of it, but what I really wanted were operational details. There, Kenny threw a curveball at us when he insisted that we had to launch from the Washington side of the river. The main reason he gave was a determination "to avoid fucking Clatsop Spit."

THE SPUR OF LAND on the south side of the Columbia Bar has caused scores of shipwrecks since the first one was recorded in 1829. That sinking—actually, more of a vanishment—was of the British barque *William and Ann*.

It was a time when the British and Americans more or less shared control of the Columbia Bar and the great river that poured into the ocean there. This Anglo-American partnership had been cemented by an 1816 deal that permitted not only peace but also a pooling of resources between the two commercial entities that controlled the fur trade in North America, the Hudson's Bay Company and the North West Company. Their shared monopoly had only been made possible by the War of 1812 and the inability or unwillingness of the American government to send some of its limited resources to defend John Jacob Astor's operations at what was then Fort Astoria. Shortly after the Scottish directors of Astor's Pacific Fur Company elected to liquidate its assets to the North West Company, the British ship HMS *Racoon* crossed the bar into the harbor at Fort Astoria, where its captain promptly renamed the place Fort George, in honor of the English monarch George III, who had reigned over the country during its defeat in the American Revolution.

In March of 1829, the *William and Ann* had approached the Columbia Bar and Fort George bound for Fort Vancouver, on the north shore of the Columbia about ninety miles upriver, directly across from where Portland stands today. Fort Vancouver had been established in 1825 as the Hudson's Bay Company's main base of operations on the Pacific coast.

The *William and Ann* by then had sailed twenty-nine thousand miles from London and around Cape Horn, and was loaded with supplies it would exchange for furs before turning back home. Just outside the bar, the barque encountered an American schooner, the *Convoy*, also loaded with goods it would trade for furs, before crossing the Pacific to Asia.

Both the global regard for the dangers posed by the Columbia Bar and the solidity of the Anglo-American deal are indicated by the fact that the captains of the two ships agreed they should cross together. The *Convoy* and the *William and Ann* sailed into the mouth of the Columbia one behind the other, with the Americans, who possessed at least a measure of familiarity with these waters, taking the lead to sound the depths and locate the sandbars that were the most notorious of the many threats ships might encounter on the Columbia Bar. The two vessels became separated, however, when the wind began to rise and the American captain responded by tacking sharply to his port side. The *Convoy's* sudden move north caused its crew to lose sight of the *William and Ann* before the schooner found safety in Baker Bay, just inside the bar and sheltered by Cape Disappointment.

As the *Convoy's* records have it, the American crew scanned the horizon for hours with no sign of the *William and Ann*, until the schooner's lookout shouted from his perch aloft, "The Britisher's in trouble!"

I was impressed, also moved, to read that the *Convoy's* captain swiftly sent a lifeboat manned by volunteers to search for the *William and Ann* and to offer assistance. The American sailors would report back that they had spotted the barque listing just off Clatsop Spit, apparently trapped in the sands. They rowed to within a quarter mile, the men at oars told their captain, before exhausting themselves in their push against the incoming tide and the shrieking winds that together had turned the bar "a terrible violent." Turning back and returning with the tide to the *Convoy*, the men said, had been the only way to save themselves.

The storm was in full rage by dark, and the *William and Ann*, less than a hundred yards from the shoreline of Clatsop Spit, was pounded by walls of water that filled her holds and rendered the ship unmanageable as it was carried out to sea early the next morning. The British barque's crew of forty-six was never seen again.

Kenny didn't know the story of the *William and Ann*, but he did know that dozens of other ships—brigs, barques, scows, schooners, and freighters—had foundered on Clatsop Spit in the years since. Unlike him, I was familiar with many of the names, the *Primrose*, the *Nisqually*, and the *Dreadnaught* among them. The two that I found most haunting, the *Leonese* and the *Rambler*, had washed up and broken apart on Clatsop Spit in the same year, 1860, just a few months apart, and in each case there had been no sign of the crew—the nine men who had been aboard the *Leonese* and the four who had disappeared from the deck of the *Rambler*.

The name of the ship wrecked on Clatsop Spit that Kenny did know, that nearly everyone in Oregon knew, was the *Peter Iredale*. She had been a four-masted British barque built in 1890 by the Liverpool shipping magnate who gave the vessel his own name. Carrying a thousand tons of ballast, a crew of twenty-five, and two stowaways, the *Peter Iredale* was bound for Portland when it attempted to cross the Columbia Bar on October 25, 1906. Amid thick mist, rising tide, and wind growing stiffer by the second, the ship had tacked east and northeast before giving up and turning to wear away from shore and wait for better conditions. The winds had turned into a squall, though, shortly before the *Peter Iredale* was driven aground on a sandbar just off Clatsop Spit. A lifeboat dispatched from Hammond had rescued the entire crew and the two stowaways, but the ship itself could not be saved.

Salvage plans were abandoned after the *Peter Iredale* broke in two amidships. The forward section stayed stuck, bowsprit pointed to the sky, in the sands right at water's edge in what is today Fort Stevens State Park. There it has remained, a hull of steel and iron worn away by weather and rust, ever since. The bowsprit fell into the surf in 1961, but the *Peter Iredale*'s scaly metal bones have endured, to become the most visited wrecked ship in the history of the Oregon Coast. Each summer, thousands of children swim in the surf surrounding it at high tide, and the hulking remains of the ship have been photographed millions of times, making it the most visible evidence available of what crossing the Columbia Bar has cost those who've done it or died trying.

Shortly before his death, my father had asked that his ashes be scattered at the *Peter Iredale*, and in the summer of 2007 I joined my mother and one of my brothers to fulfill that wish. It startled and saddened me when my mother prepared to spread the ashes without a word. A generosity of spirit I wasn't sure I had in me surfaced in an impromptu prayer:

"Here, in this place where the river he knew best flows into the ocean he loved most, we cast our sailor on the water, in hope he finds safe harbor."

My mother was quite moved, at least in part by what she understood as an expression of forgiveness. And it may have been that. Or maybe it was just a wish to forgive.

I didn't tell Ray or Kenny that story, only that a few months earlier I had helped spread my mother's ashes in the same place, also at her request, and with words I'd rather keep to myself.

Even my mother's ashes had long since washed away into the Pacific Ocean, maybe even as far as to Australia, where she was born and where my parents were married. In spite of that, there had been a kind of comfort in believing that I would make this bar crossing so close to where her remains, and his, had been scattered. Now, though, we were going to cross on the other side of the river. I felt a small measure of disappointment. Still, like Kenny, and Ray too, for that matter, it was good to know I wouldn't be dying on fucking Clatsop Spit.

ON THE OTHER HAND, DYING in the vicinity of Cape Disappointment was now a possibility all three of us had to consider. A headland as spectacular as nearly any on the planet, the cape marks the northern entrance to the Columbia Bar with a majesty that is often disguised by weather. Cape Disappointment is shrouded in fog for an average of 2,522 hours (about 106 days) annually, which is part of what makes its North Head Lighthouse so essential to ships approaching the Columbia River from sea.

During the other eight thousand or so hours a year that the view of the cape is clear, it is a thrilling sight to behold: titanic undulating basalt cliffs in which the rust orange is made more vivid by the deep brown, black, and gray of the rock above and below. From a distance, its enormity belies the size of the wind-stripped yet still towering conifers—Sitka spruce and Douglas firs—that grow along its upper ridges. Among geologists, the cape is most famous for its "pillows," the bulbous masses of basalt that have been produced by underwater eruptions. It is a spectacularly singular feature of planet Earth.

The first European to see the cape was possibly the Spanish sea captain Martín de Aguilar, who commanded the frigate *Tres Reyes* in early 1603 when it was forced off the California coast by a storm so intense it drove the ship far to the north. Somewhere above the fortieth parallel, Aguilar saw a great, raging river that may have been the Columbia. It's not possible to be certain, given that both Aguilar and his pilot died at sea a month later, leaving behind only the journal in which Aguilar noted this sighting.

The question of provenance is further confused by the fact that the Flemish cartographer Abraham Ortelius had drawn a great river spilling into the Pacific Ocean off the coast of North America in the year 1570. Where Ortelius had acquired knowledge of such a river is unknown.

It appears certain, though, that 172 years passed from the time of Martín de Aguilar's death to a more verifiable report on the location of the great river's mouth. This one came from another Spanish explorer, Bruno de Heceta, who observed the stunning headland as his ship sailed past in 1775, postulating that it must mark the entrance to a large freshwater flow. Heceta never tested that theory by venturing into what is now the Columbia because at the time he was desperately trying to conserve the energies of a crew sick with scurvy.

For nearly two centuries, the Spanish had been searching for the fabled Northwest Passage that would allow a ship to sail across North America from the Atlantic to the Pacific. Having pillaged the empires of the Incas and Aztecs, the Spaniards imagined more great cities and riches at higher latitudes and probed on both sides of the continent. Heceta's voyage had come near the end of the Spanish effort to find the Northwest Passage, and shortly before Britain took up the search.

The English captain John Meares was exploring for the Great River of the West in 1788, when he found it but failed to recognize his own success. Unfathomably, Meares concluded that the splendid headland he spotted just north of the forty-fifth parallel, halfway between the equator and the North Pole, was the entrance to a bay, not a river, then sailed away, having left behind the enduring names Deception Bay and Cape Disappointment.

So it was not until the early spring of 1792 that a ship so much as attempted to sail beyond Cape Disappointment and cross the bar. The captain was Robert Gray of Boston, whose three-masted schooner *Columbia Rediva* had two years earlier become the first American vessel to circumnavigate the globe. Convinced it was a river, not a bay, that lay beyond Cape Disappointment, Gray made at least three attempts to sail in on a rising tide across the thrust of current before being pushed back each time and then retreating. After this he sailed north all the way to the Strait of Juan de Fuca, still these many years later the disputed border between the United States and Canada. There, Gray reconnoitered with the British captain George Vancouver, who earlier that year had sailed past Cape Disappointment and decided, just as his countryman John Meares had four years earlier, that there was no river inside the headland and the huge breakers extending beyond it, but merely the body of water still known as Deception Bay.

For reasons unknown (because Gray never published an account of an accomplishment that was far more monumental than he understood), the American captain became determined to return south and try once again to prove that what he had seen at Cape Disappointment was the outside of a river mouth. On May 11, 1792, at a point well south of the cape, close by what would become Clatsop Spit, Gray launched his pinnace, or ship's boat, with a crew at oars to sound the depths of the channel. Following close behind, the *Columbia Rediva* that day became the first ship to cross the bar, and Gray the first captain to confirm that there was, indeed, a great river inside it.

Gray was foremost a merchant, not an explorer, however, and sailed less than twenty miles up the river, stopping to trade nails and other iron goods with a Chinook tribe for more than 450 animal pelts that he could exchange for a handsome profit in China, before turning back toward the ocean. It's not clear that Gray understood at the time that the river he named for his ship was the long-sought Great River of the West. Certainly, he had no sense of the river's immensity or importance, never imagined that it drained an area of nearly 260,000 square miles that included most of Oregon, Washington, and Idaho, plus all of Montana west of the Continental Divide, along with parts of Nevada, Utah, and Wyoming, or that it would become the most economically important waterway west of the Mississippi.

Because Gray did not bother to publish even a word about finding the Columbia, his discovery remained unheralded until the Americans began using it to justify their claim to the Oregon Country. The United States eventually did so with such vigor that the British were forced into the Oregon Treaty of 1846, making those who lived south of the forty-ninth parallel into US citizens.

By this time, the first two surveys of the river, one by the British in 1839 and the second by the Americans in 1841, had established that there were two separate channels of entrance into the Columbia across its bar, one to the south along Clatsop Spit and one to the north next to Cape Disappointment. What these surveys also demonstrated, however, was that both routes were perilous, owing in large part to the continuously shifting sands in the river's mouth. The American mission had found this out the hard way when one of the ships in the squadron assigned to the survey, the USS *Peacock*, ran aground on a spit of sand-encrusted bornite (copper iron sulfide) just off Cape Disappointment's tip and was totally wrecked. This firmest and most deadly of all the obstacles at the mouth of the Columbia was named then and is still called Peacock Spit.

The commanding surveyor of the American mission, Lieutenant Charles Wilkes, was astounded that "any doubt should have ever existed that here was the mouth of the mighty river." The breakers stretching "from Cape Disappointment to Point Adams, in one unbroken line" were overwhelming evidence "of a powerful flood of fresh water contending with the tides of the ocean," Wilkes wrote to his superiors. What he saw here at the mouth of the Columbia was shocking in the degree of its frightful prospect, Wilkes went on: "Mere description can give little idea of the terrors of the bar of the

Columbia: all who have seen it have spoken of the wildness of the scene, and the incessant roar of waters, representing one of the most fearful sights that can possibly meet the eye of a sailor."

No matter; the singular significance of its location and the access the river permitted to the interior of the Pacific Northwest compelled exploration and development, decided an American government that sent new survey teams on an almost annual basis. Even with newer and better charts in hand, however, one ship after another went down trying to cross the Columbia Bar. Four ships were wrecked on the bar in the year 1849 alone, and another five were sunk in 1852.

Kenny seemed to doubt me when I told him this, but my research convinced me that nearly as many ships have sunk beneath Cape Disappointment as have foundered off Clatsop Spit. The year 1913 was an especially bad one for the North Channel: three vessels were lost in a matter of months.

The most disastrous of these wrecks was that of the *Rosecrans*, perhaps as cursed a ship as any ever was. Built in Glasgow in 1884, the *Rosecrans* was commissioned into the US Army as a troop transport during the Spanish-American War, but her high operating costs so exasperated American military leaders that they sold the ship cheap to the Associated Oil Company of San Francisco, where it was converted to a tanker. In March of 1912, caught in a howling gale off the California coast, the *Rosecrans* was tossed broadside against the rocky shore of a Channel Island off Santa Barbara, drowning two of its crew. Six months after a twenty-five-foot hole in her hull was patched, the ship was gutted by a convulsive explosion of fire while loading oil at Gaviota, California. Once more the Associated Oil Company salvaged and rebuilt the ship, then made plans in early

1913 to send it north, bound for Portland, fully loaded with eighteen thousand barrels of crude oil. By then, though, the *Rosecrans* had become known as a "jinxed ship," and assembling a crew proved difficult. The company eventually managed to get thirty-six men to sign on to the *Rosecrans*, but only after hiring as ship's captain the widely admired Lucien Field Johnson, famous up and down the West Coast for having made skipper at the age of only twenty-nine. It was on Johnson's command that the ship attempted to cross the Columbia Bar in a sixty-mile-an-hour wind on January 7, 1913. After a giant wave broke over the *Rosecrans* and put out the fires that fueled her engine, the powerless ship had been driven by the gale past the North Channel entrance and hard into Peacock Spit.

It struck me while researching Peacock Spit that, though many of the hazards of the Columbia Bar were named for ships that had foundered on them, in nearly every case those particular wrecks had not involved any loss of life and were in fact most notable for the rescue operations that had saved entire crews. The people who worked the bar, and who named the places there, had in general chosen stories with a relatively happy ending, leaving the many tragedies that unfolded in these waters to the brume of history.

I on the other hand felt compelled to study all of the shipwrecks on the bar, but most especially those that involved human casualties. I knew early on that I would not even be able to list, let alone chronicle, them all, and it agitated a pang of guilt in me, a sense that I was failing to honor the sacrifices of those who had died in these waters, therefore rendering any effort I made to tell the story of the bar not just incomplete, but possibly invalid.

I cannot even do full justice to the heartbreaking story of the *Rosecrans*, but only summarize how, within a hundred minutes of striking Peacock Spit, the ship had broken in two, leaving its crew clinging to the rigging as, one by one, thirty-three men, among them Lucien Field Johnson, were swept into the surf and disappeared. Only four still had a grip by the time a boat from the US Lifesaving Service reached the wreck. One of those four disappeared when, in a fatal loss of self-control, he threw himself into the water to try to reach the rescue boat. So only three of the *Rosecrans*'s complement of thirty-seven men were carried to shore alive. Of those drowned, the bodies of only six were ever recovered.

According to the rough route Kenny had drawn on a paper napkin, we would be passing within less than a hundred feet of where the *Rosecrans* had gone down all those years earlier, and even closer than that to the best-known channel marker on the north end of the bar. The Besse Buoy was named for the thirteen-ton American barque *W. II. Besse*, which had also wrecked on Peacock Spit, this in the year 1886. Hundreds of people gathered atop Cape Disappointment to observe what looked to be a doomed rescue operation. The ship was sinking fast, but several boats were able to reach it and offload the crew before it went down. That all hands survived was cause for celebration then and encouraging to me 135 years later. What dismayed me, though, was the date of the wreck of the *Besse*, July 23. It was a reminder that, as Tom Molloy had said, conditions on the bar could change almost instantaneously, even in high summer. In the case of the *Besse*, it was a sudden gust of wind that seemed to come off the water out of nowhere that had filled the mainsail and thrown the ship against Peacock Spit.

There was no limit to what could happen out there, or how quickly it might come, I thought, and for some reason was reminded of a sailing aphorism that Ray had quoted to me on several occasions: "Any line that can tangle, will."

* * *

AFTER BREAKFAST ON THE MORNING of July 16, I drove Kenny from Astoria across the longest continuous truss bridge in North America to the Washington side of the river, Ray following in his big blue Ford van with two trimarans, a double and a single, stacked atop the trailer. We drove close to the rocky shore through villages on the east side of the Lewis and Clark National Historical Park. The town of Chinook had fascinated me ever since Tom Molloy remarked that it once was home to more millionaires per capita than any other place in the United States, wealth accumulated in the early days of commercial fishing, from canned catches of salmon, mostly. I found it these days a charming but humble burg and searched one more time in vain for some sign of its former affluence.

When I began to poke around in Chinook's past, however, I was astonished by my discovery that this little town had been the epicenter of the greatest loss of life in the entire history of the Columbia Bar. Epic snowfall in the winter of 1880, followed by record snowmelt the following spring, had nearly doubled the flow of water down the lower Columbia, raising the river to flood stage from Portland on down. One effect of this was an ebb tide at the river's mouth that extended for more than half an hour each day. These outgoing tides kept fishermen at sea for that much longer, though a handful were incautious enough to linger close to the bar, which sucked their boats in and sank them. Those that survived did so only by cutting their nets and pulling for shore.

The fishing boats of that day were not large, only about twenty-six feet in length on average, and made of wood. Propelled by sail and oar, most of these boats carried a crew of two, one man to tend the sail, the other a "boat puller" who rowed.

The fishermen then were generally gillnetters, mostly Scandinavian, who had poured into Astoria and Chinook when the canneries began to operate. They spread their woven nets horizontally in the water, strung across a rope supported by cork floats, and weighted with lead at the bottom. These nets were huge, more than a thousand feet long, twenty feet top to bottom. Most often, they were laid out on an incoming tide after dark (so that the salmon wouldn't see the nets), and on a good night scores of fish would be caught in a net by their gills. The nets would be pulled out of the water in the ebb tide, and at dawn the boats would head for the canneries. The snowmelt in the spring of 1880, though, forced the boats to spend an additional half hour out in the ocean every day.

On May 4, while the fishing boats were waiting to come in, the Columbia Bar was struck by a sudden squall of astounding ferocity. As one survivor, identified as "C. Christiansen," told the *Oregonian*, "My boat was at anchor when a heavy sea came and upset her almost alongside of James Hainson's boat. She righted immediately. My boat filled. Hainson then got in the boat, but I was entangled in the net and I could not get in until a breaker threw me in . . . We drifted opposite Megler's (fishing) station shouting for help." Hainson told him that they could never be saved in this weather, Christiansen recalled, and decided to lash himself to the boat. "A moment after, a breaker came and threw me out of the boat almost on the beach," he explained. "After a struggle with the breakers I succeeded in reaching land. I never saw anything more of Hainson." James Hainson's rigid body was found the next day, lying over the bow of Christiansen's boat.

The captain of the steamer *General Canby* reported that he had recovered four boats in Baker Bay, empty of men and gear. He also quoted survivors who had seen another four empty boats swamped in the breakers below Scarborough Hill. The lighthouse keeper at Cape Disappointment described seeing three boats "going out over the bar bottom up."

The headline on the *Oregonian*'s first story about the storm read, A DAY OF TERRORS; TWENTY-FIVE FISHERMEN LOST. It was worse than that, but at the time the dead were still being counted. Confusion reigned when a handful of boats that had been reported lost came in across the bar to the safety of Baker Bay. On May 5, still sorting it all out, the editor of the *Astorian*, Dewitt Clinton Ireland, wrote, "Many exaggerated statements were afloat yesterday concerning the loss of boats, nets and men fishing, night before last. We could not get reliable data to base anything like a correct report upon."

The statements were not exaggerated, however, merely incomplete. Dozens of fishermen at least had lost their lives on the night of May 4.

Ireland's confused reporting may have been a minor factor, but what mainly compounded the tragedy was that scores of fishermen who survived the squall of May 4 mistook what was merely a lull in the storm for its conclusion and went back out on the evening of May 5. The squall kicked up again, even more violently than the night before. Nearly as many boats and men were lost that night as had been taken by the sea the night before.

By May 6, Dewitt Clinton Ireland was simply cataloguing the losses as reports of them came in. CASUALTIES. GREAT LOSS OF LIFE AND PROPERTY, read the headline on his story that day: "Kinney's [boat] No. 6 is reported to have lost one man . . . Peter J.

Blagan, an independent fisherman, is reported lost . . . Two of J. G. Megler Co.'s boats are supposed to be among the fleet lost . . . Wm. Hume's No. 10, Mr. Geo. Adams, a noble good man, is reported lost . . . The Anglo-American Packing Co. No. 11 drifted out to sea. Men and gear supposed to be lost . . . Two boats and nets were picked up yesterday morning afoul of the brigantine *North Bend*, lying at Gray's dock . . . Hans Hansen of Geo. W. Hume's No. 28 is reported lost . . ."

Ireland continued like this for days. How many died in total I can't say with certainty. Local historians all seem to put the number at two hundred, but Ireland seems to have stopped at sixty. Whether the deaths were sixty or two hundred or somewhere in between, the loss of the fishing fleet in May of 1880 remains to this day the greatest calamity in the history of the bar, far surpassing the forty-six who drowned in the wreck of the *William and Ann*.

AFTER PASSING THE ENTRANCE to Lewis and Clark Park, we turned north up the Long Beach Peninsula, then drove through the principal place of moorage for charter fishing boats in the region, Ilwaco, before arriving at the road to the beach in Seaview. Kenny and I were far ahead by the time we rolled onto the beach (driving is legal there, and on many other oceanfronts in Oregon and Washington) and parked about thirty feet from the tide line.

Ray had proposed that, instead of crossing the bar and then coming back across it to the launch at Cape Disappointment State Park, we should make a beach landing about eight miles north at Seaview, where my car would be parked. This would prove to be the most nearly fatal decision we made all day, but at the time, riding waves ashore did not sound all that risky, and anyway I was counting on Kenny to make that call. He had told us he would know which way to vote when he saw the ocean at Seaview.

"It looks good," Kenny said as the two of us stood on the sand, our toes barely out of the water. I still had some difficulty comprehending that a day so gloomy was good, but I knew Kenny was right. The Pacific Ocean was as lugubrious as I'd ever seen it, sluggish two-foot swells coming at eight- or nine-second intervals.

Kenny was relying on a wave forecast that he'd checked again that morning, indicating that the next major wave train was nearly eighteen hours away to the southwest. The weather and wind forecasts were similarly encouraging, if unexciting: overcast all day with gusts reaching a maximum of twelve miles per hour.

By the time Ray had parked his van on the patch of gravel that speared out into the sand and stood next to us by the water, Kenny had decided that the beach-landing idea was reasonable. It would save time, avoid the risk of a second bar crossing (incoming on a rising tide that can plow the nose of a boat into a wave), and serve as a singular conclusion to our journey. Ray appeared pleased, and I wasn't objecting to or even questioning the plan. Ignorance and deference were the only excuses I had for going along with such folly. Ray and Kenny, though, were forgetting the First Law of the Columbia Bar that they'd recited to me on multiple occasions: All assumptions are incorrect. Or, as I chose to put it later, forecasts are rarely as reliable as one would like to imagine.

After we left my car along the side of the beach road and drove in Ray's van to Cape Disappointment Park, I found myself growing impatient with the delays caused by Kenny's insistence upon checking and rechecking his analysis of conditions on the bar. We parked on the side of North Jetty Road, where the gigantic rock wall begins on a half mile of shoreline in the lee of Cape Disappointment, then clambered up a sloped pile of twenty-ton boulders and stood on top to survey the water on the inside of the jetty. It was moving faster than we'd expected, and Ray looked concerned. So did Kenny, who announced that he wanted to borrow the bicycle in the back of Ray's van and ride it up past the locked gate where the road led further out toward the river.

I was tense in his absence, fearing that our plans for the day might be canceled upon his return. When Kenny pedaled back up to the gate and lifted the bike over the chain that held it shut, though, he was smiling and saying it looked a lot better out there than it did here. We were on.

At the park's boat launch on Baker Bay, the light rain was steady enough to plaster my hair to my brow, though the temperature stayed warm and produced a steam that thickened the haze surrounding us. The plan had been to do as Tom Molloy had suggested and leave an hour or so before low tide, but Ray and Kenny were both moving with a deliberation I knew made that unlikely.

The park's launch ramp was used mainly by large recreational fishing boats, though I had been told that some leaving from there were commercial fishermen. The men who ran or worked the big boats were gawking at us from the moment of our arrival. As we assembled and rigged our trimarans on the strip of grass next to where Ray had parked the van, one guy after another found a reason to walk past and ask if we were going to cross the bar "in those things." I heard derision in at least several voices, while others seemed skeptical but curious. All of them shook their heads. Ray and Kenny scowled silently at the derisive and were stoically polite to the doubtful, giving terse replies to questions about our boats, which had been seasoned by years of familiarity with the process of putting in trimarans amid myriad motorboats.

Donning our drysuits only increased the circuslike atmosphere we seemed to be creating. Mine was a red-gray-black combination that made me look, according to my wife, like a space traveler in party clothes. Much as I despised the strangulating throat gusset, I agreed with Ray that the security of knowing we could survive in the water for several hours, if it came to that, was worth the discomfort. Padding around in our drysuits, though, made us appear even more like alien life forms to the fishermen.

By the time we put our trimarans into the water, a couple of the fishermen were grumbling about the time we were taking and let us know they wanted us to clear the way.

We climbed into the Hobies out of knee-deep water, paddled a few feet away from the launch ramp, then began pedaling. The rest of the fishermen were clustered along the dock next to the ramp, watching us with expressions at once incredulous and comical. "Oh, my God," I heard one of the men say. "Pedals?"

Guffaws followed as we moved past, then a voice called out from behind us, "No guts, no glory!" followed by even louder laughter. I glanced over at Kenny in the solo Hobie, and he looked anything but amused.

As we entered the channel I heard one last voice shouting "Good luck" and wondered which one of the fishermen that was.

The rain had stopped about ten minutes earlier, and the sky already began to show signs of clearing. This produced a phenomenon I've seen only on the Pacific coast between Northern California and southern Washington and have always found immensely pleasurable.

It's a filmy, silvery light that lays like a substance on one's surroundings, magically weighting everything that it touches and somehow compressing reality in a way that creates a simultaneous sense of expansion, making what's near seem far and what's far all but unbearably close.

I'd had trouble falling asleep the night before, bothered by the thought that this could be my last night on earth, until I concluded it was that way all the time, and finally nodded off. Now, in the uncanny light of this day, as Ray opened our sail and we slid out of the channel into Baker Bay, making for the Columbia River, I felt no fear, only anticipation.

Seated in the rear position, I could see just Ray's back, until he swiveled to look at me over his right shoulder. "You and me, brother," he called. "Let's live through this."

We've both lived through a lot already, Ray, I thought to myself. *It's what we're good at.*

CHAPTER THREE

THE "NEGATIVE PIVOT POINT" OF HIS LIFE, as Ray called it, had come when he was eight years old. I admit to envying him that, because my own crippling experience of loss and abandonment had occurred at the age of only four. I don't imagine my childhood suffering was greater than Ray's, however, and it certainly was no more dramatic. But still, he got those good first eight years.

His upbringing had been actually idyllic, as far as he knew, Ray said, until that day when he was pulled out of his third-grade class in South Bend, Indiana, and brought to the principal's office, where he found his mother waiting with his newborn baby brother and her own parents. They were leaving South Bend and moving to Quincy, Illinois, Ray's mother told him. Immediately. This was, she said, for her safety and his and, especially, for his little brother's.

He remembered his mother and his grandparents as "very fearful," Ray told me, concerned "I would become combative and cause such a big ruckus that Dad would be called." Thinking back, it was difficult to separate his confusion from the distress he felt during the drive to Quincy, Ray said: "They all acted like they were saving us from a very dangerous situation, which was so far from my perception of my home life that I was enraged at the disruption. I was having a good time in third grade and felt like I had been uprooted against my will, and that Mom was betraying my dad and our family."

In Quincy, directly across the Mississippi River from Hannibal, Missouri (where my wife Delores was born and raised), Ray's mother attempted to calm her son by placing him in counseling. The explanation that his mother was merely trying to protect him from his father's bad example only served to amplify the boy's fury. "I refused absolutely to cooperate with the counseling," he remembered. "I decided to be so miserable, and to make them so miserable, that they'd let me go back to Dad."

Among the results was the inception of Ray's long and varied career as a sociopathic criminal. He quickly became, at the age of eight, "a brazen and prolific thief." His technique was to grab items off store shelves and stick them into the waistband of his pants. "I just stole anything, I didn't care what it was, didn't care about the stuff itself, and certainly didn't care if I got caught," Ray said. "It was the stealing and the being bad that propelled me." By the time summer came, he had collected a tremendous trove of items that ranged from toys to tools to electronics, along with a huge assortment of household items. "Then finally I 'confessed' to my mom and grandparents, showed it all to them, which gave me pleasure," he recalled. "They were shocked and scared that I had become such a little monster, and that gave me considerable satisfaction, and provided me with a one-way train ticket back to Dad's house, as I was causing so much pain to my grandparents and Mom that they were worried about their own health."

He was happy, at least at first, living with his dad, Ray said. At the same time, he admitted, a large part of what made him want to be back home in South Bend was that he felt so sorry for his father.

He had already figured out on some level, Ray believed, that his dad's many problems derived generally from the way he had been treated by his own father, Raymond Thomas the first. That damage, like narrative, is passed down in families was hardly news to me, but in the Thomas clan's case the story felt like it had to have been written by Eugene O'Neill.

The first Raymond Thomas was born the son of a Cornish copper miner on Michigan's Upper Peninsula. At eighteen, the young man announced he was headed to Chicago to get an education. His father replied, "You must think you're better than me," and disowned him. Raymond Thomas the first never saw his family of origin again.

In Chicago, he found employment delivering cadavers for medical school students, a job that left him with a lifelong hatred of physicians. Instead he went to dental school and became an enormously successful oral surgeon, one whose practice was made lucrative by the mobsters who passed word around that this guy was really good at fixing teeth. Among the man's proudest possessions was Al Capone's pool table, given to him in payment by one of the famous gangster's lieutenants while Capone himself was locked up in Alcatraz prison.

Working for the mob was still sort of glamorous in the Chicago of the period, and Raymond Thomas I grew wealthy and eminent, a member of the Chicago Yacht Club who owned a spectacular home in River Forest. The man named his firstborn Raymond Thomas II, and so strictly insisted that the boy follow in his footsteps that he gave his son no other choice than to attend dental school. Raymond Thomas II had no aptitude for academics in general and for dentistry in particular, however, and failed miserably. Flunking out, as his own son, Raymond Thomas III, would explain to me more than seven decades later, was "the beginning of the end for my dad."

Raymond Thomas II had good looks and charm, though, enough to land a lovely wife who was far more ambitious than he. His mom had been a successful copywriter before she became a radio actress, my friend Ray recounted, although she would become best known during the 1960s and '70s as the first female television news anchor in the Midwest. His dad, though, had never really thrived. He got jobs as a vacuum salesman for Sears and as a manufacturer's rep for Crayola, but he couldn't hold them. He liked working with his hands and was good at it, but that was hardly enough to satisfy his father, who made no effort to hide his disappointment in his namesake. Raymond Thomas II began to drink heavily and to resent his increasingly polished wife.

Ray remembered that his mother had told his counselor, who told him, that his dad was a disrespectful drunk determined to turn Raymond Thomas III against her. Yet he was still much more content living with his father than he'd been in Quincy, Ray said.

Failing at one job after another, Raymond Thomas II had decided to make a living doing what he loved. "And what he loved, and was very good at, was finding distressed antiques or classic cars at bargain prices, restoring them, and selling them for a profit," Ray said. "But he *really* loved buying old guns and fixing them up. That was his true passion."

He enjoyed working with his dad on the old cars, in particular a World War II–era Jeep that they kept for their own, Ray remembered, and got almost as much of a thrill as his dad did from turning some rusted old pistol into a well-oiled weapon in fine working order. Father and son earned most of the money they lived on, though, from the antique furniture they restored and sold. This work Ray didn't like as much, but even with that he found satisfaction in being part of their tight two-person team.

"My dad had this trailer he used to carry home the antiques and guns he bought," Ray recalled. "I was expected to come home right after school—this was fourth grade—and help him carry them into the house, then help him work on refinishing the furniture. It was also my job to answer the phone, because we had this classified ad that we were relying on for all of our business."

The father-son partnership fell apart, though, every time nine-year-old Ray wrote down a phone number illegibly or missed a call because he'd ducked out to play with a friend. "I caught hell," he recalled. This generally involved harsh words and a whack on the side of the head, but it could get worse, especially if his dad was drinking. An episode that Ray could only speak about with a tremendous effort of self-control took place one evening when, at the age of ten, he had finished taking a bath and used the towel bar to pull himself out of the tub. "I broke it off, then denied that I had done it," Ray remembered. "Because I had lied to him, he said, he took the towel bar and literally beat me senseless. I had terrible bruising all over my arms where I'd tried to protect myself and knots all over my head where I hadn't been able to."

Ray had dealt with the pain and humiliation of such brutality at the hands of a father much as I had, by hiding it from others and denying it to himself. He felt a deep anger inside, Ray said, but at the same time was confused by a parent who "would undergo a catharsis from beating the shit out of me, and initiate this reconciliation process. He'd be on his best behavior and very nice to me, and we'd do things together that were fun." The biggest difference in our relationships with our fathers was in the ways that Ray's dad was able to play on his son's sympathies. "I wasn't just my dad's worker, I was also his confidant and best friend," Ray explained. "Even when I started to hate him I still felt sorry for him. He would weep about how much he missed Mom and how she broke his heart, and this played into the secret pining I had that they would put our family together again."

Ray would shuttle back and forth between Quincy and his father's home until he was sixteen. He never lasted long in Illinois, however. To the underlying anger he felt at his mom for the breakup of the family, Ray added resentment of how consumed she had become by her career after going to work in television. "So I always blew things apart there after a few weeks or months and was sent back to my dad," he recalled.

In South Bend, where his father would live until shortly after Ray turned thirteen, there was an inevitable return to a pattern that became more and more poisonous. "I'd always start off feeling so bad for my dad," he remembered. "I had put together that his brokenness had started long before my mom left him, that it went back to the way he had been rejected by his own father. He cried at least as often as he raged. So I'd try to be the caretaker." By the age of eleven Ray was doing nearly all of the cooking and most of the housekeeping. "We'd go along for a while, everything okay, then I'd do something that failed to meet my dad's expectations and he would lose it and give me a beating," he recalled. "Every time it happened, my anger got hotter and deeper."

Knowingly or not, Raymond Thomas II provided his son with the perfect tool to express his rage when he bought the boy a BB gun for Christmas. Within a matter of months, Ray had killed every frog and bird that lived around the pond in back of his dad's house in South Bend. "I was a murderous little maniac," he told me with an almost imploring expression. "I had no moral conscience at all. I was just enjoying killing. I would make little arrangements of the frogs after they were dead and kind of study them." I was struggling to meet Ray's gaze. "Yeah, I know how that sounds," he told me. "You're maybe the only person I could talk to about it."

Ray and I had both become familiar with serial killers during our careers, and he knew as well as I did that torturing and slaughtering animals was an almost universal precursor to murder among such creatures. "I really can't explain to you how I turned myself around," he told me. "I just did."

I knew Ray well enough to be certain that he possessed genuine empathy, in fact felt the suffering of others with at least as much acuity as I did. I wondered aloud if the fact that his father had at times drawn him close and made him feel loved when he was a boy had provided some sort of protection against a truly awful outcome for him.

"That would be something if it was true, wouldn't it?" Ray mused, then shook his head. "One fucked-up deal."

I thought a while about what to say. "As long as I've known you, Ray," I told him, "there has never been anybody I'd want at my side if I was going into battle more than you."

This produced a rueful smile. "I guess that says a lot about both of us, eh?"

LIKE THE HAMMOND BOAT BASIN on the south shore of the Columbia, the launch at Cape Disappointment Park was the last place to put in on the north shore. Our entry into the river was far more measured on the Washington side, however. Here, the channel broadened so gradually into the bay, and from there into the river, that it was a bit like being poured into the current, and on this day the chop on the Columbia was not nearly so overwhelming as it had been back in May when Ray and I had launched at Hammond. I knew immediately that Kenny had done a fine job of picking not only the Right Day but also the right place.

The Jaws were visible on the horizon within minutes of our entering the river, and the sight of them lent our voyage the sense of a gradually and then rapidly building climax from that moment forward. While the South Jetty was so distant that its outer reaches disappeared into the oceanic horizon, the nearer North Jetty seemed to be extended alongside us in a way that made it collateral to our destination.

Construction of the Jaws was by far the greatest project ever undertaken on the Columbia Bar, and had both changed the character and reduced the danger of the river's mouth to degrees that are difficult to comprehend for anyone living today. Hundreds of vessels and men have wrecked and perished on the bar since the jetties were built, but those numbers would be many times greater if not for what was accomplished by a decades-long enterprise that consumed more than twenty million board feet of lumber and nearly two and a half billion pounds of stone.

Back in 1876, when the US Army Corps of Engineers decided that at least one jetty on the south side of the Columbia would be necessary to maintain even a single stable channel across the bar, the entrance to the river stretched five miles across from Point Adams to Cape Disappointment and was relentlessly unreliable. At a mean average flow of 260,000 cubic feet per second that rises to 1.2 million cubic feet per second at the height of the late-spring runoff, the Columbia's mouth carries enormous quantities of silt that have been collected along the entire 1,264-mile run of the river.

Before the jetties were built, the distribution of that silt produced sandbars, extending between what became known as the North Channel and the South Channel, that shifted constantly. The North Channel was generally the safer choice for either entering or exiting the Columbia Bar, shoaling as it did to a depth of about seventeen feet. The South Channel was both more depthless and more variable. Only ships with shallow drafts could enter by either route, but no large vessel could beat into the South Channel when the summer winds were blowing out of the northwest. At any time of the year, all ships that were heavily loaded had to come in by the North Channel, but that too was filled with sand that moved continuously. Passage was so treacherous that during the nineteenth century, sailing ships would wait as long as six weeks for conditions that permitted them to cross the bar without being caught in the sands, and many were caught anyway.

Despite its dangers, the Columbia River's commercial importance became more and more obvious to the US government after the Civil War. Oregon had become a state in 1859, and by 1880 its population was 175,000, while the Washington Territory claimed another 75,000 inhabitants. Portland, nearly one hundred miles upriver from the mouth of the Columbia, a far larger and more significant city than Seattle at the time, was just about to become the nexus of a railway system that connected it to the entire country. Both the expansion of the city's connections and the elevation of the Columbia River's importance in the public mind were engineered largely by one man, a German immigrant journalist named Henry Villard.

Villard had first gained public attention during the Civil War as a battlefield correspondent for the *New York Tribune*, an experience that turned him into an outspoken pacifist. After the war ended, he worked briefly as the Washington correspondent for the *Chicago Tribune*, then traveled to Europe to report on the Prusso-Austrian War. Villard was still living in Europe when the United States was blindsided by the worst financial crisis it had seen up to that point, the Panic of 1873. Rampant inflation, wildly speculative investment (particularly in railroads), and the demonetization of silver were among the numerous causes of a collapse that reduced bank reserves in New York City from $50 million to $17 million nearly overnight.

Villard, though, recognized that railroads would continue to be the country's main engine of economic growth, and in 1874, while living in Wiesbaden, Germany, he organized a group of investors to take control of the Oregon and California Railroad, which at that point had not extended its rail line anywhere near to California. Villard did not actually see Oregon until later that year, but during his visit, along with being stunned by the scenery, he realized that the Columbia River was the most vital natural feature west of the Rocky Mountains, draining as it did the waters of seven US states and British Columbia. He promptly persuaded his German investors to help him become president of not only the Oregon and California Railroad but also the Oregon Steam Navigation Company, so that between the two companies he had the immediate capacity to move lumber, grain, and other goods from the bottom of the Willamette Valley all the way to the mouth of the Columbia.

Villard had to have been a dazzlingly effective salesman, one fluent enough in both German and English to convince investors to put $8 million into his famous "Blind Trust," permitting him to invest the money as he saw fit. With cash in hand, he swiftly gained control of the Northern Pacific, a struggling, far-from-completed land-grant railroad chartered to connect Lake Superior to Puget Sound. Combining the Northern Pacific with his Oregon and California Railroad and his recently established Oregon Railway & Navigation Company, Villard almost instantly created a railroad monopoly that stretched across the entire Pacific Northwest, one that he centered in Portland. By 1883, when the Northern Pacific's northeast and southwest running rails were connected at Independence Gulch, Montana, Villard's empire achieved transcontinental status. Not only was the Northern Pacific now running passenger and freight trains between Portland and Minneapolis–Saint Paul, but from Minnesota it became connected to a railway system that covered the entire eastern half of the country. It was now possible to move goods in and out of the mouth of the Columbia River to and from nearly every part of the United States.

With Villard at the forefront, the business community in Portland became the main agitator for improving access across the Columbia Bar. The federal government, though, dragged its feet. The Civil War had left the country, and especially leaders in the nation's capital, feeling financially overwhelmed. Finally, after Oregon citizens raised a number of petitions for construction of the jetty recommended by the Army Corps of Engineers, the US Congress in 1884 allocated $100,000 to begin the work.

The initial plan was to build an eight-mile-wide pile dike that extended eight thousand feet at a northwest angle toward the ocean. This would have involved rows of staggered piles driven into the submerged earth with giant timbers inserted between each row, then bolted into a single structure—a dike. Doubts about how effective the pile dike would be led to the decision by the Army Corps of Engineers that the South Jetty should instead be a rubble mound, an immense wall of stacked rocks thousands of feet long that could withstand the

Columbia's current and "train" the river to flow through a narrower channel. This, it was believed, would cause the current to accelerate and flush the sandbars out of the shipping channel on the south side of the river.

Work got underway in 1885, but even with the value of US currency at the time, $100,000 was barely enough to get started. More public pressure from Portland extracted an additional $187,000 from the government, but this was still far short of what was needed.

Henry Villard was no longer around to lead the campaign to build the jetties. Until just a couple of years earlier, Villard had rivaled Jay Gould as the preeminent American magnate, while wielding a good deal more cultural clout than his New York rival. By the end of 1881, Villard had acquired influential publications that included the *New York Evening Post* and the *Nation*. His steamship *Columbia* had become the first vessel or building to use Thomas Edison's newly invented incandescent lighting system. Villard's support of higher education garnered him accolades from both sides of the country. In his adopted home state, he had paid off the debt of the University of Oregon, and the school rewarded him by naming the second building on campus Villard Hall. He also gave generously to Harvard and Columbia and was a major benefactor of New York's Metropolitan Museum of Art and American Museum of Natural History. He had married women's suffrage advocate Helen Frances Garrison, the daughter of abolitionist William Lloyd Garrison, and in spite of his wealth became a leading light of progressive causes. Wall Street bears, though, had spotted Villard's weakness, a tendency to overborrow in support of his far-flung enterprises. In 1884, the same year he put the world's second-largest ferry, a 338-foot steamboat he named the *Kalama*, into service carrying entire trains—engines, cars, cargo, and crew—across the Columbia River between Oregon and Washington, the bears organized an unrelenting attack on the Northern Pacific, all but wiping the company out and at the same time destroying most of Villard's wealth. After suffering a nervous breakdown, he had retreated to Germany, not returning to the US until several years later, and then as a mid-level executive at the Northern Pacific who would die in relative obscurity just as the twentieth century dawned.

Without Villard, the business community in Portland clamored in vain to extract more federal funding for construction of the Columbia Bar's jetties. It was not until 1888 that they were able to convince the Oregon state legislature to cough up $500,000 so that work could begin in earnest.

The federal government eventually joined in support of a project whose scale rivaled construction of the Brooklyn Bridge, completed five years earlier, and was surpassed in the US only by the creation of the Erie Canal in the early nineteenth century. Digging the tunnels for the New York subway system would not begin until 1900, and Hoover Dam would not be built until the 1930s.

A sternwheeler called the *Cascades* worked six days a week to tow barges from a quarry upriver to Astoria, where the tug *George H. Mendell* waited to pull the flat boats to the huge receiving dock that had been built at Fort Stevens. The rocks, most weighing more than twelve thousand pounds, were offloaded at the dock by more than a dozen derricks, then pulled in gondola cars out above the river mouth by five locomotives running on a pair of rail lines atop a trestle that extended across the entire planned length of the jetty. Construction of the trestle had itself been a monumental task that required a steam-powered pile driver to pound the 125-foot-long logs that were floated downriver in rafts to serve as stanchions.

A fleet of what were called mosquito launches ferried hundreds of workers to and from their job sites during the seven years required to complete a jetty that was nearly five miles long and had turned twenty-nine hundred acres of surf into dry land. The project's success was almost immediate: a South Channel that had been a highly variable twenty feet deep was now reliably more than thirty feet deep, allowing ships of nearly any size to enter the river.

For me, the difference between then and now is perhaps best illustrated by the fact that after a total of $3.8 million was allocated by the state and federal governments to build the South Jetty, the engineers and their crews had used barely more than $2 million to get the job done. The combination of work ethic, can-do attitude, and respect for public money had produced exactly the opposite of the cost overruns we consider standard today.

The success of the South Jetty did give rise to one significant unforeseen problem, however. The deepening of the channel on that side of the river resulted in a steady accumulation of silt in the North Channel, making what had long been the safest passage across the bar into an increasingly difficult and risky one. In 1913, after the wreck of the *Rosecrans*, it was agreed that a second jetty needed to be built on the north side of the Columbia Bar. Work began in 1914.

Improvements in equipment enabled the engineers and their workers to build the mounded wall of stones on the north side of the Columbia with boulders that were considerably larger than those used to make the South Jetty, many weighing more than one hundred thousand pounds. Photographs of the steam shovel that deposited these immense stones, one by one, teetering atop the end of the half-built wall, immersed in surf, make one wonder who could have possibly had the nerve to operate it under those conditions. Within three years, the entrance to the North Channel had been narrowed to two thousand feet, and the silt that had built up on the river bottom was rapidly flushed out.

Ray, though, was concerned by what he had heard about the rock at the North Jetty's base extending more than a hundred feet below the surface of the water. Because of this, he insisted that we come no nearer than three hundred feet to the jetty as we began to move almost parallel to where the wall of rocks protruded from Cape Disappointment. I shouted over Ray's shoulder that Kenny was well inside us, maybe only a hundred feet from the jetty. Ray answered that Kenny was "beyond category as a sailor" and might have decided to raise both the Mirage Drive pedals and the daggerboard and be using only the wind to advance. Kenny was falling steadily behind us, though, so it was difficult to see whether he was pedaling or not. I couldn't turn to look back at him because Ray kept giving me the rudder so that he could concentrate on the sail, and steering the boat became a consuming task.

I felt how light our craft was every time one of the fishing boats zoomed past on our left, creating wakes that struck us broadside and rocked the boat far more intensely than any of the river's naturally forming waves were doing on this day. The big boats went by one after another; the sportsmen were all out, we realized, to take advantage of the good conditions. A few came so close that I could see people on board staring at us in disbelief, but only briefly, before turning all their attention to what was up ahead.

Above us to our left the sun was rapidly burning through the cloud cover, and the sky became clearer and brighter by the minute. The wind picked up, but only slightly. The boat still felt steady enough that I used my phone to shoot some one-handed video of us coursing across the river's surface. Only when I looked at it later did I fully realize how much movement there had been in the water, even in this most gentle part of our passage. Seeing that video, I was glad I had decided a short time later to seal the phone and tuck it away, so that I had the use of both hands, one for the rudder and the other to grip a handrail. The pulse of the river picked up so gradually as we approached the ocean that I felt it only vaguely until we were close enough to see, in the distance, the fishing boats going over the bar. Observing from perhaps a half mile away how their prows were jolted upward and the boats began to bounce like spun stones across the breakers was the first real confirmation I had of what I knew was coming.

CHAPTER FOUR

IN THE LORE OF THE COLUMBIA BAR, the emphasis on the wrecks of oceangoing ships at times seems to obscure the far greater number of boats that have foundered in the river's mouth, and to neglect the hundreds of men put in the water by the sinking of those lesser vessels. There is no accurate count of how many small craft have been lost at the entrance to the Columbia River, but while the *William and Ann* is commonly listed as the first shipwreck on the bar, at least several European or American boats and more than a dozen men aboard them had disappeared trying to enter or exit the river prior to that.

The best documented of these are the two boats sent to sound the bar by the ship *Tonquin* in the spring of 1811. The *Tonquin* was owned by John Jacob Astor and carried among its passengers three senior Scottish partners of Astor's Pacific Fur Company. The ship's mission was not only to establish the first trading post on the Columbia River but to create an international emporium for the collection and distribution of the most valuable commodity on the planet at the time: animal pelts. It's nearly impossible to overstate the worth of sea otter and beaver furs in the eighteenth and nineteenth centuries. Sea otter pelts in particular brought fantastic prices in Asia, where coats or bed coverings made of them were held to be the most opulent of possessions. The density of sea otter fur is the greatest of any mammal's, nearly one million hairs per square inch. Unlike seals and other mammals that live in frigid water, the sea otter has no layer of blubber to insulate it from the cold, but rather an inner coat of fur made of shorter, softer hairs that grow under the longer hairs of its outer fur. This combination of coats, long hairs above and short hairs beneath, produces luxuriance rivaled only by mink and sable.

Well into the nineteenth century, the playful sea otters thrived along the northern Pacific coast and in the rivers that poured into the ocean there, living in what were known as "rafts" of a hundred or more. It was not even necessary to trap them, because Native tribes were already taking them by the thousands, mostly with bows and arrows, and were eager to trade their furs with European or American visitors. At the time the *Tonquin* arrived on the Columbia Bar, a pelt purchased for a dollar's worth of ceramic beads and iron nails at a village upriver could be sold for a hundred times that in Canton. Beaver pelts were almost as valuable, having been highly prized by Europeans for making felt hats since the middle of the sixteenth century. Beavers had been trapped nearly to extinction in and around Hudson's Bay and the Great Lakes yet remained abundant in the area drained by the Columbia River.

In 1811, John Jacob Astor understood the strategic importance of controlling the Columbia's mouth better than anyone alive, with the possible exception of his friend Thomas Jefferson. Astor's aims, though, were narrower than Jefferson's: Access to the Columbia and to the harbor inside its bar was the key to control of the global fur trade, he had decided. The Columbia River itself could serve as a kind of highway for canoes out of what would become British Columbia,

Montana, Wyoming, and Idaho, areas teeming with beaver, fox, and bear, while the coastline stretching from the river's mouth to lower Alaska was home to thousands upon thousands of otter rafts. On top of that, what was known as the Japanese Current (today the Kuroshio Current) was an elliptical flow of warm water that circulated not far outside the Columbia Bar and dependably carried ships along the North Pacific Gyre to and from Asia. For all these reasons combined, Astor was willing to take a huge gamble on being the first to establish a trading post at the mouth of the Columbia. To do so, he dispatched not only a first-rate ship, the *Tonquin*, under the command of former US Navy hero Jonathan Thorn, but also an overland party, led by Wilson Price Hunt, which he intended should follow the trail blazed by the expedition of William Clark and Meriwether Lewis six years earlier.

The *Tonquin* reached the mouth of the Columbia well ahead of the overland party, on March 22, 1811, and Captain Thorn wasted little time in searching for a way past the imposing—actually terrifying on that day—barrier of the bar. With a gale building out of the northwest, the line of breakers stretching from Cape Disappointment to Point Adams was six feet high. Neither Thorn nor any of his crew or passengers had seen anything like the collision of current and tide at the Columbia's mouth. It looked to them like enormous watery cymbals clashing again and again. The roar was deafening.

It may well be that Thorn, based on what little had been written about the Columbia Bar at this time, imagined such conditions were a constant at the mouth of the river. Or perhaps he did not understand how much more problematic an ebb tide was for an entrance into the Columbia. Whatever it was he believed, Thorn was not willing to risk his ship without first sending a boat to explore the bar ahead of the *Tonquin*. To this forbidding task, Thorn assigned his first mate, J. C.

Fox, and a crew of three other men, ordering them to launch in the *Tonquin*'s whaleboat.

Most of what we know about the whaleboat's fate comes from the recollections of two clerks aboard the *Tonquin*, Alexander Ross and Gabriel Franchere. Ross's account is most severe in its judgment of Thorn, asserting that the captain sent Fox and his crew into the booming sea even as the mate pleaded for their lives. According to both Ross and the Scottish partner Duncan McDougall, Thorn's reply was, "Mr. Fox, if you are afraid of water, you should have remained at Boston." After McDougall and the other Scottish partners provided a bedsheet to use as a sail, Fox ordered his men to lower the boat, telling those he left behind on the *Tonquin* that he knew he would not see them again.

By Ross's account, those aboard the *Tonquin* saw the whaleboat being tossed and turned by the "foaming surges" at almost the moment it entered the Columbia Bar. The boat was not even a hundred yards from the ship, Ross remembered, when they began to lose sight of it in the huge swells. The last glimpse they got of the "utterly unmanageable" whaleboat, Ross wrote, was of it being hurled up a soaring wave crest, then plummeting into the deep trough below. Neither the boat nor the men aboard it were ever seen again.

The *Tonquin* spent all the next day, March 23, searching for the men aboard the missing whaleboat. With the approach of evening, Thorn ordered the ship withdrawn to a safe distance from the bar, "the crew all with long faces," as Franchere described it, "even the Captain looking worried."

The wind fell off early the following day, March 24, however, and Thorn decided to probe the Columbia's mouth with a second small vessel, the *Tonquin*'s longboat, under the command of his second mate, William Mumford, with a crew that included two of the Scottish partners and several clerks, among them Alexander Ross. The longboat had barely gotten onto the bar, though, when the unrelenting chain of breakers "completely overpowered us with dread," as Ross recalled it, "and the fearful suction became so fearfully great that, before we were aware of it, the boat was drawn into them."

The men aboard the longboat spotted a group of Natives watching them from atop Cape Disappointment, signaling with their hands to row around the cape rather than try to take a direct line to shore. Seeing the waves breaking in huge rises of white water on the reef at the front of the cape, however, the terrified Mumford (according to Ross) shouted to his crew, "Let us turn back and pull for our lives! Pull hard, or you are all dead men!" They spent twelve minutes caught "between hope and despair," Ross recounted, being battered from side to side but making no forward progress at all, until at last the longboat's oars seemed to catch water and they pulled free of the breakers, able finally to row back to the ship.

The wind was even stiller and the sea much calmer on the morning of March 25. Thorn ordered Mumford to launch the longboat a second time and sound for a passage across the bar. Mumford was able to find a depth of five fathoms (thirty feet) but went no further than halfway across the bar before retreating again to the ship.

Frustrated to the point of infuriation, Thorn called on his most able seaman, third mate Job Aiken, to try the bar in the *Tonquin*'s jolly boat with a crew that included armorer Stephen Weeks, sailmaker John Coles, and two of the twenty-four Hawaiians aboard the *Tonquin*, a group dispatched to the ship's crew by the king of the Big Island,

Kamehameha. Aiken was instructed to enter the bar with a sounding line (then simply a rope with a lead weight attached to it) and to raise a flag if he found more than three fathoms of water.

Under Aiken, the jolly boat proceeded quickly through the breakers into the bar, and only minutes later Thorn and his men aboard the *Tonquin* saw the flag raised. The captain immediately ordered the ship's anchor lifted and proceeded under sail in the direction of the waving flag. A favorable wind stretched the sheets, and the *Tonquin* swept smoothly onto the bar. At that moment, the jolly boat turned and the men at oars stroked toward the approaching ship.

Accounts differ about what happened next. According to Gabriel Franchere, "We came within pistol range of the [jolly boat] and made a signal to them to come aboard, which they were unable to do, the suction of the ebbing tide carrying them away at incredible speed." The partner McDougall, who kept the ship's official log, wrote that the *Tonquin* began to drift swiftly southward after the jolly boat launched, and that Thorn countered by quickly making sail, straight for the bar. The captain "either forgot or neglected to make a signal for their return," McDougall wrote, and "by the time the Ship got abreast of them the ebb tide was making so strong ahead that we could not take them on board without heaving to or standing out to sea again." So Thorn "left them to their fate," as McDougall put it, over the protests of himself and the other partners.

Alexander Ross would insist that neither the ebb tide nor bad timing had doomed the men aboard the jolly boat, but only Captain Thorn's heartless indifference. The jolly boat had made it back across the breakers and was in calm water, Ross said, when the *Tonquin* passed it by. "Everyone now called out, 'The boat, the boat!'" Ross recounted, and all were astonished by the captain's cool reply: "I can give them no assistance."

Ross speculated that "the mind of the captain was so absorbed in apprehension, and perplexed with anxiety at the danger which stared him in the face, and which he was about to encounter, that he could not be brought to give a thought to anything else but the safety of the ship."

Even Ross would agree that the *Tonquin* was in trouble well before it completed its passage across the bar, colliding with several shoals and reefs, then tipping onto one side as waves poured over the deck. "Everyone who could, sprang aloft, and clung for life to the rigging," Ross wrote. The *Tonquin* struck against sandbars "again and again," Ross recalled, "and, regardless of her helm, was tossed and whirled in every direction."

Thorn wanted to sail out of the tempest, but all at once the wind died and the sails flapped, leaving the *Tonquin* at the mercy of surf that was battering the ship straight toward the rocks at the foot of Cape Disappointment. According to Ross, someone shouted, "We are all lost! The ship is among the rocks!" Thorn ordered that two anchors be thrown over the side to hold against the ebb tide. The anchors did not stop the ship, however, but merely slowed it, dragging on the sandy bottom as the tide pushed the *Tonquin* steadily closer to the cape.

All aboard believed the ship was certain to be broken up on the rocks, according to Ross, and, by Franchere's account, "darkness soon fell to add to the horrors of our predicament."

The drag of the anchors, though, was just enough to keep the ship from striking against the rocks beneath the cape until the tide turned and began to pull them in the opposite direction. Thorn ordered the anchors raised. Then, almost at once, according to both Ross and Franchere, a breeze rose up off the sea and the ship was able to sail into the shelter of Baker Bay, where the crew dropped anchors again just before midnight.

The next morning, March 26, Thorn was rowed to shore in the longboat by a crew that included Ross. The captain's plan was to climb to the summit of Cape Disappointment, which all agreed looked by the light of day like a smaller version of Gibraltar, and to examine the surrounding sea from there. "We had not proceeded fifty yards," remembered Ross, "when we saw Stephen Weeks, the armorer, standing under the shelter of a rock, shivering and half-dead with cold." According to Franchere, Weeks was stark naked. Ross recounted only that Weeks was so spent that he lacked the strength even to speak. They rowed the armorer back to the *Tonquin* and warmed him with food and blankets. Finally Weeks began to talk, but was "so overpowered with grief and vexation" that his words were incomprehensible, Ross remembered.

It took an hour to coax the story of what had happened to the jolly boat out of Weeks. After the *Tonquin* had passed them by, Weeks said, Job Aiken ordered his crew to escape the pummeling of the bar by rowing out to sea. The boat had barely moved, though, when a cresting wave struck it amidships and knocked the vessel onto its side. Aiken and the sailmaker, Coles, were washed overboard and disappeared. Weeks managed to grab hold of an oar as a floatation device. Clinging to the oar, head barely above water, he was able to watch as the two Hawaiians (known to the Americans, who found their true names unpronounceable, as Harry and Peter) lived up to their reputations as great swimmers and at the same time demonstrated their immense strength. The Hawaiians not only were able to right the boat, Weeks said, but had managed then to splash most of the water out of it by rocking the vessel back and forth as they swam alongside it. After they climbed in over the gunwales, Harry and Peter spotted him clinging to the oar, Weeks said, and somehow moved the boat close enough to bring him aboard. The Hawaiians, though, who had grown up swimming in an ocean that was on average almost eighty degrees Fahrenheit, were rapidly going into shock after their immersion in water that was barely more than fifty degrees. Already their hands were too numb to get a grip on him, the armorer said, so the two had used their teeth to lift him by his clothing out of the ocean and into the boat.

Peter by then was so far gone that he seemed all at once to give up, Weeks told the others. The Hawaiian lay down in the bottom of the boat and closed his eyes, as if preparing to die. Harry could only sit and shiver, leaving Weeks alone with the two remaining oars He began to row, and he kept at it, the armorer said, to avoid being pulled back into the breakers, yes, but mainly as a way to maintain his body heat. He never for a moment stopped pulling the oars, Weeks told his shipmates, even when Peter died around midnight. For reasons he did not understand, Weeks said, Harry chose that moment to lay down on top of his friend.

After hours of rowing in the dark, Weeks said, the jolly boat was thrown up onto the beach beneath the cape. He managed to climb out of the boat and to pull Harry onto the sand, and then to the edge of the forest, where "covering him with leaves I left him to die," Weeks explained.

Harry, though, had lived. The crew of the *Tonquin* found the Hawaiian less than an hour later where Weeks had left him. Harry had swollen legs and bleeding feet, and he was unconscious, but still breathing. The men warmed him in front of a huge bonfire and then carried him back to the *Tonquin* when he came to.

While the bodies of Aiken and Cole were never recovered, Peter's corpse was found still lying in the bottom of the jolly boat.

The twenty-three remaining Hawaiians staged a burial ceremony for Peter on the beach beneath Cape Disappointment the next day. Sea biscuit and pork were placed under the dead man's arms, and tobacco beneath his genitals, to nourish and comfort him during his journey to the afterlife. The Hawaiians prayed and chanted. The solemn Americans observed silently and did the grim math of their circumstances: two boats and eight lives had been lost to achieve the *Tonquin's* first crossing of the Columbia Bar. But the rest of them were still alive, and now John Jacob Astor had his trading post at the mouth of the great river.

THE STORY OF THE *TONQUIN'S* BAR CROSSING had been reverberating in my memory since the moment Ray, Kenny, and I had arrived at the Cape Disappointment Park boat ramp. I was fairly certain that from our launch point we were looking out on the exact spot where the *Tonquin* had been anchored 210 years earlier. Moreover, I had a sense from what I'd read that just minutes later we were a stone's throw from the spot where the Hawaiians had held their burial ceremony for Peter. On our voyage toward the Columbia's mouth, we were already almost certainly passing over some of the precise longitudinal and latitudinal axes that the *Tonquin* had sailed through after it crossed the bar. The shoreline had been reconfigured by the jetties, as had the river bottom, but Cape Disappointment was almost exactly what it had been back in 1811. I would feel ridiculous writing that the cape had "borne witness" to the events of that time, yet I knew that for me there was nothing that established a connection to history like geography. Knowing what had happened in a place and then being there was what most made it real to me, gave me a sense of relationship to distant events. And in some way—I didn't know what or how—being here on this water increased my wish to honor the eight men who'd died here in March of 1811.

A few weeks earlier, when I'd told Ray something like this, he'd suggested dryly that step one was surviving. Yes, I'd agreed, that was the right place to start.

Still, remembering all the details that I could of the *Tonquin*'s bar crossing, heartrending as they were, filled me with an almost tonic calm as the trimaran moved across the rolling surface of the Columbia. Our chances on this day were so much better than theirs had been back then. We knew things they had no way of knowing, especially about optimal conditions for a trip like this one, about picking the right day and the right time of day, and so forth.

Nothing had made me more convinced that I should wear a dry-suit on the day of our bar crossing than reading accounts of how the Hawaiian that the crew of the *Tonquin* called Peter had suffered and died on the ocean just outside the mouth of the Columbia. I hadn't previously considered the precise rate of hypothermia caused by cold water. Where the ocean is below sixty degrees Fahrenheit—as we could expect, even in July—the core temperature of an unprotected person drops by about one-tenth of a degree per minute, meaning it would take only a little more than an hour to lose the use of one's extremities and just about two hours to arrive at a core temperature of eighty-six degrees, the point at which nearly everyone loses consciousness. I couldn't find solid assurances of survival times in anything I read, but it was clear that the drysuits Ray and I were wearing would at least double the time we could stay alive in the water if our boat capsized.

I wouldn't have described that knowledge as comforting, exactly, but as my father liked to say of growing old, "It beats the alternative."

CHAPTER FIVE

I HAD GROWN UP LISTENING to my father's tales of his seagoing days. For me, they were the best part of him. He was always entertaining, rarely menacing when he spoke of those ten years of his life, between the ages of seventeen and twenty-seven. It only registered with me decades later how many of those rollicking tales were about violence, violence endured and violence inflicted. He was grinning, and so was I, as he reminisced about the big-necked guy from Montana, a shipmate who trained by lifting bags of grain, three of them, one in each hand and the other clenched between his teeth. That third bag, the one between his teeth, was what had made the Montanan so formidable, resulting as it did in not only a neck as thick as a tree trunk but also a jaw like an iron anvil. My father chuckled as he described how the two of them, he and the big-necked guy from Montana, had wiped the floor of a bar in Singapore with an entire US Navy crew, miming the expressions of the sailors as they shattered their fists on the big-necked guy's chin and the smile of the Montanan as the Navy guys stood stupefied, looking at their broken hands.

My dad made even the roughest events sound like rousing adventures, as when he described, for instance, being jumped at age twenty by a Filipino gang outside a bar in Manila, smashed in the face with a magnum of champagne that broke his nose, cheek bone, and eye socket, then stabbed repeatedly on one side of his belly with what he called a "penknife." He recuperated for two weeks in a hotel nearby, treating himself with wet washcloths and black-market penicillin, forced to stay behind when his ship left port without him, staying on in Manila in the hope the next Merchant Marine vessel would take him aboard. I was mightily impressed as I studied the small, faded scars under the left side of his ribcage.

My father truly was a tough guy. The first fight between adults I ever saw was at age seven, when my dad took me to the Jones Stevedores locker to help me weld together a sculpture I'd made out of tin cans and wire hangers for a school art contest. I won several art prizes as an elementary student, and at that time this made me feel more embarrassed than proud. To be an "artist" simply didn't compute where I was coming from; art was something only girls were good at, as I understood it, and not in the least a manly activity. I remember my dad shaking his head and wincing slightly when he came home from work and my mother displayed some framed award I'd been presented at a school assembly. I did love to draw and paint and make things, though, and was excited that my dad had brought me to the Jones locker to help me finish up my latest project, thrilled that he wanted to do something like this with me. The two of us were standing at a workbench when a man I remember only as younger and larger than my father stepped up behind us and began to make what I just vaguely understood to be insulting remarks. The man started to talk about my mother, whom he'd seen out with my father. I wouldn't have recognized a sexual innuendo at that age, but I recall feeling that something wrong was happening, that this big guy was mean and nasty and dangerous, and was trying to start a fight with my dad by saying bad things about my mom. My father said not a word. He just turned and listened for a few moments, then reared back. My memory is probably exaggerated—I was only seven—but it seemed to me my father went so far back on his right heel that his knuckles nearly touched the floor before lunging forward to land his fist right in the center of the big man's jaw. The guy went down like a felled tree, unconscious even before he flopped onto his back on the cement floor. It was the most awesome, terrifying event I'd ever witnessed, and I'm pretty sure the several grown men who were in the locker with us felt similarly.

My dad pulled me out of the locker a moment later, my sculpture only half complete. Next to him in the front seat of his pickup truck, I started to cry, upset by what had happened and that we were leaving with my work unfinished. My father reached over to cuff me behind one ear, told me to "dummy up," then drove home without another word, quaking with rage the entire time.

He had a streak of sadism in him that was melded somehow to his machismo. The first time he ever took me down to the waterfront to bring a ship into port, I remember walking along the edge of the dock amazed and frightened by how far down it was to the deep green water of Coos Bay. I was staggered by the thickness of the ropes the longshoremen were using to tie the big ship off, feeling small and helpless among all these rough men with their calloused hands and coarse language. All of a sudden my father swept me off my feet and spun me out over the edge of the dock, thirty feet above water that looked as if I could sink in it forever. He turned just that one revolution and then deposited me back on my feet on the dock, chortling at my white-faced panic. I can't imagine what he thought he was doing. I just know that he repeated pretty much the same maneuver the following summer when he taught me to swim by tossing me out of a boat in the middle of Loon Lake. I flailed and kicked and thrashed my way back to the side of the boat in sheer terror before my father pulled me out of the water, wearing a satisfied expression. When I reminded him of this event years later, my dad told me, "Well of course I'd have jumped in to save you if I had to." No doubt, but I didn't believe that at all back then, when for me it had been the purest sink-or-swim experience of my life.

I struggled even as a young boy to understand how my father could be such a genuine he-man and at the same time such a bully, a bully to me and to my two younger brothers. Those two aspects didn't fit together in my mind, and even now, so many years later, I was still trying to sort it out.

He'd left to go to sea halfway through his senior year of high school. It was early 1944, about five months before the D-Day Invasion. American soldiers were fighting in Italy and on the Marshall Islands in the South Pacific. The US was just about to launch its first Victory ship, delivered by the Oregon Shipbuilding Corporation in Portland. These were huge cargo carriers manned mostly by Merchant Marines, intended at first to move military supplies, then later in many cases made over into transport ships to bring the troops home. Apprentice Seaman Grade Seven Howard Sullivan got most of his training on the job, having been rushed through the Cadet Corps along with thousands of others to fill the depleted ranks. Seven hundred thirty-three Merchant Marine ships were sunk during World War II, and the 9,521 men who perished were the highest proportion of casualties in any US military service.

I don't recall him ever saying he'd gone to sea to get in on the action. It was to get off the farm, though he made that sound more his parents' idea than his own. Just months earlier, he'd hoped to go to college; his high school football coach had written a letter to an old friend who was on the staff at the University of Southern California to say he had one helluva fullback up north at Dos Palos High School, and it looked like he was going to get a tryout, my dad recalled. The family was in desperate straits at the time, however, in real danger of losing the 220 acres they had worked as sharecroppers to acquire after moving from Oklahoma to the San Joaquin Valley in the mid-1930s. So it was agreed that Howard, the oldest of the four children, would join the Maritime Service and send home half his paycheck each month. My father told this part of his story in different tones at different times, occasionally with pride that he'd taken on such adult responsibility as a teenage boy, but more often as further evidence of how little importance his parents had placed on him other than in terms of what he could contribute to the family coffers. He'd grown up valued mainly as a farm animal, my father believed, up at four a.m. to milk cows, shoveling shit in the barn or forking hay in the field until after dark, an Okie child of Okie parents in a world of Okie hurt, even if he did spend the second half of his childhood in California. This was what fed the bitterness in his heart as it ate him away from the inside out, and that for some reason he would want me to suffer for as much as he did.

At sea, though, as a young man, he found his way. Having become a Merchant Marine so late in the war, he was in relatively little danger. The battle for the Atlantic Ocean had long ago been won, and no US cargo ships were sunk by U-boats in 1944 or 1945, while just two were destroyed in the Pacific theater by kamikaze attacks. He saw the machine gun mounted on the first ship he went aboard used just once, my father told me, when the Navy gunners who operated it used a whale for target practice. After the war, he saw the world and enjoyed many adventures, from hunting Kodiak bear off the southwest coast of Alaska to becoming infatuated with a Chilean prostitute in Santiago.

I loved hearing his stories, even after I had begun to hate him, and wished many times I'd known the young man he remembered himself to be. His capacity for hard work and the quickness with which he learned resulted in steady advancement through the ranks of the Merchant Marine. He was a chief mate at twenty-six and all but certain to soon become the only American ship's captain under thirty. But it was not to be.

At twenty-two, he'd fallen in love with a beautiful girl he met in Sydney, Australia, where they married, then carried her off to the United States. My mother told me that all she knew about my father's family was that they owned a "ranch" in California. But it was hardly her idea of a ranch when she finally saw it; the only livestock were dairy cows. And my grandparents had sold that land anyway shortly after my parents married, using the money to buy a pair of motels in Phoenix, Arizona. The story I heard was that my grandmother was unable to say no to anybody who had a hard luck story, especially if they came from Oklahoma. Word got around and before long both motels were filled with nonpaying guests. I wonder if it was that simple, but one way or another my father's parents lost the motels and moved with a couple who had been living in one of them to Coos Bay, Oregon, in 1951, while my mother was pregnant with me.

My father had stopped sending his parents part of his paycheck after they sold their California land and bought the Phoenix proper- ties. When my grandparents were forced to unload the motels at a loss, however, their situation became more tenuous than ever. Then my grandmother began, at age forty-four, to die of breast cancer.

My mother grimly remembered agreeing that it would be necessary to relocate from Los Angeles, which she loved, to Coos Bay, which she hated. She was the prettiest woman in that small town on the Oregon Coast from the day she arrived, and way too overdressed, in the opinion of those who ridiculed her Aussie accent and accused her of giving their husbands ideas. The only good friend she could ever make there was a redhead named Frances who starred in all the local theater productions, wore low-cut dresses, and was dismissed as a "floozy" by the same women who so resented my mother.

She made one mistake even worse than agreeing to move to Coos Bay, my mother told me, and that was agreeing to live with her husband's family. It was a crowded house. My father's youngest sister was still in high school, unhappy about where she was and how she'd got there. His famously voluptuous older sister had run off to New York with some charmer who, in a fit of drunken, jealous rage, had shaved her head and sent her home, where she pushed to the front of the line of local women who found my mother offensively attractive. Both my aunts doted on me, but nothing like the way my grandmother did, a dying woman pouring out all the love left in her on her first grandchild, a love she'd never been able to give her oldest son. When he came home and saw that, it was one more source of hurt for him, the beginning, I think, of his resentment of me.

At least I wasn't all he resented. His younger brother, the one who'd stayed home while he went off to sea, had gotten that college football scholarship my father had dreamed of, and in fact made third team All American. Now he was in graduate school, working hard to pay his own way, but sending not a cent to the house in Coos Bay where my father paid the rent, even though he was only there two or three months of the year.

My mother wanted him home more, wanted not to be left to fend for herself in a house where her husband's dying mother was teaching me to call her "Mommy." She made him give up going to sea, a decision she realized later in life had been bad for them both. As a ship's captain, he might have been home for only a few months out of the year, but there's a good chance it would have been a happy few months. Or perhaps that's wishful thinking. All I know for certain is that he felt profoundly aggrieved by being made to give up his future as the master of his own ship, and brooded about what might have been for the next two decades. That brooding grew darker the more he drank, and he drank a lot. And then, invariably, he would release his discontent in an explosion of violence. All too often, it exploded on me.

My grandmother had protected me for as long as she was able. A story I heard from my aunt, later confirmed by my mother, was that when I was two and a half my dad made the mistake of giving me a smack in my grandma's presence. She had sprung to her feet, slapped him hard across the cheek, and warned, "Don't you ever touch that child like that again." My father, cowed by a woman who was six months from dying at age forty-six, surrendered me into her arms without a word.

I was just three and a half when she died, and utterly unable to accept or understand what that meant until my mother, to her immense regret, led me into the back of the funeral home to see my grandmother's body in her white wicker burial casket. My response was to stop speaking for three days.

I was a precocious child who had started walking at seven months and talking shortly after turning a year old, voluble and sweet-natured, according to my mother, but "your personality changed after that," she said. A second event a short time later, she believed, pushed me even deeper into myself. Four months after my grandmother's death, my brother Brady was born. My mother had become seriously ill with septicemia immediately upon giving birth, so I was sent away for two weeks to stay with my grandmother's closest friend while my mother recuperated and took care of her new infant. I have no memory of that time, just that I was terrified of the woman's husband for the rest of my childhood. The main thing, though, was that I apparently believed I had been traded in for a new baby and this devastated me. When I finally came home, my mother recalled getting down on one knee to hug me, and being answered with a slap on the face. My father responded by giving me the first whipping with a belt I'd ever received. This time I stopped talking for an entire week.

The whippings from my dad continued, month after month, year after year. My mother apologized many times during the last years of her life for not stopping them, defending herself mainly by explaining that she was still an "alien" in the United States back then, in a time when a married woman couldn't even open a bank account without her husband's name on it, and feared she would lose me altogether if she tried to take me out of the country back to Australia. That's part of the truth, I'm sure.

What I remember best about all of that is the realization that struck me at about age six, when time slowed down during and immediately after one of the beatings I got from my dad. It had happened more or less the way it always did, with some offense I'd committed resulting in an explosion of his rage that was far out of proportion. I'd see his eyes go snake-flat, then a snarl begin to curl his lips, and knew I was in for it. But on this occasion, as I lay sobbing afterward I was struck by the clear recognition that he hadn't been giving me these beatings "for my own good," as people said

85

back then, but simply as a way to vent his bottled-up fury. He had actually hated me in those moments. This thought was so dreadful that the agony it caused is still with me. And that was when I began to hate my father back.

Yet I still loved and needed him. It took me many years to find someone who put resonant words to the impossibly complex nature of what Ray and I and so many others are stuck with—the deep emotional bond we feel to the men who abused us. In the preface to his book *I Don't Want to Talk About It*, the family therapist Terrance Real wrote of his own father: "His violence should have pushed me away from him, and consciously it did. But in some more primitive way it only drew me closer. As he raged, out of control, even as he beat me, I never lost touch with him."

Neither did I lose touch with my father, and our closest point of contact was me listening to stories of his days as a seaman. What they provided was something like tangible evidence that he had been, and so perhaps still could be, a better man, one who was funny and free and far from the agonies he knew ashore.

He also liked to follow whatever was in the news about the maritime world, and would occasionally read me part or all of some article about a wreck or a rescue of a ship at sea. One in particular stands out, because it was so close to home. I was in the third grade in January of 1961, just days before John F. Kennedy would be inaugurated as US president, when suddenly my father and most of the other adults I knew seemed consumed by something that had happened north on the coast at a place called the Columbia Bar. I understood that three boats had been sunk and that seven men had died in the course of a Coast Guard rescue mission, but not much more. My father collected every bit of information about it he could on the waterfront and wanted to share it when he got home, soon exhausting my mother's interest and leaving only me to hear him describe, among other things, his own near brush with death on the Columbia Bar as a young merchant marine. It's one more tender reminder of how deeply I craved connection with him that I listened so attentively.

As I prepared with Ray for our own trip across the bar, I began to research whatever it was that had happened there back in early 1961, going so deep into the cascade of catastrophe that I became, I daresay, the world's leading living authority on those events. Curiously, even perhaps ironically, the main lesson my newly acquired knowledge imparted was one I could have understood as a boy: Even the right day can be wrong.

JANUARY 12, 1961, HAD BEGUN as a fine day for crossing the Columbia Bar. At noon, the forecast from the Coast Guard's floating beacon, the *Columbia* "lightship" (a 128-foot vessel mounted with a 15,000-candlepower lantern), from its position five miles outside the entrance to the bar was of waves six feet high and a southwest wind steady at eight to twelve miles per hour. Fishing boats and freighters had been making their way out of the river into the ocean without difficulty all morning.

By the time the thirty-eight-foot crab boat *Mermaid* set out from its moorage at three that afternoon, the winds had picked up considerably, with gusts up to forty miles per hour. Sea waves were now ten to twelve feet. "Rough but passable" was how the National Weather Service described conditions on the bar. A small craft advisory had been issued, but the Weather Service was already planning to call it off at 5:00 p.m. It didn't look that bad out there.

The two brothers who worked the *Mermaid*, thirty-year-old Bert Bergman and his twenty-seven-year-old brother, Stan, undoubtedly felt they had little choice but to go out that afternoon. Crabbers suffer a short season during the year's worst weather. On the Oregon coast, harvesting Dungeness crabs is legal into the summer. It's just that crabs are not only more plentiful but both meatier and tastier if taken in fall or winter. Good restaurants would rather serve crabmeat frozen in January than caught fresh in June, and will pay a heftier price for it. Commercial crabbing on the Oregon coast is almost never permitted before December, and in years when the state delays the start of crab season to January, the taverns in Astoria echo with the bitter complaints of men who wonder how they'll buy their kids Christmas presents.

Dungeness crabs look, like most crustaceans, as if they might be some prehistoric insect: five sets of whitened legs extend from a purple carapace that is on average about eight inches wide, with large claws on the front legs that are used both as weapons and for tearing apart food. They like to live in beds of eelgrass on the ocean floor and are caught commercially in heavy iron baskets covered with wire mesh that are called "pots." Commercial crab pots are heavy and must be dropped onto and lifted off of the sea bottom with hoists. The bait inside the pot is generally some sort of meat, poultry, or fish; salmon heads and frozen chicken wings are favorites. Crabs crawl into the pot for the bait and can't get back out. The pots are expensive, and crabbers can't afford to lose many of them. And crabbers *will* lose their pots if they leave them in the ocean long, especially in a stormy sea that can cause pots to quickly become "sanded in," that is, buried so deep into the wet silt on the sea bottom that even the sturdiest winch can't pull them out of the ocean. The Bergman brothers were facing just such a predicament that afternoon.

It was almost exactly 4:15 p.m., about an hour after the *Mermaid* had launched, when a call came into the Cape Disappointment Coast Guard station that the crab boat's rudder had broken and that the *Mermaid* was, as the Coast Guard log put it, "drifting in dangerously breaking surf" on the Columbia Bar. The call was made by another crabber, Roy Gunnari, captain of the *Jana Jo*, who was coming in off the ocean because of concern about the worsening weather.

The officer in charge of Station Cape Disappointment, Boatswain's Mate Doyle Porter, was visiting his wife at the nearby hospital, where she had just delivered their baby. That left a twenty-six-year-old petty officer named Darrell Murray in charge at "Cape D," as the Coasties called the station then, and still do. Murray decided to dispatch two Coast Guard boats: a thirty-six-footer designed for sea rescues and a forty-foot utility boat that was not nearly as floatable in heavy surf but considerably speedier running flat out. Murray took the helm of the forty-footer with a crew of two others, and gave a barely qualified coxswain named Larry Edwards charge of the thirty-six-footer, also with a crew of two more men aboard.

Murray's thinking was that he could reach the *Mermaid* first in the forty-footer, help get it out of the breakers, then turn over the tow to the thirty-six-footer that was designed for such missions. This might have worked out better if not for the delays. The *Mermaid* was unable to communicate directly on the Coast Guard's frequency, so everything had to be passed back and forth through the *Jana Jo*'s skipper, Gunnari. How much time this cost, Murray couldn't say for certain, but at least half an hour.

After he had crossed the bar, Murray steered the forty-footer to the vicinity of Buoy No. 7, where the *Jana Jo* had last reported seeing the *Mermaid*. But the crab boat was nowhere in sight. It was growing dark fast, and that, combined with the wind-driven spray off the high waves, reduced visibility to nearly nothing.

Gunnari used the sounding lines from the *Jana Jo*'s navigating system to conclude that the *Mermaid* had drifted out across the bar to the northwest of Peacock Spit. Steering the forty-footer in that direction, Murray was able finally to get Bert and Stan Bergman on the Coast Guard's 2,183-kilocycle frequency. He told the brothers to turn their spotlight on the clouds overhead, and when they did, he saw the *Mermaid*'s location immediately. The crab boat was now well north of the bar. When Murray reached the *Mermaid*, he conferred with the Bergmans at close range, trying to convince them to come aboard his boat for safety. The Bergmans, though, refused. They were convinced, correctly, that Murray intended to let the *Mermaid* drift until it either sank or washed up on the beach. The boat was their livelihood, with every penny the brothers had tied up in it, and they could not accept its abandonment. Though his own boat was not designed for such a job, Murray agreed to take the *Mermaid* in tow with the brothers still aboard and try pulling it to the lightship. A line with a steel pendant at one end was passed and the tow got underway at almost exactly 5:00 p.m.

The thirty-six-foot rescue boat that had been dispatched from Cape D along with Murray's boat was intended to make up in buoyancy what it lacked in speed. Neither the *Mermaid* nor the forty-footer were anywhere to be seen when the thirty-six-footer arrived at the entrance to the bar, Edwards reported from the helm of the rescue boat. The young coxswain was already dealing with a communications issue created by a weak radio signal that filled the air with static, and his boat had been swamped by a series of huge swells as it crossed the bar, taking aboard hundreds of gallons of spray and green water by the time it passed out of the river into the sea.

Edwards and his crew spotted the lights of Murray's forty-footer and the *Mermaid* soon after they had crossed the bar, and accompanied the other two boats to Buoy No. 1, which marked the outside of the North Channel. The radio static was so bad by now that Edwards could barely hear Murray speaking to him from a short distance away. He sent one of his crewmen to check and learned the radio's antenna was broken. Edwards went to inspect his boat's stern compartment himself, and was alarmed by the amount of water sluicing around inside it. He suspected the pounding breakers on the bar had opened a seam in the boat's rear end. He reported the situation to Station Cape Disappointment, where Doyle Porter, having returned from the hospital, advised him and his boat to stand by.

With reports of waves approaching thirty feet on the bar, Porter decided that neither the forty-footer under Murray's command nor Edwards's damaged rescue boat was capable of towing the *Mermaid* to the lightship. He called Station Point Adams to request that they dispatch the biggest and best boat under Coast Guard command on the Columbia, the fifty-two-foot *Triumph*. Self-bailing and supposedly self-righting, with a 205-horsepower diesel engine, the *Triumph* had been involved in more major rescue operations than any other vessel on the bar. Warren Berto, the commander of Station Point Adams, sent the fifty-two-footer out under the command of John Lee Culp, a thirty-one-year-old petty officer he considered the most capable coxswain currently working on the Columbia Bar. Culp was given a crew of five that included one last-minute volunteer, a twenty-one-year-old and relatively inexperienced engineman named Gordon Huggins, who, though about to go off shift, had convinced the senior engineman assigned to the *Triumph* to let him take the veteran's place aboard the fifty-two-footer.

The *Triumph* got underway at five after five, but by then conditions had deteriorated even further. The wind was gusting up to sixty miles per hour, and even on the inside of the Columbia Bar the swells were huge. Pushing against gale and tide, the *Triumph* needed more than two hours to get from Point Adams and across the bar to Buoy No. 1. It was seven thirty in full dark by the time the fifty-two-footer took over the tow of the *Mermaid*, passing a four-inch manila hawser line that the Bergmans secured by tying it to their boat's bow rail.

Berto, at Station Point Adams, and Culp, at the helm of the *Triumph*, exchanged a series of radio communications about the conditions on the bar. Towering swells were breaking across most of the North Channel by then, and the wind was steady at about forty miles per hour out of the southwest. Berto got the impression Culp had decided he should tow the *Mermaid* out to the lightship, but Culp instead determined that the turning tide made taking the crab boat in over the bar a better bet and proceeded in that direction.

By this point, Station Cape Disappointment had lost much of its ability to communicate with either of the boats dispatched from there. The broken antenna on Edwards's boat filled the air with ear-piercing shrieks when any transmission was attempted. The radio equipment on Murray's boat, meanwhile, was so soaked with seawater that it became inoperative, requiring manual keying of messages. Only by such laborious and time-consuming transmissions were the forty-footer and the thirty-six-footer able to decide jointly that it would be best to "ease up to the bar, observe conditions, then decide whether to cross," as Murray recalled it, or turn back and make for the lightship.

The *Triumph* was not far away as it moved in toward the bar, but the darkness and increasingly thick curtain of spray made it impossible to remain in visual contact with the two smaller boats.

Going mostly on feel, Murray decided conditions on the bar were rough but navigable and steered his boat into the breakers. One of Murray's two men, Acie Maxwell, was standing outside the cabin at the control station with his lifejacket on. The Coast Guard was still using World War II vintage kapok lifejackets. These were excellent for floatation, but in the enormously turbid waters of the Columbia Bar they needed to be not only secured around the torso but also buckled to the thighs, or run the risk that the lifejacket would be stripped off a man who had gone overboard. The kapok jackets were so bulky, though, that a man wearing one over full foul weather gear found it almost impossible to work in close quarters. For this reason, neither Murray, at the helm, nor his second crewman, Terrance Lowe, who was inside the cabin working the radio, was wearing a lifejacket, though Murray had kept his close at hand.

The black buoys that marked the North Channel were stenciled with odd numbers, 3, 5, 7, and 9, while the red buoys that marked the South Channel were even numbered. Murray was approaching Buoy No. 7, in the middle of the bar, when the forty-footer was struck by three successive huge swells. "One of the weirdest breaks I've ever seen," he would say. "It was a piggyback. We started to broach on [the second] one, I got it straightened out, and the next thing I knew we were going up again." From the top of a wave that the captain of a passing freighter estimated at fifty feet high, Murray's boat was plunged almost straight down into a trough of foam.

The moment the big wave caught his stern, Murray shouted a warning and reached for his lifejacket. He managed to actually slip it on before the bow of the boat dug in and flipped the forty-footer.

Maxwell had been thrown clear as the boat capsized. Wearing his fully strapped lifejacket, he surfaced in the water and saw the forty-footer floating upside down right in front of him. He swam to the stern and climbed onto it, clinging to the propeller shaft.

Lowe, not wearing a lifejacket, was still inside the cabin of the capsized boat, immersed in flooding water. After a moment of disorientation, he found the exit door and worked his way out through it into the water of the bar, then surfaced just ten feet from the overturned forty-footer, close enough to swim to the stern and join Maxwell there, clinging to a blade on the propeller's opposite side.

Murray was the one in real trouble. Directly under the boat, fully submerged in water, his lifejacket had snagged on some metal projection he was unable to identify. After losing precious seconds in a struggle to pull the lifejacket free, Murray finally shrugged his way out of it and began to swim, ignoring what felt like a dislocation of his left shoulder. It was his good fortune that he chose the long way out and up, swimming nearly the entire length of the boat underwater before surfacing some thirty to forty feet astern. He had swallowed seawater and was coughing for air, thoroughly exhausted and without his lifejacket, but, after only a moment of despair, he spotted his boat's life raft floating just feet away. Made of canvas-wrapped balsa wood and painted Navy gray, these World War II–era rafts were impossible to steer but nearly unsinkable. After swimming the short distance to the raft, Murray couldn't pull himself in, so he simply clung to the side, paddling one-handed back toward the boat. He heard Lowe and Maxwell shouting to him and shouted back. But he was barely moving,

Murray remembered, until a breaker lifted the raft and carried him right to the stern of the boat. That the man would later describe his survival as "miraculous" is hardly surprising. Maxwell and Lowe pulled Murray out of the water and wrapped his arms around the one remaining propeller blade.

Edwards, still at the helm of the thirty-six-footer, had lost sight of the forty-footer, but had no idea Murray's boat was capsized. The young coxswain had pressing problems of his own to contend with. In addition to an inoperable radio, these now included a stern compartment that was half flooded, making the boat more and more sluggish in the water, as both rudder and engine began to slowly fail.

Edwards decided his best hope was to head for the lightship and had just begun to turn the thirty-six-footer in that direction when he saw the overturned forty-footer, and then the three men clinging to the propeller at the stern. He made one neat pass around the capsized boat that permitted his men to pull Maxwell aboard with a thrown line, then approached for a second pass just as a breaker caught him and heaved his boat into the overturned forty-footer. This opened a second gash in the rear of the thirty-six-footer, and the stern compartment began to flood even faster as Edwards's panicked crew threw lines toward the propeller of the capsized forty-footer. Murray would remember that they threw at least a dozen lines before he and Lowe each caught one and were pulled aboard the rescue boat.

Murray took the helm of the thirty-six-footer and began to steer it toward the lightship. He was so physically spent, though, that within seconds he had to surrender control of the boat back to Edwards. It was the decisions that the "non-rated" coxswain Edwards made during the next three hours that saved them all.

The key moment came when Edwards tried to throttle down in the face of an oncoming breaker and felt his engine falter. Knowing he could not risk doing this a second time, Edwards determined to go full throttle the rest of the way, pounding through one wall of water after another. His already-battered boat took a terrible beating, and so did the men on board, but the thirty-six-footer kept moving, even as its rear end sank steadily deeper.

More than an hour passed before Edwards's boat made it to the lightship, and by then the vessel's stern was awash, its rudder all but gone, and its engine room filled with water. Yet somehow Edwards managed to circle the lightship for another two hours, maneuvering to come alongside. He finally did, just in time for the lightship to drop the Jacob's ladder by which the six men on board the thirty-six-footer began to ascend. One of them was washed off the rope-and-wood ladder by a wave, then retrieved by the lightship's chief engineer. Another fell between the lightship and the sinking boat, only to be pulled out of the ocean by a lightship crewman whose legs were held by two other men. All six had made it aboard the lightship just before the thirty-six-footer broke its lines and sank in seconds.

The men on the *Triumph* would not be so fortunate. The fifty-two-footer's tow of the *Mermaid* had been hampered not only by the high winds and rough sea but also by the way its heavy rope was attached to the crab boat. Without the steel pendant Murray's forty-footer had used to secure its towline to the bow of the *Mermaid*, the four-inch nylon rope that the *Triumph* had sent to the crab boat was simply knotted to the *Mermaid*'s steel rail. The way the *Mermaid* listed from side to side in the surf not only slowed the tow but also began to create a sawing motion of the steel rail against the manila hawser.

For this situation, local historian Finn J. D. John would blame the faceless bureaucrat who had decided Coast Guard boats no longer needed to carry drogues aboard. Drogues were a special kind of sea anchor that could be used for steadying a boat in tow and, in Finn's estimation, would have enabled the *Triumph* to pull the *Mermaid* directly behind it, rather than allowing it to yaw to one side and take the sea on its beam.

The Bergmans no doubt would have liked to have a drogue aboard their boat; instead they strung a line of crab pots behind the *Mermaid* in an attempt to create the same sort of drag such an anchor might have provided. While a drogue would have helped, a towing bridle aboard either the *Mermaid* or the *Triumph* might have saved both boats, and the men aboard them. In the absence of that single metal piece, less than thirty minutes passed before the towline between the *Triumph* and the *Mermaid* parted. John Lee Culp and his crew were able to retrieve the hawser from the water and send it back to the *Mermaid*, where the Bergmans again secured it to the rail, only this time running the big rope through a rubber tire to prevent chafing.

This improvement only delayed the inevitable, and at almost exactly 8:30 p.m. Culp informed Point Adams station that the towline had parted again. The *Mermaid* was drifting into the breakers off Peacock Spit, Culp told the Coast Guard commanders at the Point Adams and Cape Disappointment stations: "I'm going in to get them."

These were the last words anyone who lived through that night ever heard from Culp. What happened next, like what had happened to Murray's forty-footer, was a product of the Columbia River Bar's extraordinary characteristics.

Waves that pulse in off the ocean tall and deep are compressed at the bottom as they hit the shallower water at the big river's mouth.

The Columbia's current then essentially pushes the bases of the waves backward, at the same time as the tops of the waves lunge forward even higher. During a storm at ebb tide like the one on the evening of January 12, 1961, such leveraged motion can generate shockingly huge breakers, some as high as sixty-five feet, with a heavy undertow beneath them. Should a breaker of that size and nature strike the stern of even the biggest boat at the right angle, it can raise the vessel's back end out of the water at the same time it drives the bow down toward the sandy bottom of the channel. This can result in what's known among sailors as a "pitchpole"—flipping a vessel end over end.

It happened to the *Triumph* just moments after John Lee Culp advised his Coast Guard commanders that he was "going in" after the *Mermaid*. Culp and three of the four men who were on the deck of the *Triumph* with him crashed upside down into the sea with their boat right on top of them. Only one man, Joseph Petrin, was thrown clear. He surfaced in the sea very near to the *Mermaid* and was pulled aboard by the stunned Bergman brothers.

The novice engineman, Huggins, was not on the deck, but down below in a watertight compartment. He understood what had just happened only when he found himself sitting on the engine room's overhead with the deck planking falling on him from above. The inexperienced man's first impulse was to move down the companionway and try to get out through the watertight door. As the Coast Guard's Board of Investigation's report would dryly observe, "Fortunately, he could not open it."

Huggins remembered the axe stored near the door, found it, and tried to chop his way out. His inability to do so again saved his life. The engine had stopped running and the lights all were out. Huggins sat for a time in the dark as the room he was in slowly filled with water. Then, all at once, he felt the boat begin to roll again. The fifty-two-footer was self-righting, as advertised, just not as promptly as promised.* In a matter of moments, Huggins found himself standing right side up again, as the water in the room ran down into the bilge. When he pushed on the companionway door this time, it fell off its hinges and he climbed out onto the deck.

After realizing everyone else was gone, Huggins thought about trying to drop the boat's anchor but realized he did not know how. The *Triumph* was down by the head, he noticed, and listing starboard. For an hour, Huggins, wearing a fully strapped lifejacket, simply sat and waited alone aboard the sinking ship.

Then the *Triumph* went into another steep roll and the young engineman was washed into the sea. The waves tossed him violently for a few moments, Huggins remembered, then, to his amazement, he felt his feet touch bottom. He was able to stagger, then crawl up out of the breakers onto the beach north of Cape Disappointment, where he lay face down, exhausted. Huggins recalled that after some time—he couldn't say how long—he saw lights, sat up, and began shouting.

He was the only member of the *Triumph*'s six-man crew who would survive the night.

At that moment, though, Joseph Petrin was still alive, aboard the *Mermaid* with the Bergmans, where all three of them had watched the *Triumph* tumble upside down into the Pacific Ocean. Petrin got Porter on the radio but was in such a state of shock, the Station Cape Disappointment commander said, that he could only get out, "Chief,

---

* The Coast Guard's investigative panel's report speculated that, most likely, the door to the forward compartment had come loose and allowed it to flood.

a big breaker hit us and the fifty-two-footer went down. I am the only one left."

Chief Berto, at the Point Adams station, had already dispatched two more thirty-six-foot rescue boats to the scene. The cutters *Yacona* and *Modoc* also set out for the bar from Astoria and Coos Bay, and two planes were dispatched from the Coast Guard air station at Port Angeles, Washington.

One of the two thirty-six-footers sent by Berto was diverted to pick up the most experienced coxswain in the region, John Webb, now serving as commander of the North Head Light Station. Webb had volunteered to take the helm of the rescue boat. The lifeboat driven by a coxswain named Paul Miller got to the *Mermaid* first, however, arriving at about 9:15 p.m. The bar was too rough to try to come in, Miller told Porter and Berto, or to take the three men on the *Mermaid* aboard his boat. So he would put the crab boat in tow and make for the lightship.

Now the fourth coxswain of the evening to attempt pulling the *Mermaid* to safety, Miller tried to avoid tearing the hawser by rigging his rope through the *Mermaid*'s starboard bow chock. The problem this created was a persistent veer to port that made it nearly impossible to maintain forward progress. Therefore, neither Miller's boat nor the *Mermaid* had moved much of a distance by a bit past 9:30 p.m., when both vessels were met by a wave estimated at between twenty-five and forty feet. The Coast Guard boat was rolled, but managed to ride over the top. The wave broke right on top of the *Mermaid*, however. Aboard the thirty-six-footer, the crew felt a jolt as the taut towline snapped. When they looked behind them, the crab boat was gone.

About three hundred yards away, Captain Kenneth McAlpin, who was trying to take the SS *Diaz de Solis* outbound across the bar, had been observing the towing operation from the ship's helm. He watched as the Coast Guard boat rode over the top of a huge swell that broke directly over the *Mermaid*, McAlpin recalled under questioning later, then saw the crab boat be thrown end over end and disappear from sight. He assumed, and so did the Coast Guard investigators who took his report, that the big wave had driven the *Mermaid* straight to the bottom.

McAlpin illuminated the area with his searchlights and maneuvered his ship to create a lee for Miller's lifeboat to search the area. No sign of the *Mermaid* or the three men aboard it was found. After fifteen minutes, the searchlights of the *Diaz de Solis* burned out, and McAlpin decided he could no longer justify the risk of remaining in the area. He steered his ship back across the bar and made rendezvous with the Columbia Bar Pilots vessel *Peacock*.

The *Yacona* and the thirty-six-footer helmed by Webb arrived on the scene moments later and joined Miller's boat in a search that went on until daylight, aided until first light by flares dropped out of the two planes sent from Port Angeles. As the Coast Guard's investigative report would tersely put it, "The water side searches all produced negative results."

Scores of volunteers were by then searching the beaches above the North Jetty. At 10:45 p.m., one group heard Huggins's calls for help and found him, alive and relatively uninjured, about three-quarters of a mile to the north of the jetty. He would spend the next four days in the hospital being treated for shock.

A little past midnight, a second group of searchers discovered John Lee Culp's body very near to where Gordon Huggins had been found. The body had no lifejacket on it, but a kapok lifejacket with all but the leg straps fastened was found on the beach just feet away.

The search continued for the next week, until, on January 19, the body of Bert Bergman was found on the beach eighteen miles north of Cape Disappointment.

The bodies of the other five young men, all in their twenties, presumed to have died aboard the *Triumph* and the *Mermaid*—Stanley Bergman, John Hoban, Joseph Petrin, Ralph Mace, and Gordon Sussex—were never found.

CHAPTER SIX

UNTIL I BEGAN DIGGING INTO the Coast Guard investigative panel's report on the *Triumph/Mermaid* disaster, I had mostly lost track of what a large place in my youthful imagination was occupied by those events. The "tragedy at sea," as it was described in the *Coos Bay World*, was what first got me reading the newspaper. What I most remember being fixated on at the time was that the dead were all young men. More than sixty years later, I can recall reading that one of them (John Lee Culp) had been posthumously awarded the Coast Guard's highest honor, the Gold Lifesaving Medal, and thinking for perhaps the first time seriously about the concept of bravery. Like many before and since, I wondered if I would be brave if called upon. I doubted it.

Now, as a man of nearly seventy in a small craft approaching the Columbia Bar, what I asked myself was how much reading those long-ago newspaper articles had to do with my being where I was. At least a little, I believe.

It occurred to me that all of this had been happening in Coos Bay at virtually the same time Ray was being pulled out of his third-grade class in South Bend and moved to Quincy. Even back in 1961, we had been on some sort of parallel tracks that led us to each other and this moment. Parallel, but wide apart.

Ray had fought back against being bullied years before I had. Our natures and characters may have had something to do with this. But the natures and characters of our fathers themselves was probably a bigger piece of it. My own dad was not quite twenty-five when I was born, and still a bull of a man when I entered my teenage years. He was forty-three and I was eighteen when I finally struck back against the violence I had endured since early childhood. We fought to a draw that evening, in a brief brawl that bloodied us both and broke several pieces of my mother's furniture. I give my dad credit that he was the one who stood down—literally sat down—to end the fight. I can remember like it happened last night standing over him, weeping and raging as I demanded he get back on his feet and "finish it." I'm fairly certain one of us would have killed the other if he had. Instead, he just sat silently, seething but still, as I demanded again and again that he "get up," until my tears overwhelmed my fury and I went off to cry in the arms of the girl I loved. It was the first and last time I would sob in the embrace of a woman. Remembering, I find it easier to forgive myself for marrying at the age of nineteen.

My father never laid a hand on me in anger again. We did have one more altercation, however, one so disturbing that I suppressed the memory of it for years. But I'll come to that later.

Ray was just fourteen when he scared his dad off. This was only a little more than a year after his dad gave him his worst beating ever. It seemed significant to us both that Ray's frog slaughtering was the catalyst for his father's explosive violence. The beating wasn't for killing amphibians, though, but for abandoning his post at the telephone and then lying about it. "The lying apparently enraged him," Ray said in a way that saddened me, because I understood all too well the need to find a reason for the abuse one suffers as a boy. "My dad cornered me in the downstairs bathroom and he was hitting and kicking me, and he was a reasonably large guy, so I was really beaten up."

Even as he was growing to hate his father, he still held pity for the man close to his heart, my friend admitted. "It tore me up to see my dad literally falling apart in front of my eyes," Ray explained.

Ray Thomas II was at once rescued and destroyed, though, in 1965, when Ray Thomas I died without a will. Even if it wasn't what the deceased had intended, all of his considerable assets went to his only child. "My dad got my grandpa's big house, his Cadillac, and $700,000 in cash and other liquid assets, which was a whole lot of money in those days," Ray said.

He and his dad left South Bend and lived on the River Forest estate for a time, Ray remembered, before Ray Thomas II decided to sell that place and fulfill what his son called "a lifelong dream" of returning to Laurium, Michigan, the Upper Peninsula town Ray Thomas I had fled from as a young man, to buy the mansion that had once been home to the big boss who owned the copper mine where his grandfather was employed.

Restoring the mansion was the nearest thing to work his father did for the next number of years, Ray remembered, though Ray Thomas II also bought huge quantities of collectible weapons and spent hours restoring them in a room dedicated to that purpose. Mainly, though, Ray Thomas II seemed to be consumed by what his son described as the man's "Dean Martin lifestyle." By this Ray meant that his father drank heavily, drove convertibles, and took a second wife, Sandy, "a Fredericks of Hollywood–mail-order-wearing hottie who was about fifteen years younger than him, had a platinum blonde beehive hairdo, and was just out for a good time," as Ray described her. Sandy drank, too, and had a temper every bit as nasty as that of Ray Thomas II. The couple's bar fights were notorious throughout the region. "They'd knock over furniture and break mirrors and windows," Ray remembered.

His dad's preoccupation with Sandy and with spending his inheritance at least gave young Ray plenty of free time and resources for making trouble, and he did a lot of that. Small animals continued to suffer for a time. Ray and the best friend he made in Laurium, Tommy Williams, decimated the chipmunk and bird populations in a one-mile radius around the Williams family's camp on the Little Betsy River in Keweenaw County. "BB guns, slingshots, blow guns, wrist rockets, things I'd buy from the JC Whitney catalog," Ray recalled his inventory of weapons.

I had met Tommy when he'd visited Portland, a basic blue-collar guy who still lived in Michigan, who was as simple as Ray was complicated, and to whom Ray felt an undying loyalty. "Tommy's family would take me in when things were really bad at home," Ray recalled. "He was always by my side."

When I asked what ended the carnage around Tommy's family's camp, Ray seemed to struggle for a moment to answer. "At first it was, *There's no more birds in the area, so now I've got to go further to find birds to shoot.* And then I thought, *Maybe I shouldn't be doing this.* It wasn't a moral sense, more a sense of finite resources. It was more like, *Don't you want to have birds around?* So I stopped doing that. This was like in eighth and ninth grade."

Right around the time the animal annihilation ended, Ray and Tommy and some other friends started making bombs with the gunpowder they emptied out of shell casings stolen from the Laurium mansion's weapons room. "We liked to blow up mailboxes and trash cans because the tight fit of the lid or cover created maximum destructive force and shrapnel," Ray remembered. "Afterward we would look in the snow for twisted bits of metal and smell the explosion smell on them, like they were trophies."

Though most of the neighborhood knew he was a terror, Ray received a good deal of sympathy and support from other parents. "My friends were very afraid of my dad and so were their moms and dads, who would forbid them from being at my house," Ray told me, by way of explanation. He remembered a sleepover with one of his friends in the summer after seventh grade, Ray said. "I had not told my dad because he was out drunk. I had bunk beds, and my friend was in the top bunk when my dad came home and found him there. My dad threw a bottle of Jim Beam at the wall just above my friend, covering him with broken glass and whiskey. My friend was so petrified that he refused to move a muscle all night, even though he'd pissed the bed. At about five in the morning I snuck him out. He never wanted to come back in my house after that." Other neighbors ordered their sons to stay out of the mansion on the hill after an episode in which Ray Thomas II chased his son down the street with a saber.

Young Ray achieved both a measure of autonomy and a sort of stealth rebellion by making copies of all his father's keys. "I started stealing his guns and his cars," Ray remembered. "He was drinking all day by then, so he didn't notice usually. But he caught me a couple of times. Once was the incident I told you about with the Walther P38. I'd left it on a table while I went to take a pee and he came in and found it. I think he may have been going through the d.t.'s at the time, but anyway he got the idea I was gunning for him and that was when he tried to scare me by firing the pistol right next to my head."

His dad continued to beat him, Ray said, even as the man's health declined. "He was drinking martinis all day, plus he had diverticulitis, and he had all these injuries from falling down drunk, so he was on crutches. He'd beat me with the crutches when he'd catch me stealing from him, or when he suspected I'd taken one of his cars for a joyride."

Ray Thomas II was still investing his dwindling inheritance in lifestyle—buying a new Cadillac convertible, a Chris-Craft yacht, dressing up in cashmere sweaters and keeping a lot of "broads," as he called them, Ray remembered: "A part of me wanted my dad to return to the things he used to do with me, but he was preoccupied with being a 'swinger,' in the old sense of the word."

The deterioration of Ray Thomas II was only accelerated by Sandy's leaving him. Her departure was hastened by the evening when, after a terrible fight, she'd passed out drunk and Ray Thomas II had decided it would be amusing to play tic-tac-toe all over his young wife's naked body with a Magic Marker. When Sandy came to and saw what her husband had done, "she didn't think it was at all funny," Ray remembered. "She took an alarm clock and threw it as hard as she could and hit him right in the head. He fell down unconscious on the spot. He had on this big cast, but the cast broke when he fell and he lay on the floor all night with his leg at a terrible angle with the circulation cut off."

His dad was in a new cast for a whole year after Sandy's exit, but he never stopped drinking and never ceased tormenting his son. The turning point came one evening when his dad was insisting that he call some friend and confess about something he'd done wrong, Ray said; he couldn't even recall now what that was. "I just remember that he had me cornered, and I had the phone in my hand, and he was trying to make me call my friend, and all of a sudden my circuits blew and I hit him in the forehead with the phone as hard as I could. I must have hit a bleeder, because it opened his head up. There was blood all over and I ran out of the house, breaking the glass in the door when I slammed it, in the middle of winter. And after that he told me never to darken his doorway again."

So at fourteen Ray became a vagabond. "I lived with Tommy Williams's family for almost a year, and with the home economics teacher from my school who lived on our street, and in between I would stay a night or two or three at some friend's house." Learning that people, neighbors, could be so caring and kind was something of a revelation, Ray allowed, but it didn't make him behave a whole lot better. "I kept stealing things," he said. "I went through a period when I was stealing cars and I really liked doing that. I would take them for joyrides and, again, I really didn't care about being apprehended. I'd just leave them wherever."

He wasn't out to hurt people, Ray said, but he did. He seemed to do his worst when he was living on the street, as he had been when he stole a car from a parking lot, spun donuts until he damaged the transmission, then drove it up against the building wall and revved the engine until the tires began to smoke and the rubber came off the rims, then ran off into the night. "That car belonged to some working stiff," Ray told me. "All the cars I stole belonged to working people, which I feel terrible about now, but not then."

He got caught more than once, of course, and usually ended up in some foster home, Ray remembered: "I lived in four different foster homes, and I'd behave for a while, but then I'd either run away or do something criminal and get thrown out."

Ray Thomas II had by then very nearly exhausted his funds, and decided to put what he had left into the purchase of the oldest and most famous bar and restaurant in nearby Calumet, the Michigan House, where he took up residence in an apartment on the top floor. "I don't know how, but he managed to run it for about twelve years," Ray recalled. "I'd usually end up on the street after I got thrown out of a foster home, but I still had all my dad's keys, and I started staying in the attic of his building. I could use his bathroom when he was gone, or the big washtubs and sinks in his basement laundry room if he was home."

One day when he was sixteen, though, his dad caught Ray inside the apartment. "He was furious and came at me," Ray recalled, "and I reacted just like a cornered rat. I hit him before he could hit me, and I just beat him with my fists, down to the ground, and then kicked him four or five times, broke his ribs, gave him a concussion. It was as bad a beating as he'd ever given me. Maybe even a little worse."

There was no room in the attic for Ray after this. "I'd sleep at people's houses, or outside if I couldn't find a bed, or in a car." On the couple of occasions when he encountered his father, he was astonished, Ray recalled, by the realization that his dad considered him the whole problem. "He would look at me without a shred of realization about the awful stuff he'd done to me and the terrible effect it had on me. What he thought about was how awful I had been to him. And how deeply it had hurt him. He would look at me with such pain. I didn't get it. I still don't get it. I don't know what he did with what he'd done to me. He'd relegated it to me being so bad, I had deserved it."

Ray was still refusing to go back to Quincy and his mother, preferring to take his chances on the streets. Then the minister at the local Presbyterian church took him in, and he lived with the preacher's family for the last part of his sophomore year in high school. "I'd behave pretty well there, but not out on the streets," Ray said. He was still regularly stealing from his father, which was how he came to be at the Michigan House one evening when he spotted a beautiful 1966 Buick Riviera in his dad's parking spot. Half an hour later, he was driving the hot-wired car at high speeds on the back roads of Houghton County. "I was showing off for a friend of mine," Ray remembered, "when I lost control on a big, sweeping curve and went into a skid, hit a telephone pole, and broke the Riviera in half." He and his friend were banged up but not badly hurt and abandoned the car right there, Ray said, but he wasn't going to get off with being sent to a foster home this time.

"The police thought it was my dad at first," Ray remembered, "because it turned out he'd driven it off a lot in town, supposedly for a test drive. But he told them it was me, it had to be me, and they eventually got it out of me. So I was charged with unauthorized use, reckless driving, fleeing the scene of an accident—all this stuff. And the judge who heard the case in Houghton County court decided I should be declared an incorrigible child."

He was now a ward of the court and looking at a long stretch in juvenile jail, Ray said, when the minister came to his aid, convincing the judge that the boy should be placed at the Fort Wayne Children's Home, a residence for unwed mothers and problem boys. "So one day I'm picked up by the police and they took me forcibly from Michigan down to upper Indiana," Ray recalled.

He was enraged during the whole drive there, Ray said, but "the home turned out to be fat city for me. Along with living in the same building with all these hot girls who were pregnant, I was getting regular sleep, regular meals, and a regular wardrobe for the first time in my life that I could remember." Meatloaf and mashed potatoes and steamed vegetables for dinner, eggs and bacon with hot *and* cold cereal for breakfast: Ray recounted the meals he ate at the Fort Wayne Children's Home with an avidity that made the menus sound like song lyrics. "I was still growing but already six feet tall," he remembered, "and I weighed one twenty-five when I went in there. In four months I gained forty pounds and grew another inch. I was thriving."

He repaid the minister and the people who ran the home by being such an exemplary student that he was soon allowed to spend most of his junior year at the public high school in town. "I was really trying to behave," Ray said, "but I needed money, so I started buying cigarettes during lunch hour at the public school and selling them at the children's home. I made a killing. Then every time I made enough money I'd buy a Greyhound bus ticket and take off for a trip somewhere. I did that three times, so I was still considered a problem child."

Nevertheless, the following summer he was discharged to the custody of his mother to finish high school in Quincy. "And I kind of pulled myself together," Ray remembered. "I was starting to develop a moral sense. I don't know how. But I didn't want to cause people pain anymore. I began to think about the difference between right and wrong, and to feel a stirring of honor and empathy. Maybe it was all arrested development, I don't know, but being out of the orbit of my dad changed me. Even my mom saw it.

"But I had to stay on top of it, like you do, like we both do, even now."

CHAPTER SEVEN

A PAIR OF PASSERSBY marked the latter stage of our approach to the Columbia Bar.

Just before the first of these appeared, I had begun to wonder at what point Ray and I (and Kenny, wherever he might be; behind us was all I knew) would be officially within the Jaws. We had been moving along next to the North Jetty for at least half an hour, and the inside of the South Jetty, where it protruded from Point Adams, was increasingly visible. So we were between the two jetties, but still sailing in relatively smooth waters. The inside of the entrance to the Columbia Bar, I knew, the point where the jetties were most widely spaced apart, was almost exactly a distance of two miles across. The outside of the entrance, where ships came into the river off the ocean, and where the collision of tide and current was truly felt, was only a little more than half a mile wide.

We were at a point where the distance between the jetties was maybe a little more than a mile, I was guessing, not quite "in" the Jaws, I had just decided, when Ray pointed sharply off to his right in the direction of the North Jetty. For a moment I saw nothing, then spotted the fin moving through the water about sixty or seventy feet off our starboard side. It took another second before I recognized the large silver-gray shape moving under the water, beneath the fin, and realized I was looking at a great white shark.

It was the first one of these I had ever seen live. I knew great whites were all along the West Coast of the United States. About the only time one heard of such a sighting, though, was when a shark attacked a surfer. Two of the last three such attacks had happened in the surf off Seaside, the resort town just south of where I live, so I knew great whites were in the neighborhood. The most recent shark attack in Oregon had happened there in December of 2020. It was pretty typical, though it could hardly have seemed that way to a twenty-year-old apprentice electrician named Cole Harrington, who was just sitting on his board waiting for a wave when the great white struck. As is nearly always the case, the shark dropped Harrington in the water and swam away after getting a bite of his wetsuit and realizing this wasn't the meal it was looking for.

Other surfers saved his leg with a tourniquet, and Harrington was flown by helicopter to a hospital in Portland that would discharge him a few days later with stitched-up wounds on his foot, ankle, and leg, and a story that could be verified by scars for the rest of his life.

Ray told me later it was the first great white he had ever seen also, and that made the sighting seem especially significant, though precisely how, I wasn't prepared to say. The main thing I was thinking at the time was that, if our trimaran capsized, we'd have more to worry about than simply managing to stay afloat until a rescue boat came for us.

Earlier, I had worried briefly that some water beast could tip the trimaran over. My concern then had been mainly about what was likely the great white's main prey in these waters, sea lions. We'd seen several of them surface for air already, one not ten feet from our boat. Ray called over his shoulder that I should smack it in the face with a paddle if it swam any closer.

Two summers earlier, in Portland, Ray and I had traveled upriver on his jet skis to Willamette Falls, perhaps the most neglected natural wonder in Oregon, a large and spectacular cascade that is only visible from the water. We abruptly found ourselves slaloming through sea lions in the bubbling foam under the falls; there were at least a dozen of them in the water there, feasting on spawning salmon. The creatures were huge—the bulls over five hundred pounds—and quite aggressive, even obnoxious, I'd say. So Ray's apprehension had a basis.

On both the Willamette and the Columbia, there was considerable contention over proposals to start culling the burgeoning sea lion populations, because they were decimating salmon runs. The whole idea made even more sense to me when I realized that their abundance on the Columbia must be attracting more sharks into the river's mouth.

The very next time I was in front of a computer I did a search for "sea lion vs. great white shark" and was not entirely surprised to learn that adult sea lions, males in particular, are a potential meal that great whites most often pass up. The big bulls can and will fight back, and they are faster and more agile swimmers than sharks. Sea lions actually eat smaller sharks. So great whites tend to limit their hunting to sea lion pups or smaller females.

It wasn't long after we spotted the shark that I saw the big freighter headed toward us, incoming off the ocean across the bar. I blame Ray for the way my breath caught in my throat. Before and during our first two training sessions in the trimaran, Ray had backed up his warnings that I couldn't "cramp up or crap out" on the bar, and not be able to pedal full speed, by employing the image of some large freighter coming full speed straight at us as it entered the river's mouth, and he and I needing to be able to pedal out of the way to avoid being crushed.

For a minute or two, when the freighter, coming from the north, began to swing in to port off the ocean, the ship looked as if it were headed our way for sure. The freighter's left turn wasn't nearly as sharp as it had seemed for that first minute, however, and when it actually came through the Jaws into the center of the South Channel, the ship was nearly a thousand feet from us.

It was a big but rusted old bucket, built before the days of container ships, and I was taken aback when it got close enough for us to read the white letters painted on the port side of its bow: MATSON. When I was a boy, the Matson Lines had more or less made my father's career. First in Coos Bay, then in Portland, the San Francisco–based shipping company had regularly insisted that my father be placed in charge of the loading of its freighters. This was part of what made my dad a legend of sorts on the West Coast waterfronts, that and having been at twenty-nine the youngest longshoreman ever elevated to the position of Walking Boss, an honor he still holds. It's not easy to explain what a walking boss is to people who have never worked the waterfront. A walking boss is a foreman, but the job is a little more than that. My dad's work was akin to being a director of operations, supervising all the various dockworkers, from the ones wielding grappling hooks to the ones operating cranes, and at the same time planning how the cargo would be placed and fitted into a ship's holds. The people who ran Matson Lines knew that my father regularly got more cargo—from logs measured by footage to grain measured by tons to trucks and tractors measured by units—into the holds of its ships than any other walking boss on the West Coast. He was driven about it, and he drove "the men," pushing them to help break his own records for footage or tonnage or units or whatever it was.

Part of what made him such an epic figure on the waterfront, along with his reputation as a fearsome fighter, was that he had only been a longshoreman for a couple of years before being promoted to walking boss. Others who got that coveted job had waited, on average, a couple of decades. My dad, though, had climbed just as rapidly as a stevedore as he had as a sailor. Hard work, a keen mind, and an obsessively competitive nature had raised him above other men at sea and on shore.

The more I heard of Ray's story, the more I wanted to tell him how mine was different, and yet the same. My father stayed married to my mother for almost fifty-five years, and he loved her the whole time. This love wasn't always reciprocated. A familial theme during my childhood and adolescence was that my father wasn't good enough for my mother. She was beautiful and she was smart, very smart. In a different time, this one, say, she could have been a CEO. Instead, the only alternative to being a housewife she knew was to work as a secretary. Men in suits were hitting on her constantly, but, as far as I know, she never met one she thought was man enough to replace Sully, as she called my dad. Yet she despised everything about him that was uncouth, and there was quite a bit of that, especially when he'd been drinking.

She started confiding in me about her dissatisfaction with him when I was twelve or so, regretting the lost opportunities she'd had to leave him when I was little and bemoaning all that her life, and mine, might have been. She filed for divorce three times. They separated, but then after one or three or eight months, she'd let him come back home and the marriage would go on. My mom stayed beautiful, and on a purely physical level, my dad was a match for her. He was as handsome as Kirk Douglas, with almost as cleft a chin, and carried a big-bellied beefcake quality well into his sixties. I knew on some level from a pretty early age that my parents had some powerful sexual chemistry between them. And I knew also, on some level, that this played a part in my mom's taking him back after their separations.

But her dissatisfaction remained, and she resented being dependent on him. Most people don't realize how much money a walking boss makes. The top ones earn as much as $400,000 per year these days, and my father's income was commensurate to that in its time. After moving to Portland, we lived in an upscale suburban neighborhood where the other dads went to work in suits and ties. Mine wore Frisco jeans and Pendleton shirts with Red Wing boots. He came home from work sweaty and dirty (he went down into a hold to show the men what hard labor was supposed to look like for at least part of every day), and often only after having spent a couple of hours at a bar playing pinochle or poker and knocking back shots of whiskey. One of his haunts was Portland's notorious Lotus Cardroom, where some of the city's most nefarious characters played stud poker at the back corner table. I remember him coming home one time with knife slashes on the back of his hand and forearm that were wrapped in a bloody white T-shirt, exulting, or so it seemed to me, as he described how some guy he'd caught cheating had come out of his chair with a switchblade that he flicked open as he stood. My dad and two others at the table had taken the knife away from the cheater and held him for the cops, but not before he'd drawn blood from each of them. It was the kind of disreputable triumph that he seemed to find most life-affirming. I listened, at once frightened and entranced. He was my father, but at the same time seemed like someone out of a movie. My mother, though, recoiled from him then, as she so often did, and sent me out of the room with an expression on her face that suggested she was ashamed this was the man who had sired me.

A good deal of the trouble I had with my dad, I came to realize when I was older, was the jealousy he felt about the particular way my mother doted on me. It was almost as if she was trying to make me into the man she wished she'd married. And he resented the hell out of that. It must have started before I was aware of it, because I understood even as a boy, at seven or eight at the latest, that my father saw me less as a child to be nurtured than as a rival to crush. Upon reflection, I find it significant that my dad never physically abused my mom, even as he was giving me one brutal beating after another.

Ray couldn't relate to any of that, except to the being beaten part. My father was a formidable man in many ways, and Ray's wasn't. But of course, what we had in common, what had bonded us at the beginning of our friendship, was the way violence, mostly paternal violence, had shaped us. At times in our relationship it had felt as if only the two of us could comprehend the poignancy of our upbringings.

That wasn't true, of course. Hundreds of thousands of men of our generation were beaten by their fathers. This is the main fact obscured by Millennial attacks on baby-boomer men (for having hogged so much of America's wealth, mainly) and what, for me, makes those attacks so shallow and dishonest. As I recently pointed out to my son Gabriel, born in 1997, on the cusp of Gen Y and Gen Z, he has heard his father tell him that he is loved just about every day of his life while growing up. I never heard it from my father even once. There's no real way to account for such disparity in measuring which generation got the lousier deal, but it certainly deserves consideration.

Yes, it was easier for Ray and me and Terrance Real and others of our generation to buy houses, but don't damn tell me it was easier to *be*, because it wasn't, not for us.

The ambivalence toward our fathers that Ray and I had struggled with was heightened by the complexities of historical context. We each had admitted to the other that we felt we were fundamentally sturdier than our sons because of what we had endured, but also perhaps less sensitive because of it also. My wife once told me that Gabriel was "a more evolved version of you," and perhaps that was true. And perhaps I was only a more evolved version of my own father, who had been beaten himself as a boy, no doubt more severely than he had beaten me.

Many of those seamen who died crossing the Columbia Bar, it had occurred to me more than once already, were raised in circumstances rougher than my own, rougher than Ray's, rougher even than my father's. It hadn't gotten easier for most of them aboard ship. Those who entered the mouth of the river in the nineteenth century faced disciplines that included flogging, along with being tarred and feathered or keelhauled (dragged with a rope beneath the ship). Their main rations were salt beef, moldy cheese, and hard biscuits, much of it lost to the rats and other vermin in the holds. Even a minor wound often resulted in gangrene and amputation. Many just lived, as long as they could, with the gonorrhea and syphilis they caught from prostitutes in the ports they visited. "Work hard, live hard, die hard, and go to hell after all," as Richard Henry Dana Jr. wrote of the sailors' code in *Two Years Before the Mast*.

It was suffering as much as anything else that I felt the need to honor, the suffering of those who had endured so much of it only to die in the cold water as young men.

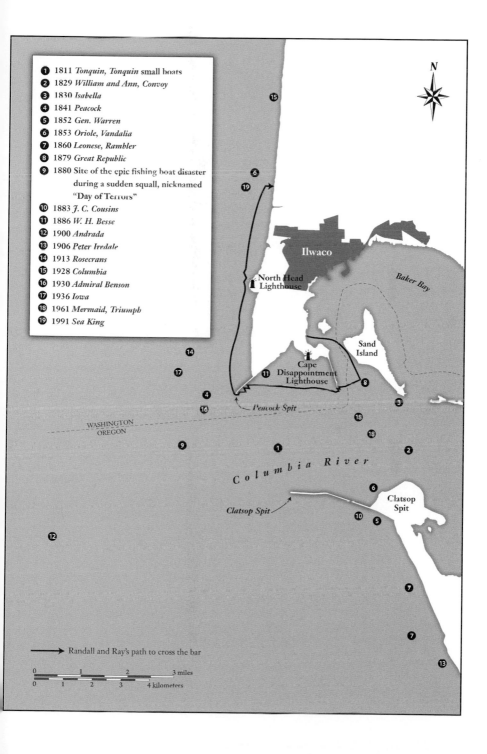

1. 1811 *Tonquin, Tonquin* small boats
2. 1829 *William and Ann, Convoy*
3. 1830 *Isabella*
4. 1841 *Peacock*
5. 1852 *Gen. Warren*
6. 1853 *Oriole, Vandalia*
7. 1860 *Leonese, Rambler*
8. 1879 *Great Republic*
9. 1880 Site of the epic fishing boat disaster during a sudden squall, nicknamed "Day of Terrors"
10. 1883 *J. C. Cousins*
11. 1886 *W. H. Besse*
12. 1900 *Andrada*
13. 1906 *Peter Iredale*
14. 1913 *Rosecrans*
15. 1928 *Columbia*
16. 1930 *Admiral Benson*
17. 1936 *Iowa*
18. 1961 *Mermaid, Triumph*
19. 1991 *Sea King*

Ilwaco

Baker Bay

North Head Lighthouse

Sand Island

Cape Disappointment Lighthouse

WASHINGTON
OREGON

Peacock Spit

Columbia River

Clatsop Spit

Clatsop Spit

→ Randall and Ray's path to cross the bar

0   1   2   3 miles
0   1   2   3   4 kilometers

Lieutenant Jonathan Thorn (1779–1811), the former US Navy hero who was made captain of the *Tonquin* in 1811 when businessman John Jacob Astor set out to control the mouth of the Columbia and monopolize the global fur trade.

An etching of John Jacob Astor by Alonzo Chappel, circa 1864. Astor (1763–1848) sent the *Tonquin*, with Thorn at the helm, to establish the first trading post for his Pacific Fur Company on the Columbia River and expand his business.

A memorial in Astoria, OR, dedicated to Concomly, the Chinook chief of the Native group on Baker Bay who, in 1811 and 1812, greeted the Astor expeditions when they arrived both by land and by sea.

Captain George Flavel (1823–1893) first crossed the bar in 1850 and went on to dominate the bar—and make a fortune—as one of the earliest Columbia River Bar pilots.

ASTORIA, AS IT WAS IN 1813.

Astoria was the first American trading post in the region. In 1813, it had been recently taken by the British, who arrived on the *Raccoon* with help from Concomly in crossing the bar.

The Flavel House Museum, built in 1885 in Astoria, was George Flavel's home for the last decade of his life, and now serves as a historical site for the Columbia River and the town of Astoria.

Randall and Ray approaching the mouth of the Columbia River in the Hobie Adventure Island trimaran on July 16, 2021.

A Coast Guard boat navigating the mouth of the Columbia River below Cape Disappointment Lighthouse.

Randall, two and a half years old, with his parents.

Randall's parents at their wedding in 1950.

Ray, nineteen, with his father in 1971.

The *Admiral Benson* stranded just inside Cape Disappointment, on what is now known as Benson Beach.

The *Columbia*, right, in the shelter of Baker Bay, just inside the bar.

The *North Bend* aground on Peacock Spit, 1928.

The mouth of the Columbia River, where the bar is formed by Peacock Spit (above right) and Clatsop Spit (below left).

The *Great Republic,* which, in 1866, departed San Francisco with over a thousand people on board and wrecked on the bar after several failed rescues by George Flavel's pilot boats.

The North Head Lighthouse, still a beacon to thousands of vessels approaching the Columbia Bar each year.

The *Peter Iredale* in 1906, when it ran aground on a sandbar just off Clatsop Spit.

The remains of the *Peter Iredale*, where Randall spread the ashes of first, his father, and later, his mother.

Construction of the North Jetty began in 1914, one year after the wreck of the *Rosecrans*. The South Jetty, built years earlier, had been immediately successful in making the bar safer for ships of any size to cross by increasing the depth of the channel.

The South Jetty on the Columbia River.

The *Triumph*, right, towing a schooner off the coast of Oregon. The *Triumph* was at the center of a failed Coast Guard rescue in 1961, which left five of the *Triumph*'s six-man crew dead.

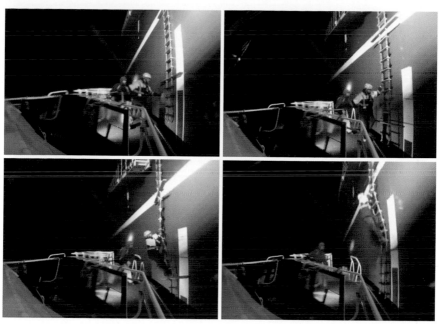

A Columbia River Bar pilot climbs a ladder from a pilot boat to a barge, which he will guide across the bar.

A tanker in rough waters on the bar.

Kenny, Randall, Ray (left to right) on the shore at Seaview shortly after Randall and Ray survived the near-death experience of their beach landing, July 16, 2021.

A Columbia River Bar pilot boat guiding a log barge.

Scenes from the Coast Guard's failed attempt to rescue the crew aboard the fishing boat *F/V Sea King*, just outside the Columbia Bar, resulting in the loss of three lives.

A US Coast Guard boat off the coast of Cape Disappointment.

Coast Guard rescue training on the bar.

AGAINST RAY'S INSTRUCTIONS, I began using my control of the rudder to steer us a bit nearer to the North Jetty, to take a better look at it. What struck me first about the rubble mound at closer range was how many of the giant boulders at the waterline were crumbling along their edges. I had read that back in the 1930s engineers had observed that the base of the North Jetty was being steadily eroded by the river's more rapid current and was in danger of failing. This had impressed me in print, but seeing for myself where those gigantic rocks were still being broken by water was significantly more impactful.

The power of the Columbia's flow is difficult for a human mind to apprehend. The best illustration of it I ever heard came from Tom Molloy, who was recalling the time he'd served as second in command aboard a Coast Guard buoy tender. The buoys had to be lifted and reset every year, Molloy told me. He had not really understood why until the first time he supervised the replacement of a buoy his boat had tethered twelve months earlier. The chains they had used seemed ridiculously heavy, Molloy recalled, case-hardened steel with links a full inch in diameter. When they raised the buoys to remove and replace the chain, Molloy recalled, the diameter of the links was barely a quarter inch. Three-quarters of an inch of steel had been worn away by the river's current in a single year.

The Army engineers who at first urged that the North Jetty needed repair or even replacement were largely ignored for a few years, especially after they began to suggest that some sort of additional structure must be added to protect the rock wall. The costs were prohibitive and the jetty was holding, the politicians who held the purse strings told the public.

It took the most politicized shipwreck in the history of the Columbia Bar to change their minds.

Utility on the cheap was the hallmark of the SS *Iowa*, and likely what doomed it. One of eighteen "type 1019" steel-hulled cargo ships built by the Western Pipe and Steel Company of San Francisco in 1919 and 1920, the *Iowa* was notable mainly for how underpowered it was. Twenty-eight hundred horsepower was enough to move the 410-foot, 5,742-ton vessel through shipping lanes in normal conditions, but nothing near to what it would take to pass over the Columbia Bar into the Pacific Ocean in the teeth of a sixty-mile-per-hour gale.

On the evening of January 11, 1936, the *Iowa* had left the Weyerhaeuser pier at Longview, Washington—a town created to provide millworkers with homes—loaded with more than two million board feet of lumber stacked on her decks, holds filled with hundreds of cases of canned salmon, wooden matches, tons of flour in barrels, and thousands of bundles of cedar shingles. A pilot had been aboard to guide the boat through the shoals of the lower Columbia but disembarked in Astoria.

The *Iowa*'s captain, a Brit from Liverpool named Edgar Yates, was a licensed Columbia Bar pilot himself and felt confident he could take the ship out of the river into the ocean without assistance. Gale pennants that warned of winds between thirty-nine and fifty-four miles per hour had been flapping in Astoria for the previous thirty-six hours, but conditions were not yet considered severe. Ships had been coming and going across the bar without apparent difficulty all day.

It was after midnight when the *Iowa* approached the bar, however, and conditions, as they so often do in these waters, were intensifying rapidly. The wind speed now easily exceeded the sixty miles per hour that classified the weather system on the bar as a hurricane, and seas were growing rougher by the second.

What happened to the *Iowa* shortly after it passed over the Columbia Bar will never be known exactly, because there was no one alive to tell. The wind speed was seventy-three miles per hour by the time the *Iowa* made it into the ocean. At that point, or very soon after, Captain Yates faced a harrowing choice: Should he turn back to port and recross the bar to make for safe harbor, or push the *Iowa* directly into the squall? It would be difficult later for the captain's critics—and there were many—to fault him for deciding that a return to Astoria was too dangerous. Heaving broadside to the huge seas for the minutes it would take to turn the *Iowa* around would have created considerable risk of a rollover. Instead, at some time shortly after 3:00 a.m. on January 12, 1936, Yates chose to head at full speed right into the tempest. His problem was that full speed for the *Iowa*, even under ideal conditions, was twelve miles per hour, and conditions on the ocean in the early morning hours of January 12, 1936, were far from ideal. The ship's single-screw propeller simply couldn't turn fast enough to make headway into the screeching storm and a strong northerly current.

At 3:45 a.m., the *Iowa*'s radio operator sent a distress call to the Coast Guard that the ship had become "unmanageable" and was adrift in the vicinity of Peacock Spit.

The cutter *Onondaga* was dispatched from Astoria to assist the struggling *Iowa*, but the Coast Guard vessel was overmatched by the Columbia Bar also. Towering waves did significant damage to the *Onondaga*'s upper works as it crossed out of the river's mouth; two of the cutter's lifeboat stations were destroyed completely. The *Onondaga*'s captain ordered that his crew carry on with their mission, but the cutter could make little or no headway once it passed into the ocean and would not reach the *Iowa* until almost another eight hours had passed.

The only eyewitnesses to the *Iowa*'s demise were a pair of lighthouse keepers and a meteorologist stationed at North Head, all three watching through telescopes as the massive breakers pushed the ship inexorably toward the shoals beneath Cape Disappointment. When the *Iowa* failed to respond to radio calls, the meteorologist, Nino Sunseri, tried using a shuttered signal lamp to send queries in Morse code. Nothing came back, Sunseri would say later, though he thought he had seen a flicker of light in the *Iowa*'s pilothouse before it was obliterated from view by the squall.

At daybreak, Sunseri and his colleagues could view the *Iowa* clearly through the telescopes at North Head. The storm had subsided slightly, but the ship was still being bashed by big waves, listing to nearly tipping point in the winds. All of the *Iowa*'s lifeboats were gone, the men at North Head saw, and so were the ship's upper works, along with the lumber that had been stacked on its deck. It was still early morning when the men at the North Head telescopes recognized that the *Iowa* was being broken in two amidships. The only sign of life he saw on the ship, Sunseri said, was a sailor who emerged from the pilothouse to try making his way to the foremast, apparently hoping to climb into the *Iowa*'s rigging. A wave that broke over the ship seconds later swept the man into the ocean, and he was gone from sight after that. Only moments later, the pilothouse itself was ripped loose and catapulted into the sea, the meteorologist remembered.

By the time the *Onondaga* got within sight of the *Iowa*, all that showed of the ship in the surf was its masts and king posts. The cutter could come no closer than fifteen hundred feet to the spot where the *Iowa* had gone down, but it was obvious even from that distance that survivors were unlikely. Unable to launch its own lifeboats, the *Onondaga* dropped anchor to wait for surfboats from the Point Adams and Cape Disappointment stations. The three Coast Guard boats that arrived a short time later were able to cruise around the *Iowa* long enough to pull two bodies out of the ocean and to determine that none of the thirty-four men who had been on board the ship was still alive.

All that day and into the night, 250 volunteers from the Civilian Conservation Corps camp at Fort Canby searched the twenty-eight miles of shoreline between Cape Disappointment and Willapa Bay. Four more corpses were found, bringing the total to six, meaning that the bodies of twenty-eight men were still unaccounted for.

Recovering those bodies would be made near to impossible by the winter gales that rolled in one after another for the rest of January. During the few and short breaks in the weather over the next several weeks, the Coast Guard dispatched amphibious aircraft from its base in Port Angeles to perform flyovers, but this resulted in nothing. The Coast Guard considered sending dive teams to check the wreckage of the *Iowa* for bodies, but the monstrous breakers made that into a suicide mission. There was nothing really to be done except watch as the sea dragged the *Iowa*'s aft section deeper into the water and smashed the forward section against Peacock Spit, gradually crushing it to smithereens.

The bodies of two *Iowa* crewmen did wash up days later on the beach near Oysterville, Washington, miles north on the Long Beach Peninsula. In mid-March, one more body was found on the peninsula near Klipsan Beach, then another one, described as "unidentifiable," was discovered in the sands at Seaview. That brought the total recoveries to ten. The other twenty-four bodies of the *Iowa*'s crew were never located.

The newspapers in the Pacific Northwest, meanwhile, had been covering the sinking of the *Iowa* more fervently than they had any other shipwreck in the history of the Columbia Bar. Portland's *Oregonian* had reported as early as January 13 that "a death patrol" was scouring the beaches north of Cape Disappointment, then over the next few weeks quoted an assortment of politicians and labor leaders looking to assign blame for the disaster.

The Portland city council adopted a resolution that the Port of Portland furnish "whatever information" it could obtain about who was responsible for sailing the *Iowa* across the Columbia Bar under such terrible conditions. The commissioner who had written the resolution told the *Oregonian* that there should be an investigation into the possible removal of Peacock Spit. This prompted a state representative from Portland to demand that Peacock Spit be removed by WPA (Works Progress Administration) labor.

The editorial page of the *Astorian* expressed astonishment at how little leaders inland understood about the Columbia Bar, mocking the "Portland officials" who had demanded the demolishment of Peacock Spit. "It would be about as simple to order that no more gales blow at the mouth of the Columbia," one editorial observed. A second editorial responded to the suggestion that WPA labor be used to remove Peacock Spit by suggesting that perhaps also the Cascade Mountains should be "smoothed" so as to ease the passage of rain clouds into the high deserts of Central Oregon, or that the Columbia Gorge's Multnomah Falls might be moved to the hills of Northwest Portland, to be more easily enjoyed by the public.

The furor was hardly quelled by the US government's public inquiry into the wreck of the *Iowa*, commencing on January 31 at the federal courthouse in Portland. The committee had heard from an assortment of "expert witnesses," its report stated, and based on their testimony could draw some general conclusions. The most significant of these was that no blame should be placed on the *Iowa*'s skipper. "It is reasonable to assume that Captain Yates, with all his years of experience, was not unskilled, negligent or careless," a section in the report's summary read. "It was impossible to foresee the rapid and intense changes that took place in such a short space of time, and after reaching a point when to turn back was impossible, control of the vessel was beyond human hand or the seamanship of man." In short, the caprices of the Columbia Bar alone had killed the men aboard the *Iowa*.

The editors at the *Astorian* weren't buying it, publishing an editorial that described the shipwreck as "a sorrowful tragedy and a wholly unnecessary one." While "criticism of the dead is not a pleasant matter," the editorial went on, in this case it was warranted, because if the *Iowa* had sat in port for another twelve hours that night, as it should have, the wreck would not have happened. "It is safe to say that no bar pilot would have attempted to take a vessel out that Saturday night," the editorial asserted. Certainly, no bar pilot was disagreeing publicly.

The families of the dead concurred with the *Astorian*, not the government, and filed multiple tort claims against the States Steamship Company, all of them based on the argument that States Lines was responsible for the wreck of the *Iowa* by having given command of a poorly maintained ship to the headstrong and heedless captain Edgar Yates. District Court Judge James Alger Fee would decide the case in San Francisco without a jury. His ruling was that States Line had mounted a persuasive defense. Against the claim of failure to properly maintain the *Iowa*, the company showed that the US Marine Inspection Service had certified the ship's boilers and hull two days before Christmas, 1935, and found both to be in good condition. As for allegations regarding Captain Yates, States Line showed evidence that the *Iowa*'s skipper had taken an average of fourteen ships a year across the Columbia Bar for the past seven years without incident. The company had no reason to imagine he would have sailed into the sort of seas that had taken the *Iowa*, Judge Fee ruled, but then decided that, under the circumstances, the baby should be split. States Steamship Company was ordered to pay $10,624 in claims for lost cargo, and $340,000 ($10,000 per man) for the loss of lives.

The dead Captain Yates received little sympathy in the final decree issued by Judge Fee. "In light of all the circumstances, the captain's recklessness was the sole cause of the disaster," Fee wrote. "He misjudged and failed. He expiated fault by going down with his ship, according to the traditions of the sea."

The words "misjudged and failed" reverberated in my mind for weeks after I read them in Fee's judgment. Captain Yates was sixty-eight years old when the *Iowa* went down, just a year younger than Ray and I were as we joked about being the old men on the sea. Oceangoing for nearly a half century, Yates was widely admired on the West Coast for his ability to navigate rough seas in a lumbering tub like the *Iowa*. Yet a single misjudgment and failure had cost the man not only his entire reputation, but also his life, and had resulted in the deaths of thirty-three other men.

I would have preferred otherwise, but I identified with Captain Yates. He wagered on himself one time too often, underestimated the ocean and the river, and suffered the supreme loss for it.

What the words "misjudged and failed" should evoke in me, I decided after repeating them any number of times, was a firm conviction that the mouth of the Columbia River should never, under any circumstances, be approached without a sense of deference.

Remember to be afraid, I began to tell myself. *Be as afraid as Captain Yates must have been when he knew the* Iowa *was about to become a wreck.*

REMEMBERING TO BE AFRAID was difficult, though, when the river beneath us was still undulating so smoothly. Ray must have felt the absence of tension, because he turned to look at me over his shoulder for the first time in some while and said, "Don't relax."

The ease of our progress at this point, I knew, was in large degree a function of how the Jaws had transformed the Columbia Bar. Before the jetties were built, the bar had been both wider and longer. With them in place, the new V-shaped entrance had compacted the drama of a crossing into a relatively small space at the outside of the entrance to the river's mouth. For big ships, this was a threat only in extraordinary weather. For small boats—and ours was surely the smallest that had been out there in some time—it meant a slow build to a brief but intense experience of precarious passage.

That the North Jetty in particular still worked so marvelously to keep the channel on this side of the river entrance clear owed a good deal to the wreck of the *Iowa* and its aftermath. Once the politicians in Portland had accepted that removal of Peacock Spit was not an option, the pressure to find other ways of making the Columbia Bar safer for ships mounted.

A voice that rose above the cacophony of posturing and pandering in Portland was that of Astoria's harbormaster Frank Sweet. He was convinced that the disrepair of the jetties, and of the North

Jetty especially, had at least something to do with the wreck of the *Iowa*, Sweet told the *Astorian*. The gradual narrowing of the North Channel was due in part to the reduced effectiveness of the jetties on both sides of the river, Sweet said. Outgoing ships were being forced to hug the North Jetty, Sweet explained, at exactly the point in a bar crossing where the current pushed them closer to the dangerous shoals extending seaward from the west end of Peacock Spit.

The *Oregonian* threw its weight behind Sweet's opinion with a huge article that ran under a red-letter banner headline on the front page of its Sunday, February 9, 1936, edition. PEACOCK SPIT . . . REMNANT OF THE COLUMBIA BAR, read the red letters.

After explaining why the removal of Peacock Spit was all but impossible, the *Oregonian* article did a decent job of describing what construction of the jetties at the Columbia's mouth had accomplished. Among other things, the jetties had moved the Columbia bar further out to sea, the article explained. As a result, Peacock Spit, which had once projected right into the North Channel, was at least marginally outside of it these days.

The problem was that the combination of current and tide was wearing the jetties away. The pounding of the sea had flattened the top of the South Jetty to a point where breakers crashing over it at high tide were setting in motion "destructive currents" that resulted in unfavorable shoaling in the South Channel. This problem had been only belatedly addressed four years earlier by a project to place a new cap of much heavier rocks atop the rubble mound of the South Jetty, an undertaking that was to be completed by the end of 1936.

But this still left the considerable problem of a North Jetty that was breaking down from the bottom up, worn away at its base by the Columbia's ceaseless current.

After years of inaction, there was finally an agreement at both the state and federal levels that something had to be done to either shore up or protect the North Jetty. The first thing the Army Corps of Engineers tried was the construction of four pile dikes on the north side of the Columbia. One came off the riverbank in Chinook, while the other three extended off the edge of a huge pile of silt created by the original construction of the jetties, now known as Sand Island. All four dikes ran perpendicular to the shoreline, each extending two thousand feet into the river to push its current away from the North Jetty.

The dikes helped but still weren't enough to fully protect the North Jetty, so in 1938–39 the Corps of Engineers constructed what they called the A Jetty, a rubble mound extending southward from the base of Cape Disappointment a full mile into the river. The A Jetty worked splendidly, not only protecting the base of the North Jetty but also scouring sediment that was accumulating on the North Channel's south side. Still, to this day, the boulders of the jetty break down over time and have to be regularly blasted loose with dynamite and replaced with new ones fitted into the opening the explosion has left.

The accelerated flow at the Columbia's mouth created by the North Jetty was enough to deepen the channel to forty feet. The Corps of Engineers had predicted a depth of fifty feet, however, and the bar pilots were insisting that in an era of ever-bigger ships, the channel had to be at least forty-eight feet deep to prevent scraping bottom with the new, deep-drafted vessels. They were soon proven correct when the hull of an oil tanker was punctured, spilling its load into the river.

In 1953, the government agreed to spend $8.5 million on a dredging operation that would give the North Channel a depth of forty-eight feet. The work was done then and has been done ever since by US Army engineers.

The dredging was of little moment to us in the trimarans, of course. Our boats had drafts of less than a foot, and even though the kick-up fins and the daggerboard each extended another eighteen inches below the water's surface, the Hobies were unlikely to touch even the shallowest sandbar on the north side of the Columbia. The main effect of the jetties we would feel as we approached the Jaws was the increased speed of the current, something that each of us understood had actually made the collision of river and ocean more rather than less turbulent, and that could and probably would toss vessels as light as ours in any and all directions during our crossing of the bar. This was why it had been so important to choose the Right Day, one on which both the wind waves on the river and the swell of the ocean's incoming tide were far reduced from what they might have been on a wrong day.

But then, as Ray and I were about to learn, and Kenny to be reminded, forecasts are predictions, predictions just educated guesses, and educated guesses about as reliable as the weather on the Columbia Bar.

CHAPTER EIGHT

AMONG THE OUTCOMES OF THE *IOWA* WRECK was that the catastrophe and its aftermath focused attention on the control over the mouth of the West's most significant watercourse by a small group of men: the Columbia River Bar Pilots.

It was a push from the bar pilots that had impelled Frank Sweet, among others, to demand that repairs and improvements to the jetties at the entrance to the Columbia be undertaken immediately, and it was the pilots' insistence that the bar channels be dredged more or less annually that had pressured the state and federal governments into coming up with the money to pay for it.

At the same time, a realization of just how influential and exclusive "the club" of the bar pilots had become concerned certain Portland politicians. This concern grew into an outcry in January of 1939, when a bill was introduced in the Oregon state legislature to revamp the commission that oversaw the pilots, establishing that a maximum of eight be licensed at any one time, and ensuring that at least one "experienced river pilot" serve on the three-person commission that administered those licenses. Immediately there was criticism that the bill was intended to take control of the bar away from the public and give it to "the club."

This wrangle over how much power over the Columbia Bar should be held by the pilots would go on for more than a decade, and is still not entirely done, nor will it be so long as the pilots have the authority to decide whether conditions are bad enough to close the bar to shipping—a choice that, each time it is made, or not made, can cost hundreds of businesses millions of dollars.

What the back-and-forth mainly generated in 1936, though, was much greater curiosity outside Astoria about who the bar pilots were and how they had become such a significant political and commercial force.

Part of what people would learn was that, in the centuries-long saga of the Columbia River Bar, the story of the bar pilots was, to a remarkable degree, a narrative created by the life and career of a single person.

CAPTAIN GEORGE FLAVEL HAD NOT BEEN FIRST, only foremost. For a half century before his arrival on the Columbia Bar circa 1850, other pilots had established themselves as indispensable to the establishment of commerce at the mouth of the great river.

The most legendary of these was Concomly, the Chinook chief who led the tribal group located on what was already known among Europeans and Americans at the dawn of the nineteenth century as Baker Bay. The first British fur trader to regularly work the mouth of the Columbia, Charles Bishop, described Concomly during the last years of the eighteenth century as a second-rank chief. Almost a decade later, the Lewis and Clark Expedition concurred in that opinion.

The elderly one-eyed headman was a unique combination of character traits, however, a "shrewd old savage," as Washington

Irving would describe him in his largely fanciful book *Astoria*, who was at the same time a warm personality. In 1811 and 1812 Concomly greeted the Astor expeditions, arriving first by sea and then by land, with kindness and assistance. Shortly after the *Tonquin* anchored in Baker Bay, Concomly saved the lives of John Jacob Astor's Scottish partners, Duncan McDougall and David Stuart, when they ignored his advice and tried to cross the five-mile estuary inside the Columbia Bar by rowing the ship's longboat with a crew of eight into a gathering storm. Wind waves capsized the longboat, spilling the Scots and their men into the frigid water. They floundered and gasped until being pulled aboard two large Chinook canoes that Concomly had sent after them with his best paddlers aboard. The chief had a large fire built to warm the white men and dry their clothes, then insisted that they spend the next three days sheltering in a tribal longhouse as the gale subsided.

Comcomly had been just as generous with the English when they had arrived fifteen years earlier, but as Charles Bishop observed soon after, beneath the one-eyed chief's welcoming manner was a profit-making purpose. Bishop recounted the rough and devious ways in which Concomly had persuaded the tribes upriver to sell him furs at bargain rates, then charged the British three, four, even five times that amount in manufactured goods.

Though less warlike than other chiefs, Concomly was a canny businessman every bit as committed to amassing wealth as any of the tribal headmen. And with the arrival of the Europeans and Americans, his location at the mouth of the Columbia provided him with splendid opportunities for enrichment.

Nearly all the Chinook tribes of the lower Columbia were seagoing people who paddled out of the river into the ocean in their enormous canoes. Concomly, though, by virtue of living there year-round, knew the river's bar better than any man alive. He had demonstrated both his ability and his willingness to assist the arriving white men early on, guiding the *Racoon* across the bar and into Baker Bay when it arrived in 1813 to claim Fort Astoria for the British. Soon Concomly was piloting nearly every ship that arrived at the mouth of the Columbia. The wily old chief offered this service free of charge, but only on the condition that he serve as middleman between the upriver tribal groups and the white fur traders arriving out of the Pacific. He soon became the richest member of the richest tribe in North America.

Attitudes toward the Natives were hardening in the region during the second decade of the nineteenth century, though. The single-biggest factor was the way the north-coast Clayoquot* tribe had exacted revenge against the *Tonquin* after a series of abuses inflicted on them by other European and American fur traders visiting Vancouver Island. The *Tonquin* had headed there in early June of 1811, less than three months after crossing into the mouth of the Columbia. It took the ship about a week to reach Nootka Sound, where Captain Thorn's plan was to trade for otter pelts at several Clayoquot villages. The *Tonquin* was anchored at a place called Woody Point on June 14, when the captain was offered otter pelts at a price he thought far too high. The Clayoquot chief, insulted by Thorn's counteroffer, ordered his warriors to leave the ship, and to take their pelts with them.

During the night, a Native woman came aboard the *Tonquin* and warned Thorn that the Clayoquot were going to attack the

* The tribe today prefers "Tia-o-qui-aht"; I'm using the name as it appears in historical texts that were written, obviously, in English.

ship the next day. Thorn did not believe her. The following morning, when the Clayoquot paddled two large canoes up beside the *Tonquin*, and the chief agreed to the price for the pelts that Thorn had offered, the ship's captain waved them aboard. Forty Clayoquot men climbed onto the deck of the *Tonquin* with war clubs and knives hidden in the furs. Just as their numbers began to concern Thorn, the Clayoquot pulled their weapons out of the bundled otter pelts and attacked. Thorn was dead minutes later, most of his crew along with him. Only five sailors aboard the ship managed to barricade themselves belowdecks, where they broke out the pistols and muskets stored in the hold. Their bullets drove the Clayoquot off the ship, but as they stood at the *Tonquin*'s gunwales and surveyed the bodies of their shipmates floating in the pink water below, the four of them who were uninjured knew they were not nearly enough to set the sails on the big square-rigged ship. A decision was reached to make a run for it in the *Tonquin*'s longboat, try to outrace the Clayoquot to the safety of Fort Astoria. One man, who may have been ship's armorer Stephen Weeks, chose to stay aboard the *Tonquin*. Whether this was because he had been too badly injured to make the journey or was simply intent on avenging his dead shipmates will never be known for certain. Either way, the last white man aboard the *Tonquin* waited until hundreds of Clayoquot were either on the ship's deck or in canoes next to it, then lit a match to nearly a thousand pounds of gunpowder, blowing to bits not only the *Tonquin* but also a reported two hundred Clayoquot. According to Joseachal, the British Columbia Indian who had served as Thorn's interpreter, the four men who had attempted to escape in the longboat were forced to shore by a storm, then captured by the Clayoquot, who brought them back to their village, and there slowly tortured each one to death.

In the aftermath, hatred on both sides of the settler/Native divide ran deep. At the mouth of the Columbia, a tipping point was reached in 1829, when the head of the Hudson's Bay Company's outpost at Fort Vancouver, John McLoughlin, received word that the vanished *William and Anne* had gone aground near the Clatsop village at Tansy Point two months earlier. There was no sign of the crew, McLoughlin was informed, and the Clatsop refused to surrender the cargo from the wrecked vessel. Incensed by the tribe's defiance and strongly inclined to believe the Clatsop had murdered the *William and Anne*'s crew, McLoughlin sent a hundred men to demand relinquishment of the ship's cargo and to launch an all-out attack if the Natives refused. The Clatsop would not yield, and McLoughlin's troops opened fire, killing just one member of the tribe but sending the survivors scattering into the forest. It was the beginning of the end for the Clatsop and for Concomly.

The old chief had managed for decades to hold on to both his wealth and his influence by continuing to pilot American as well as British ships across the bar. Complaints within the Hudson's Bay Company about Concomly's avaricious schemes had mounted for years, though, until finally the company retained its own pilot in 1830. Concomly died just months later.

THIS FIRST WHITE MAN to pilot ships across the Columbia Bar was James Scarborough,* an Englishman who had come in across

---

* Some local historians identify Alexander Lattie as the first white pilot on the bar, but Lattie did not begin working at the mouth of the Columbia until 1831, a year after Scarborough.

the river's mouth initially as the second mate aboard a ship called the *Isabella*. After being hired by the Hudson's Bay Company as its Columbia River pilot, Scarborough settled into the frontier community so completely that he married a Chinook woman, who took the name Elizabeth Ann, and shortly after laid claim to 643 acres on the north bank of the river. He worked two decades for the company, through the last years of the "joint occupation" agreement by which the Americans and British had agreed to share control of the region, and for a time after the signing of the Oregon Treaty of 1846 that formalized English surrender of all land south of what is today the border between Washington State and British Columbia.

Scarborough was still working for the Hudson's Bay Company in 1848, when what was now the United States' Oregon Territory issued its first official bar pilot license to an Irishman named Selah E. C. Reeves. How broadly connected the West Coast was in those days is indicated by the fact that Captain Reeves's specialty was bringing ships north from San Francisco, then into the Columbia across the bar. He ran three ships aground in the mouth of the river within a matter of months, but it was a longboat capsizing in San Francisco Bay that killed him in 1849, only a little more than a year after he had been licensed as a bar pilot.

That same year, Jackson George Hustler became the first American bar pilot on the Columbia. Hustler was a large figure. He had worked as a harbor pilot in New York City, then come west during the California Gold Rush. After less than a year in the Sierra Nevada, he had enough money to purchase the schooner *Mary Taylor*, a ship he knew from New York, and bring her north to Astoria, where she became the first vessel to regularly guide ships across the Columbia Bar.

In the long view of history, though, Hustler looked to have been merely setting the stage for George Flavel. An Irishman brought up in Virginia, Flavel was already a shipmaster at age twenty-seven when he first arrived on the mouth of the Columbia at the helm of the brig *John Petty*. Soon after, he went to work for Hustler to learn pilotage of the bar. By virtue of his ability and his ambition, Flavel swiftly separated himself from both Hustler and other would-be pilots. Over the next twenty years he would build both a great reputation and a great fortune.

In the surviving photographs of him, Captain Flavel is an almost-handsome man with a high brow and curly dark hair. His expression is sternly dour in every picture, though, and the faraway and forlorn expression in his pale eyes is discomfiting.

Whatever it was that gave him such a gloomy aspect, Flavel would prove again and again that he was simply superior to any other at the job of piloting ships on the Columbia River, and especially at its mouth. He studied and charted the bar like no one before him had, and by the age of thirty knew the currents, the tides, and especially the shoals at the mouth of the river better than anyone.

It was the role Flavel played in the shipwreck that cost more lives than any since the *William and Ann*, though, that boosted his reputation beyond that of all others who had worked at the entrance to the great river.

THE *GENERAL WARREN* WAS a schooner-rigged side-wheel steamer built in Portland, Maine, in 1844. The ship was named for Joseph Warren, the American general who was famous for sending Paul Revere on his midnight ride of April 18, 1775, and also for dying valiantly two months later in the siege of Boston at the Battle of Bunker Hill. The vessel was something of a novelty when it first appeared on the Columbia River around the same time that Captain Flavel did. Few steamers had been seen on the Columbia before then, and crowds would gather on the banks of the river to watch the old "kettle" pass by, leaving a trail of black smoke behind her. The *General Warren* had been lavishly designed and outfitted, with carved woodwork and velvet furniture in its lounge, where at the top of a grand staircase hung a painting of the general himself. More than a few had criticized the side-wheeler as unseaworthy, though, by the time an Oregon City–based shipping firm purchased it and put the steamer to work hauling loads of both cargo and passengers between Portland and San Francisco.

The *General Warren* was loaded with fifty-two persons, seven hundred live hogs, and grain to capacity when it set off from Portland on January 28, 1852, with Captain Charles Thompson in command. It had been announced as the ship's last voyage.

Flavel piloted the boat downriver and across the Columbia Bar, then disembarked at sea to the *Mary Taylor*. All looked well. As happens on the Columbia Bar, however, what had been only an overcast sky all afternoon turned into a startlingly sudden gale before the *General Warren* had so much as left sight of land. The side-wheeler was sluggish even with a spread of canvas to assist its steam engine, and soon was barely moving in the sea's steepening waves. The temperature began to plummet, and rain turned to snow that blew into the eyes of the men on deck until it nearly blinded them. They were able to see the fore-topmast being torn loose by a huge gust, though, and then watch it cartwheeling across the ocean surface before disappearing beneath the swells. The ship's strained timbers began to separate, and water seeped into the hold, soaking the grain and clogging the pumps.

After a night spent sleepless on the bridge, the captain at daylight ordered the ship put about and brought back toward the bar. Signal flags were raised asking for Flavel's return; he wanted Captain Flavel, no one else, Thompson indicated. But it was 3:00 p.m. before the *Mary Taylor* could reach the *General Warren* again and put Flavel aboard. The tide was already turning, and the ebb was strong by dark. Amidst mountainous waves, Flavel refused to make the bar crossing until conditions improved. "Absolutely out of the question," he told the insistent Captain Thompson. "You'll have to ride out the storm. Possibly by morning I can take you in. The bar is breaking clear across. You haven't enough steam to cross before dark."

He would stoke the engines with bacon fat and anything else that burned, the *General Warren*'s skipper told Flavel, urging him once more to steer the ship back to port. Flavel shook his head. "I know the bar," he said. "You can never make it. It is suicide to try."

The few crewmen aboard who would be alive the next day recalled that panicked passengers surrounded Flavel, at first pleading and then demanding that he change his position. Even with shaking fists in his face, though, Flavel refused. Captain Thompson joined in with the passengers, insisting to Flavel that his ship could not stay afloat much longer. Passengers began to taunt Flavel as a coward.

Finally, the pilot yielded. "Very well, if you insist on going, I will take you in, but I refuse to be responsible for what might happen."

Flavel signaled the *Mary Taylor* to sail in close by the wallowing *General Warren*, but the winds were too much for the schooner, and it was blown out of sight in minutes.

With the ship barely advancing and water filling its holds, Flavel ordered that the side-wheeler drop anchor. The captain, though, refused, insisting that his vessel must be beached immediately if there was any chance to save it. At Thompson's insistence, Flavel ran the *General Warren* aground on Clatsop Spit in the full dark of 7:00 p.m.

Captain Thompson ordered that a keg of whiskey be brought on deck and opened, to warm and calm the passengers and crew. Flavel resisted adamantly. "We will need clear heads if we are going to save those aboard," he said, and persuaded Thompson to help him roll the keg of whiskey overboard.

The *General Warren* was breaking up fast. Most of its lifeboats had already been crushed or swept away. The crew huddled at the front of the ship, some praying, some cursing, some singing. Captain Thompson called for volunteers to man the one undamaged lifeboat and, after a considerable time, nine men, passengers and crew, stepped forward. Because he knew the bar best, Flavel was asked to take command of the lifeboat. He agreed, and the lifeboat was put over the side in seas so high that it was nearly swamped before the men could get to the oars. As they began to row, Thompson cried out to Flavel, imploring him to come back. "If I live, I will return," Flavel called in reply.

The tide had turned to flood by then, and with its aid Flavel was able to get the lifeboat across the bar through icy swells in what was now a blizzard. The lifeboat made it to Astoria less than three hours after it had put in off the *General Warren* and tied up next to the barque *George and Martha*. Flavel persuaded the barque's captain to give him the ship's whaleboat and a crew to man it so that he could get back to the *General Warren*.

The whaleboat, with Flavel on the steering oar, reached the spot where the *General Warren* had been run aground before light the next morning. The ship, though, was gone. All that could be found of it were pieces of the hull and the corpses of the drowned floating in the sea.

Among the bodies recovered later that day was Captain Thompson's. The discovery that made the greatest impact, though, was of a dead and frozen young married couple on the beach, hands tightly clasped. The bride still had on her wedding ring.

The forty-two lives lost with the *General Warren* were, and still are, the most in a Columbia Bar shipwreck since 1829. The publicity was enormous. Press coverage made Captain Flavel famous up and down the West Coast; even East Coast papers published stories about the wreck and how Flavel's heroism had saved the lives of nine aboard the *General Warren*. The city of Portland presented Flavel with a medal in a public ceremony.

In the glow of his fame, Flavel partnered with Captain Alfred Crosby to buy the sixty-four-foot schooner *California*, and the two brought it north to compete with George Hustler's *Mary Taylor*. It was no contest. In less than a year Hustler was working for Flavel.

Soon after, another shipwreck, this one with Flavel aboard, lifted the bar pilot's reputation even higher. The barque *Oriole* had been carrying supplies for the construction of the Cape Disappointment Lighthouse on September 19, 1853, when the wind died while the ship was crossing the bar. Sails sagging, the *Oriole* drifted until she struck hard onto the south sands adjacent to Peacock Spit. An outgoing tide pulled the ship seaward, scraping and striking her bottom against the sand until the *Oriole*'s rudder was broken and her hull stove in. Moments after the passengers and crew put out the lifeboats, the barque slipped off the sands and sank. The ship's lifeboats struggled in the surf, but Flavel saved them all by ordering the boats chained together, then guiding them back and forth through the shoals all during the night, until they were picked up the next day by the *California*. The *Oriole*'s captain, Lewis Lentz, praised Flavel to the skies, and was quoted in the newspapers declaring that the pilot had saved all their lives.

His legend cemented, Flavel became the clear favorite of nearly every skipper who brought a ship onto the Columbia Bar. By the years of the Civil War, Flavel would own almost absolute control of traffic at the mouth of the river. His timing could hardly have been more favorable.

There had been four white residents in the outpost of Astoria in 1844, six years before Flavel's arrival. Gold and silver strikes in the Northwest during the 1850s and 1860s doubled and then tripled the number of vessels coming and going across the bar. In 1867, the introduction of salmon canning made a boomtown of Astoria. Scandinavian gillnetters and Chinese fish-packing workers poured into town. Astoria's population would be twenty-five hundred by 1880, and the county's was more than seven thousand. Portland and other cities upriver were demanding more and more goods, and sending huge loads of timber from Oregon's forests and grain grown in the Willamette Valley back the other way.

Astoria was well on its way to becoming what Portland's *Oregonian* called "the most wicked place on Earth for its population." In the late nineteenth century, at a time when churches outnumbered saloons by at least three to one in every other of the state's towns, Astoria had twelve churches and forty-two saloons. Astor Street was a rip-roaring carnival of sin, lined with saloons, dance halls, and "boarding houses" that everyone in town knew were bordellos. "Crimping" was a thriving local industry. Crimps were on sailors from the moment they stepped off a ship, taking control of their wages in exchange for lodging and entertainment. At the same time, they accepted fees from the brothels and barrooms where the seamen were lodged and entertained. A good many crimps also worked with bar owners and brothel madams to "shanghai" sailors—to get them so drunk or drugged or groggy from a blow to the head that they could be loaded onto a ship in need of crew and put out to sea before they came to, long after the crimp had pocketed his pay from the ship's captain.

What were known as "sailortowns" had sprung up in seaports all over the globe, from London and Liverpool to Amsterdam and Antwerp, in South America, the West Indies, East Africa, and Australia, all of them pretty much alike—waterfront districts of cities crammed full of bars, brothels, and tattoo parlors, with shops selling nautical equipment and with ad hoc houses of religion interspersed. On the US West Coast, San Francisco's Barbary Coast was the best known sailortown, but Astoria's was no less robust and unruly. And unlike most other port cities, Astoria had not one but three streams of transient workers passing through steadily. Along with the seamen off the ships in the harbor, the fishing and logging industries produced an unending flow of untethered men looking for whiskey and women, along with places to toss dice or play poker. The wink-and-nod system of law enforcement was most apparent in the way the city enforced its gambling ordinances: once a month, on the same day of the month, the men who ran the card parlors were cited and fined, always the exact same amount, so that it became a kind of local business tax. Places were only closed if someone got shot or stabbed, and even then they almost always were open again before the end of the week.

What the city had become was evident to all in 1883, when a fire that had started in a sawmill burned up most of the waterfront: all that the citizens of Astoria seemed determined to save were the barrels of whiskey they rolled to safety.

George Flavel stood amidst this bedlam of vice as a pillar of rectitude, a teetotaling, churchgoing family man whose only failing seemed to be that he lacked a sense of humor. He worked six days a week at least, seven if need be, and was cleaning up, charging $12 per foot for vessels with drafts of less than twelve feet, $13.50 per foot for those drawing twelve to fifteen feet, and $15 per foot for ships that drafted over fifteen feet. Captains paid what they decried as his obscenely high prices because Flavel kept the standard of service high. Every vessel that went down without him aboard—and there were more than a few—was an advertisement for what Flavel offered.

In 1865 a tugboat captain from California, Paul Corno, showed up at the entrance to the Columbia to challenge Flavel. Quickly recognizing and exploiting the resentment of Flavel that had by now spread across Oregon, Corno convinced the state's pilot commission to revoke the licenses of Flavel and his associates, leaving Corno's tug, *Rabboni*, the only legal pilot boat on the Columbia Bar. Flavel replied by obtaining a pilot license from Washington State and operating the *California* from that side of the river. Corno's tugboat *was* faster by far at towing sailing vessels out of the Columbia's mouth. Those barques and schooners, though, were being rapidly replaced by steam ships that needed to be guided, not pulled, and whose skippers placed their trust in Captain Flavel and his experienced pilots. In ten months, Corno and his tugboat returned to California.

As Flavel grew wealthier, he began to diversify, buying an interest in the schooner *Halcyon* and commanding her in carrying ice between

Vancouver, B.C., and San Francisco. He invested the profits from that in the barquentine *Jane A. Falkenberg*, captaining her for a time on runs up and down the West Coast, while maintaining his ownership share of the schooner *Columbia*, and with it a near monopoly on bar passage.

The complaints of gouging—even extortion—against Flavel increased. But between 1852 and 1875, eight ships would be lost when they tried to cross the bar without Flavel's services. "Proceed at your own peril" was the implicit motto of his business, and fewer and fewer captains declined to heed it.

The state of Oregon, concerned about both Flavel's hegemony and the vessels being lost at the Columbia's entrance, offered a subsidy of $30,000 to anyone who would maintain a steam vessel dedicated to pilot service across the bar. Flavel saw this not as a provocation, but as an opportunity, and promptly paid $40,000 for the tugboat he called *Astoria*. Six years later, Flavel retired his sailing ship *Columbia* and replaced it with a tug that took the name.

The state squeezed Flavel as best it could, restricting pilotage rates on the Columbia Bar to ten dollars per foot of draft to a depth of ten feet, and an additional two dollars per foot above that. He continued to get richer.

During the 1870s, Flavel became the central figure in an increasingly vicious rivalry between Astoria and Portland to be the premier port of the Columbia. The famous bar pilot was bitterly attacked in the pages of the *Oregonian*. A front-page article reported that Flavel was turning an ungodly profit of $50,000 per annum. "This bloodsucker at the mouth of the river," an ensuing editorial described him.

Flavel's defenders, who were not just in Astoria, retorted that the captain won out against other companies and skippers because his service could not be bettered, and because all admired the resolute fearlessness of a pilot who was always willing to put out in the worst weather if that was what it took to bring a ship safely to shore.

A bill was submitted to the state legislature by Portland politicians to renew the authority of the pilots commission to license those who led ships across the Columbia Bar, and to set maximum fees and to increase regulations, adding one, clearly targeted at Flavel, requiring that all ships accept the services of the first pilot to reach them as they approached the mouth of the river, rather than signal for the pilot they wanted. Flavel's allies and admirers killed the bill in the state Senate after it had passed in the House.

The single-greatest controversy ever to engulf Flavel took place in 1883, two months after the Astoria waterfront fire, when the venerable pilot was moving into retirement. Construction was just about to begin on Flavel's new mansion, by far the grandest home the Oregon coast had ever seen, a magnificent Queen Anne (which some called "Carpenter Gothic") topped by a four-story tower with a cupola that served as the aerie for an eagle-eye view of ships coming in and out across the Columbia Bar. The place was 11,600 square feet, with six fireplaces, each with its own uniquely hand-carved mantel. The inlaid hardwood floors, enormous stained glass entrance panel, the copper bathtub and flushing toilet in the central bathroom all were firsts for the region, and a match for any house in Portland.

The grandeur of the home, though, would only inflame the resentments of those who hated Flavel already. But even before the house was finished, the strange circumstances surrounding the sixty-six-foot schooner *J. C. Cousins* had become a new line of attack on the captain.

George Wood, yet another skipper determined to compete with
Flavel for preeminence on the Columbia Bar, brought the *J. C. Cousins*
north in 1881. She had been built as a rich man's pleasure craft, and
was a magnificent ship, trimmed with the rarest of hardwoods and
outfitted with first-rate chandlery. The schooner worked the bar as a
pilot vessel under Captain Wood for thirty months, longer than any
other ship had managed to hold its own against the Flavel operation.
Then one afternoon in October of 1883, the schooner was seen by
both people onshore and the crew of the tugboat that had taken the
name *Mary Taylor* behaving oddly.

Earlier that day, the *J. C. Cousins* had been spotted at anchor just
off Peacock Spit, apparently waiting for approaching ships in need of
pilotage. That was normal. Just a few hours later, though, the crew of
the *Mary Taylor* saw the boat sailing through heavy breakers inside the
South Channel, in spite of the clear and easy water just yards to its
north. The *Mary Taylor*'s captain would recall watching the schooner
cross the bar back out into the ocean through that same choppy water
during the late afternoon, then, a few miles offshore, suddenly tack
and turn back toward the Columbia's mouth. He lost sight of the ship
in the gathering darkness, the captain said, but there it was again the
next morning, still sailing under full-rigged masts, but apparently
headed nowhere in particular.

Then, at about 1:00 p.m., the *J. C. Cousins* came in across the
bar by the same rough route it had left through earlier and ran hard
aground on Clatsop Spit, flipping onto one side. Observers had to
wait several hours for low tide, and all during that time saw no sign of
life aboard the ship. When the tide ebbed and the would-be rescuers
finally reached the *J. C. Cousins*, they found no sign of its crew—not
a soul aboard.

Many theories of what had befallen the "ghost ship" circulated in the months afterward, but the one that gained greatest currency involved a mysterious Mr. Zeiber, a stranger in Astoria who had only just joined the crew of the *J. C. Cousins*. Someone had hired Zeiber to murder the other men aboard the ship, this story went, and the same person or persons had taken him off the schooner during the darkness of night before it ran aground.

Flavel's enemies naturally pointed fingers at him. Who else had so much to gain from the wreck of the *J. C. Cousins*? they demanded to know. No evidence was ever offered to support this accusation, but when several seamen returned from ports of call in East Asia claiming to have seen Zeiber there, the charge against Flavel lingered. The captain offered a pretty solid defense: He had sold his interest in the pilotage operation a year before the mystifying abandonment of the *J. C. Cousins*, forced into retirement by hands that were now so arthritic he could barely open or close them. His opponents whispered that the deaths of the *J. C. Cousins*'s crewmembers were part of the deal Flavel had made with his former partner Asa Simpson, but only those who wanted to believe this did.

It must have amused Flavel that so many of those who had vilified him for behaving like a medieval lord were soon the very ones openly urging his return to piloting ships across the Columbia Bar. His successors had impressed no one. Portland grain shippers who had long loathed Flavel put the tug *Pioneer* in service on the bar, but the boat never turned a profit and was sent off to Puget Sound in 1887. Another tug, the *Escort*, also worked on the bar for a time, until it was obliterated by a boiler explosion, also in 1887.

Other pilots inevitably were compared to Flavel, and rarely favorably. Captain Charles Johnson, bringing in a ship with his boat the *Albercorn*, had been killed when he ran his vessel aground in the spring of 1888. A year later, another new Columbia Bar pilot, Captain James Hill, was killed by the wreck of his tug *Fearless*.

The state of Oregon put its own schooner, the *General Moody*, into service as a pilot boat on the bar, until the ship crashed into North Head in early 1890 and sank on the spot. The state's replacement schooner, the *San Jose*, lasted all of twenty-three days on the bar before it was declared unfit for its duties as a pilot vessel.

Flavel was not entirely absent from the bar in these later years of his life. He ran a series of salvage operations on ships that had wrecked crossing the bar without his pilotage, the most famous being the *Great Republic*. It was one of the four original Pacific Mail steam-ships constructed in 1866 of white oak and chestnut, with copper and iron fastenings. At 378 feet in length and 4,750 tons, the *Great Republic* became the largest passenger vessel on the Pacific coast after it began running between San Francisco and Portland in 1878. The side-wheeler carried thousands of Chinese workers during the next year, usually crammed into miserable steerage quarters, delivering them to meet the demand for labor from mine owners and railroad companies. Four enormous boilers fed a vertical steam engine that was capable of propelling the *Great Republic* from Astoria to Portland in a then-unheard-of five hours and fifteen minutes.

The *Great Republic* was carrying nearly 900 passengers, 346 of them in steerage, when it departed from San Francisco on April 16, 1879. Crew included, more than a thousand people were on board. The *Great Republic* arrived at the mouth of the Columbia River at about midnight on April 18. A pilot boat awaiting the ship put aboard Thomas Doig to bring the side-wheeler in. Doig at first told the captain they should wait for daylight to cross the bar, but by 12:30 a.m.

had changed his mind and decided to steer the ship into Astoria at high tide. The sea was calm and most of the passengers were sleeping in their berths when Captain James Carroll told pilot Doig he thought they were getting too close to Sand Island. Doig, by his own account, disagreed and said the ship needed to go further out into the river. The early ebb tide was now pulling the ship hard toward the island, Carroll said, and he ordered Doig to "port the helm." The pilot, however, let the ship run for another few minutes, just enough time for the tide to bring the ship against the shoal of Sand Island. The *Great Republic* had been moving so slowly that "the jar was hardly noticeable," according to Doig, and he and the captain agreed it would likely come off at the next high tide with the help of four soon-to-arrive tugboats, two of them Captain Flavel's.

The next morning's flood tide was a small one, though, and the tugs could not pull the ship off the sand. The barometer had begun to fall and he could sense a storm coming, the captain recalled. He ordered that most of the passengers be put off on Sand Island and ferried to Astoria aboard the tugs. A handful of passengers and all of the crew, however, were forced to remain on the ship.

At dusk, a southwest gale blew in that brought heavy chop with it and pushed the *Great Republic* up even higher onto the island. Crushed against the shore, her steam pipes broke and disabled the engine. Then the hull began to come apart. Water flooded into the lower compartments and the bilge pumps were soon so clogged they couldn't send it back out.

Captain Carroll had arranged for Flavel to have three tugs there at the next high tide. While they waited, he set the crew to dumping coal overboard to lighten the ship. By the time the flood tide came, however, the seas were so heavy that the tugboats could not get close enough to the *Great Republic* to throw her lines and try to pull the side-wheeler off the island.

At 6:00 a.m. on Sunday, April 19, the captain ordered the few remaining passengers and the crew to put ashore on Sand Island aboard the *Great Republic*'s lifeboats. The second-to-last of the lifeboats left the ship at 10:30 a.m., but within seconds of setting out, its steering oar broke and the boat capsized. Eleven of the fourteen men aboard drowned, one of them Carroll's first officer. (Twenty of the twenty-seven horses aboard the *Great Republic* drowned also.) The captain and the pilot remained on the ship until 5:00 p.m., when the two of them lowered the last lifeboat and came ashore safely.

Captain Flavel headed up the salvage operation that made a desperate effort to pull the *Great Republic* off the sand, but the seas were so heavy that the boat quickly broke into three pieces. The bow was beached, but the two aft compartments of the ship disappeared beneath the waves. With them went the *Great Republic*'s treasure tank, filled with gold and silver from the Comstock Lode and the San Francisco and Carson City mints. That trove of ore and coins, worth millions even at the time, is still somewhere on the floor of the ocean just outside the river's mouth. Perhaps nothing speaks so persuasively of the danger of the Columbia Bar as the fact that there has never been a serious effort to recover the treasure of the *Great Republic*; no one has considered the difficulties and risks worth the hundreds of millions of dollars that treasure is worth today.

In the aftermath of the wreck, Thomas Doig's pilot license was suspended for one year, and when people grumbled that if Flavel had been there instead of Doig the *Great Republic* would still be afloat, few cared to disagree. And if Flavel enjoyed little success in salvaging the *Great Republic*, he did far better after the *Queen of the Pacific*, blinded by fog and smoke from nearby forest fires, ran aground on Clatsop Spit in 1883. Flavel and his tugs were able to rescue all aboard, and the ship itself, along with most of its cargo, saving the shipping company approximately $737,000. The company, however, refused to pay the $65,000 salvage bill they had been sent. The case went all the way to the US District Court in Portland, where Judge Matthew Deady not only awarded the salvagers every penny of what they demanded, but gave Flavel himself $10,000 of that money, declaring that "the enterprise and gallantry displayed by him on September 5th 1883, was such as would reflect great credit on a much younger and abler man than himself."

Flavel by then was done with even his tugboat business. His enormous wealth gave him plenty to manage in retirement. He invested heavily in his community, one of five incorporators of the Astoria and Winnemucca Railroad Company, and was the main organizer and initial president of the First National Bank of Astoria.

By the time he died in 1893 at the age of seventy, Flavel's imprint was so deep on Astoria that it is omnipresent even today. His mansion is a museum and a major tourist attraction, standing right on the curve where Highway 101 becomes the city's main drag, Commercial Street. The Columbia River Bar Pilots still list Flavel as first among them and have continued to honor his insistence that no one should be permitted a license to pilot ships on the Columbia Bar without having first served as a ship's captain.

Yet history has not been truly kind to George Flavel. Joseph F. Halloran, editor of the *Astorian* in the 1880s, wrote a memoir that described the captain as "a grave, saturnine sphinx; sour, dour, cold and crabbed, turning to gold all he touched without a friend and suspicious of all." And thanks in large part to a 1993 *New Yorker* article by

Calvin Trillin, Flavel is perhaps best remembered both in Astoria and beyond for the decline and fall of his family's fortunes. After a brief summation of his "stranglehold" on the bar, Trillin's article dispensed with Captain Flavel to focus on the last of the family's line in Astoria, the captain's unmarried, childless sexagenarian great-grandchildren, a brother and sister. The story really was about the great-grandson, Harry Flavel, a peculiar fellow who at twenty had gotten away with hacking another young man with a hatchet, and then at fifty-eight was convicted of stabbing a second young man with a large knife or bayonet. The motif of the article was the pleasure taken by those in Astoria who had enjoyed seeing the arrogant and out-of-touch Flavels brought low, their family fortune spent and their reputation ruined.

It was an entertaining piece that I read with weary sadness. The life-saving heroism George Flavel had displayed during the wrecks of the *General Warren* and the *Oriole*, unmentioned in the *New Yorker* article, was no longer what the people of the city that once called him its first citizen remembered about the man. All of that had been eclipsed by the legend of his greed and rapacity, and by the descendants who squandered the wealth and status the captain had left to them.

MY FATHER HAD COLLECTED a fair few stories about Captain Flavel back in the 1960s and '70s, when he worked regularly in Astoria, where he was sent to supervise the loading of outgoing ships, and he admired the legendary bar pilot. Inferior men begrudging a better one was a theme he returned to regularly in books and movies. He passed more than a little of that inclination on to me, and that perhaps had at least something to do with the upwelling urge to defend Flavel that I felt. At the same time, I recognized a connection to a certain obdurate childishness that abided in me. What made this particular slice of my psyche childish was how stubbornly it resisted understanding that a man could be at once fine and flawed.

Having Howard Sullivan for my father had certainly complicated that part of growing up. Along with enjoying the sea stories he all but sang, like shanties, and the outdoor activities we did together—hunting, fishing, camping—the main sphere we shared was sports. Ray hadn't been a good athlete as a boy—too loose-jointed, he said—but I was. Yet I was never good enough, it seemed, for my dad. I avoided playing catch with him because he would burn the ball in, throwing as hard as he could when I was eight years old, and I used the new glove he bought me mainly for protection. In the small coastal town where I was growing up, youth sports were a very big deal, a pipeline to the high school varsity teams whose wins and losses the entire community celebrated and suffered passionately. We started playing in an organized league representing our elementary schools when I was in fifth grade. That first year, I scored every touchdown our football team made. In basketball, there were several games in which I outscored the entire other team. High school coaches came to watch me play, and I got my first taste of something like celebrity. "The little hero," my mom called me. But all I got from my dad was criticism, for how I hadn't thrown a block that would have helped a teammate or had hogged the ball when I should have passed it. It was a kind of double life I lived, as the golden boy at school and as a defective wretch at home. The two realities converged finally in the spring of that year, when my class began swim lessons at the local pool. On the third day, one of the instructors, previously impressed that I already knew how to stay afloat, saw me undressing and observed the belt bruises on the backs of my legs. I remember vividly the expression of shock on his face. He told me to put my clothes back on, then called my mother and told her to come get me, that he couldn't let the other kids see me that way. I was so used to them that I barely knew the purple stripes on my legs were there. My mother was deeply upset and ashamed, but my father never acknowledged so much as having heard about anything happening at the swimming pool. The main thing that concerned me was that word would spread—and it did—and that everyone would know what I wanted to keep secret.

Yet at the same time, I remained grateful to my father for having protected me a year earlier. When we were in fourth grade, my class took some test I found remarkable only because of how closely we were monitored; our teacher brought in another teacher to make sure there was no whispering or any other communication between one student and another. Some days later, I noticed that not only my teacher but all the other teachers as well were looking at me strangely—staring at me, actually. It was an IQ test we had taken, and I had gotten the highest score in the history of the school district. I had no idea at the time what it was all about, just that the school, or maybe the school district, had decided that I should jump from fourth to sixth grade. My mom, feeling I think an obligation to do what was best for me, went along with it, but my dad objected resolutely. Absolutely not, he said. I'm sure some part of it was that he didn't think I'd be able to compete successfully in sports against boys two years older than me, but I remember him saying he wasn't going to let me be made into someone the other kids saw as a freak, or someone who thought of himself as something special. I've appreciated his intervention in this instance ever since, because I know that skipping two grades in school would have been terrible for me, and for pretty much the reasons my dad gave for stopping it from happening.

We moved to Portland a year later, shortly before I turned twelve, and for me things went downhill. I was relocated from a working-class town where most of the men were fishermen, loggers, longshoremen, or mill workers to a social environment that had produced what the *Oregonian* described as "Portland's country club high school." As I've told my own kids, moving from Coos Bay to Portland just before I turned twelve was far more jarring than moving from Oregon to New York City in my early twenties. In suburban Portland, I didn't know how to speak or dress or act. The worst part, though, was being a late bloomer. I entered puberty more than a year later than most boys, and it made me miserable. I stopped growing, still looked like a boy when classmates were turning into young men, and was, among other things, uncomfortable in the locker room. I hung on in sports, my one way of standing out from the crowd, but only by exerting a fierce combination of grit and intelligence. *Both* my parents helped me through it, because each had experienced the same thing. I found it difficult to imagine, looking at these two extraordinary physical specimens, but they'd matured later than their peers also. My mom spoke a lot more about it, but simply hearing my father acknowledge that he knew what it was like, that he too had wondered "when the hell I was going to catch up," was tremendously reassuring. I was able to convince myself that the change would come, eventually.

And eventually, it did. Right around the time I turned seventeen, testosterone began surging through me like the crude oil of an uncapped well. I became bigger, stronger, and faster on the field almost overnight, but the main thing I noticed, and enjoyed, was girls looking at me in a whole new way. This improvement in my situation soared when I caught the eye of the girl I'd most admired from afar, the one with the best legs and prettiest eyes in the entire school. For two years, while I was sneaking looks at her in the hallways, she'd been dating a guy from the class ahead of us, one who happened to be the student body president. When "Mr. Perfect," as I called him, went off to Harvard, though, Karen sent a friend to say she'd like to meet me. In short order, she was my girlfriend, not his.

The apogee of my splendid senior year in high school came at a big football banquet where I was presented with a trophy while my girlfriend and my father watched from the seats. I had told Ray about it, about how for the first and only time in my life I saw my father looking at me with pride. I couldn't recall another occasion, I said—which made even that memory more sad than fond for me, because I'd done a lot of other things to be proud of that seemed somehow not to matter.

Right after football season ended, I was playing basketball in the gym with a group of ex-teammates from the class ahead of mine, guys who had already graduated, the kind for whom being starters on the varsity football and/or basketball squads in high school would be the high point of their lives. One of them was Bill Swanson, whom our football coach had never called by his name, but had addressed, in front of us all, only as "Stud." There was a loose ball and I snared it, but Swanson reached in with excessive aggression to snatch it away from me. I tore it loose from his grip, my whole upper body twisting, swinging an elbow that fortunately only brushed his chin, although in that moment I was perfectly prepared to break his face. He stepped back with a stunned but, I must admit, bemused expression and said, "Sullivan's gotten big." *You're goddamn right*, I thought. I was just about ready to really hurt somebody.

Only in one of my conversations with Ray about our fathers did I go very far into the past, telling him how, right after we moved to

Portland, my father had initiated a new form of abuse masquerading as discipline. When he'd bring out the belt, he'd offer me a choice between "five bent over or ten standing up," and I'd always take the ten lashes standing up. I refused from the first to cry or cringe (though God knows I'd done plenty of that when I was younger), but pretty soon I denied him the satisfaction of any expression on my face at all. That was the best I could do to fight back. He put away the belt a year or so later and after that all the beatings he gave me were in eruptions of drunken rage. He went pretty quickly from whacking me open handed to punching me with a closed fist. Only when, shortly after my eighteenth birthday, we got into the brawl in which I frightened him with my own capacity for violence, did all that end. But still it wasn't over.

I don't think of myself as someone who blocks anything out, but when Ray told me the story of being cornered in his father's apartment and exploding into a savagery that left Ray Thomas II crumpled on the floor, a memory came back to me, one I realized I had been denying for decades. It happened about two years after that first fight I had with my father, when I was twenty and he was forty-five. The catalyst was something absurdly insignificant: I was over-celebrating having cleaned out him and his pal at the poker table the night before. But my father heard me jeering and that set him off. I saw his eyes narrow and go as cold as a pond freezing over, then that familiar snarl curling his lips, and before he could say a word or take a step forward I had punched him as hard as I could right under the ribs on his left side. I recall consciously, deliberately, thinking that I was hitting him right where, years earlier, I'd seen those tiny, faded penknife scars. He doubled over, then lifted his head just enough to show me an expression I'd never seen on his face before, one that combined surprise with hurt, as if I'd just done something that was shockingly vicious. Then the lips started to curl again, and he rose up to take a swing. I was on him in an instant. He outweighed me by thirty pounds, but I was three inches taller, at least as strong, and a lot quicker. I don't think I could have brought myself to hit my father in the face, but I had him in a headlock even before we went to the floor. On the ground, I began to squeeze, rolling him onto one side and then twisting, digging in my heels to build leverage. I could feel his neck being strained to the breaking point, knew it was just about to snap, that he would be a dead man if I applied just a little more torque, when I heard him whisper, "Please son, don't. Son, don't."

And I let him go.

Afterward—hard to believe, I'm sure—we both played off what had happened as roughhousing that had gotten out of hand. In very little time, I blotted out the memory of that moment when I held him helpless, right at the edge of the end of his life. I'd come so close.

Only looking back on it a full fifty years later did it occur to me that what I'd heard from my father was him pleading not just for his own life but for mine as well, begging me not to destroy my future in an insane act of patricide. At least, I think that's what I heard. Hoping that's true isn't enough, of course. I have to believe it.

CHAPTER NINE

WHILE NO FIGURE TO RIVAL GEORGE FLAVEL arose again on the Columbia River Bar, Captain Charles Gunderson is among those who came closest. His career on the bar was a long and eventful one, spanning the eras of hand-nailed wooden ships and welded steel freighters and culminating in the formation of what became the Columbia River Bar Pilots Association.

Back in the 1880s, Gunderson had been trained by Captain Flavel personally and he figured into many of the most dramatic stories of shipwrecks and rescues from that period. Gunderson was present at the sinking of the *W. H. Besse*, but it was his work on the lifeboat that saved the crew of the *Fern Glen* in October of 1881 that began his legend. The British clipper had been tossed onto Clatsop Spit at four in the morning when her captain mistook the Tillamook Rock Light for the Point Adams Light. The steamer *General Canby* attempted to take off the *Fern Glen*'s crew but was driven back by the heavy surf, forcing Flavel's tug *Columbia* to launch its lifeboat, with volunteers that included Gunderson aboard, to save the British seamen.

On December 12, 1900, Gunderson had put one of his colleagues, Captain Peter Cordinier, aboard the British barque *Andrada* just north of the river mouth to bring that ship into port. The *Andrada* never made it across the bar, though what happened to it will never be known for certain, other than that it was caught in yet another of those sudden gales that have caused so many deaths on the Columbia Bar. After Cordinier was put aboard, the *Andrada* was seen again only by the captain and crew of another British barque caught in the hurricane-force winds that had arisen so swiftly. The *Ardermurchan*, sailing south from Vancouver, British Columbia, bound for Liverpool with a cargo of canned salmon, had been swept into the gale about fifty miles southwest of the Columbia's mouth. The wind had thrown the *Ardermurchan* so far onto her side that the ship's lower yards were dipping into the sea when the crew saw the *Andrada* on an opposite tack, keeled over with her rail in the water. The *Ardermurchan*'s captain saw the other ship's flags signal, "Andrada: We are in distress," and sent back, "We are in the same condition." Just moments later, the gale blew the two ships so far apart that the *Andrada* disappeared within seconds, the *Ardermurchan*'s captain remembered.

The *Ardermurchan* survived, but only after a near mutiny when the junior officers and crew demanded that the masts be cut away. The ship's captain had stopped them only at the point of a pistol. Instead, the captain ordered all five thousand cases of salmon dumped overboard, and with that the ship righted and was able to make it safely into port.

The *Andrada* was never seen again. No part of her, or of the bodies of those who had been aboard, was ever found.

Gunderson and the other pilots took up a fund for Cordinier's wife and four children, then continued to put aboard ships coming in and out across the bar. In 1903, he and a group of other pilots paid $13,000 for the sleek schooner the *Joseph Pulitzer*. In 1909, when the Port of Portland assumed control of Columbia Bar pilotage and purchased the *Joseph Pulitzer* for $12,000, Gunderson was one of the five men the port hired to continue bringing ships in and out of the river's mouth.

After the Port of Portland relinquished its authority over the bar in 1914, Gunderson was the leader of the group that formed what became the Columbia River Bar Pilots Association. He was also serving as the president of the Oregon Pilot Commission in 1923 when he helped put into service the most storied vessel ever to work the bar.

This was a ship that had become world-famous under the name of its builders, King & Winge of Seattle, who had produced it as their masterwork in 1914. Designed as a halibut schooner, the *King & Winge* was 110 feet long with two sixty-foot masts. Made with four-by-four oak frames seamed close together and covered with two layers of sheathing, the ship was extraordinarily stout. The steel plates for breaking ice that fitted to her bow gave the *King & Winge* a look of majestic formidability, a vessel far too grand to be a fishing boat. That, at least, had been the opinion of Captain Olaf Swenson, who, with his partner C. L. Hibbard, chartered the *King & Winge* before it was finished, then took her north to the Arctic for a hunting and trading expedition that the two planned as the basis for a motion picture.

Their plans turned in the harbor at Nome, Alaska, where *King & Winge* anchored close by the *Bear*, a cutter that had been dispatched by the US government to assist in the rescue of the survivors of the world-famous Stefansson Expedition.

Formally the Canadian Arctic Expedition, but renamed by the newspapers for the famous explorer who headed it, Vilhjalmur Stefansson, this was a fleet of three ships that the government of Canada had sent to search, survey, and map the Northwest Territories' Parry

Islands. Stefansson, the son of Icelandic immigrants who had been born in Manitoba and raised in North Dakota, was world-famous for his 1913 book *My Life with the Eskimos*, in which he described the four years he had spent in Western Canada as part of an expedition sponsored by the American Museum of Natural History. The Canadian Arctic Expedition was a far more complex enterprise, and Stefansson was more loner than leader. When the main ship, the *Karluk*, became marooned in the ice, Stefansson and five other members of the crew left it. Stefansson's story was that they had gone to hunt fresh meat for the *Karluk*'s crew, but this was disputed by some who had remained aboard the ship; they accused Stefansson of having abandoned them because he knew the *Karluk* was doomed. Whatever the truth, it was a fact that the *Karluk* had been carried off by moving ice until it was stuck fast in the frozen water and slowly crushed.

When the two other ships that were part of the expedition reached safety, word of the missing *Karluk* and the twenty-five men who had been aboard it turned into international news. The public debate over whether Stefansson was a hero or a villain made headlines throughout North America.

It was a time when not only explorers but ships themselves could become central characters in the narrative of world events. Newspapers across the globe reported on the search for the *Karluk* and crew, but it was most closely followed up and down the Pacific coast in a time when the interconnection of the waterfronts stretching between San Francisco and Anchorage was felt deeply, owing in large part to the shared sense of separation from folks "back East" that pervaded the region.

A failed effort by the *Bear* to find the *Karluk* and the abandoned men was part one of the story, and when they read it, Captain Swenson and his partner Hibbard recognized an opportunity for heroism that would generate enormous publicity. The two immediately proposed joining the *Bear* in a second try to rescue any survivors who might still be out there on the ice.

Most of those who had been aboard the *Karluk* were already dead. Four had made it as far as Herald Island, where they died together. Another group of four had tried for Wrangel Island but succumbed along the way. The remaining members of the expedition had stuck with the *Karluk*'s captain, Robert Bartlett, who got them to Wrangel Island. After Bartlett and his Inuk hunter set out across the sea ice to Siberia to seek help, the men left on Wrangel Island slowly succumbed to the elements. Three were dead by the time the *Bear* and the *King & Winge* reached the island and took the remaining survivors aboard. It was one of the most celebrated rescues of the time and made the *King & Winge* known to most of America and to mariners worldwide.

The ship would become even more famous four years later, when it was witness to one of the great disasters in maritime history, the sinking of the passenger steamship the *Princess Sophia*. Late in the evening of October 23, 1918, the ship had left Skagway, Alaska, for Vancouver, British Columbia, with 268 passengers and a crew of 75 aboard. Running three hours behind schedule, the *Sophia* was headed at full speed south down Lynn Canal when it was met by a stiff southwest wind and an obliterating snowstorm. Because visibility was nonexistent, the captain ordered that the crew use a method of dead reckoning that involved blowing the ship's whistle and calculating its location within the canal based on the time it took for an echo to return. The result was that the *Sophia* had drifted more than a mile off course by two in the morning when it struck hard into the tip of an underwater mountain known as Vanderbilt Reef.

A wireless distress call was received in Juneau, and a flotilla of boats and ships launched from various locations to try to reach the Sophia in time to save those aboard. One was the *King & Winge*. By the time the US Lighthouse Service tender *Cedar*, which was to lead the rescue operation, arrived at Vanderbilt Reef, the *King & Winge* was already there, circling the *Sophia*, which was sitting entirely out of the water at low tide, but was unable to get closer than a few hundred feet to the stranded steamer.

The *Sophia*'s captain, Leonard Locke, had decided that the rough seas made evacuation impossible and so, in consultation with the captains of the *Cedar* and the *King & Winge*, agreed to wait for high tide, hoping either that the rising water would lift the ship off the reef or that the lifeboats could be put in at first light. The gale-strength winds, though, rose steadily at the same time the water did. The rising tide lifted the stern of the *Sophia* off the rock, but the gashed bow remained stuck on the rock, and the ship was spun nearly 360 degrees, then washed off the reef with her whole bottom torn open. The *Sophia* sank within an hour with all 343 passengers either drowning aboard or dying quickly in the nearly frozen sea. The only survivor was an English setter found a couple of days later paddling in Auke Bay, outside Juneau.

The wreck of the *Princess Sophia* remains to this day the greatest maritime disaster in the history of Alaska and British Columbia, and was among the most intensely covered tragedies of the early twentieth century in American newspapers, not quite on a par with the sinking of the *Titanic*, but close, given that so many of the dead were women and children, the families of soldiers and sailors.

The captain and crew of the *King & Winge* were featured in many stories for having pulled the floating bodies of the dead from the water and carrying them to Juneau for burial.

The glory days of the *King & Winge* seemed far behind it by 1923, however. The schooner was now in the hands of a criminal gang that had been using her as a rumrunner since the advent of Prohibition. After the ship was seized at sea, however, the Columbia Bar Pilots were able to buy her cheap, considering the quality of her construction. A new two-hundred-horsepower diesel engine was installed, and the name was changed to *Columbia*. In this fresh incarnation, the ship became fabled all over again, this time for the strength and durability it displayed in leading tens of thousands of ships across the Columbia Bar during the thirty-four years it served as a pilot boat.

Captain Gunderson would be long retired by the time the *King & Winge* version of the *Columbia* was removed from service on the bar. He prided himself on never having lost a ship, and was grateful that his name had so rarely been in the news. Bar pilots, it seemed, only received newspaper coverage when something terrible happened to them or to a ship they were aboard.

The year Gunderson retired, 1925, the first bar pilot since the formation of their association died on the job. Captain Kenneth P. T. Wood fell from the rope-and-wood ladder he was using to climb aboard the steamer *Knoxville City*, disappeared into the big waves below, and was never seen again. A year later, in one of the stranger mortalities ever suffered on the bar, a pilot at the helm of the steamer *West Nigeria* somehow lost his bearings in the fog and crashed into the bar pilot office at the foot of Eleventh Street in Astoria. A retired pilot approaching the office on foot suffered a heart attack at the moment of collision and died on the spot.

Just as strange and far more absurd was the attempt in 1929 by the National Geographic Board to soften the reputation of the Columbia Bar by issuing a decree that the completion of the jetties had made the entrance to the river "the safest in the world." Just a few weeks later, on June 16, 1929, the Quaker Line's freighter *Laurel*, headed outbound across the bar carrying seven million board feet of lumber to New York and Philadelphia, was overwhelmed by huge breakers that disabled her steering then swept the ship onto Peacock Spit, where it was battered by the big waves until it broke in two the next morning, right at the spot where a nineteen-year-old seaman named Russell Smith was standing. After Smith was pulled to his death by the wave that was breaking across the *Laurel*'s bow, the other thirty-two men on board crowded onto the ship's after section.

The Coast Guard cutter *Redwing* arrived just in time to collect the twenty-four men who were steering the *Laurel*'s lifeboats through the lumber that had spilled into the sea and was being tossed at them by the waves like giant spears. The other eight members of the ship's crew, though, were forced to wait until the following morning to be rescued.

The delay was caused by a distress signal that came in from the steam schooner *Multnomah* stating that after its boiler had failed in the heavy seas, its hull had begun to take in water, the ship was tipped sideways, and six hundred thousand feet of lumber had spilled from the deck. The Coast Guard sent its cutter to remove the fifteen passengers aboard the *Multnomah*, then helped make temporary repairs to the boiler that enabled the ship to chug back to Astoria, where within a day it was declared no longer fit for sea duty.

The *Redwing* got back to the *Laurel* in time to take off seven of the eight men aboard, but the Coast Guard had been unable to convince Captain Louis Johnson to leave his ship. The Coasties stood by, even sending planes that snapped pictures of Captain Johnson on the bridge of the *Laurel*, where he remained for the next fifty-four hours, until an even more powerful gale blew in and separated the two halves of the ship by a distance of eight hundred feet. Soon after that, the Coast Guard saw a white flag raised from the *Laurel*'s bridge and sent a motor lifeboat that fought through crashing seas to the side of the broken freighter. Johnson slid down a manila rope into the arms of his rescuers.

The Geographic Board stubbornly refused to retract its "safest" declaration for nearly another half year, until after the *Admiral Benson*, a three-thousand-ton steamship carrying thirty-nine passengers, a crew of sixty-five, and a cargo of citrus fruit, ran aground on the sands near Peacock Spit just after dark on February 15, 1930, and found itself stranded about four hundred yards west of where the *Laurel*'s remains were still visible in the fog. Coast Guard lifeboats from the Cape Disappointment and Point Adams stations took off the passengers. The crew remained aboard the *Admiral Benson*, hoping to refloat her, but a rising gale persuaded Captain C. C. Graham to let his men be taken off also. Graham had remained aboard the ship alone for the next four days, until the heavy seas began to pull the ship's riveting apart, cracking the decks and flooding the engine room. After Graham signaled for assistance, his rescue became one of the more spectacular in the history of the bar, effected by a nearly thousand-foot-long cable the Coast Guard strung between the ship and the shore. Hundreds of people watched from Cape Disappointment as Graham pulled himself hand over hand, just above the waves, to safety.

Just a few weeks later, the former *King & Winge*, now the bar pilot vessel *Columbia*, was crossing the bar when it was struck by a wave that tore off its stack and starboard davits. The now widely mocked Geographic Board quietly withdrew its statement about the Columbia Bar being the "safest in the world" ocean entrance to a major river.

The *King & Winge* iteration of the *Columbia* was sold in February of 1958, replaced by a new sixty-five-foot pilot boat that was stable in all but the heaviest seas. Pilots were still boarding the incoming ships they would take across the Columbia Bar the same old way, though, assisted by a pair of "mates" who rowed a dory boat through ocean waves from the *Columbia* to the ship, then stood by as the pilot climbed up a rope-and-wood Jacob's ladder. The pilots disembarked from ships they had taken into the ocean by the same ladder, and again were rowed in the dory back to the *Columbia*. "Idiot sticks" was what those who manned the oars called them, so overmatched were they by heavy seas.

The gallows humor that the pilots and the crewmen aboard the *Columbia* used to soften the sense of danger they experienced constantly was tested beyond its limits on September 30, 1962, when Captain Edgar Quinn stepped off the Jacob's ladder that had been dropped over the side of the Japanese ship *Olympia* into a dory with Donald Nelson and William Wells at the oars. Amid waves whipped up by winds upwards of fifty miles per hour, the crew of the *Olympia* watched as the dory was swamped within seconds after the pilot Quinn came aboard. His crew had lost sight of the boat within seconds, the *Olympia*'s captain said when he called the Coast Guard.

The dory rolled over several times, and when it capsized the second time, Wells disappeared. Captain Quinn and Donald Nelson, who was training as a pilot, were able to right the boat each time it flipped, and "did the best they could with the flimsy oars," as an *Oregonian* article the next day put it. This was just enough to get within sight of land in a boat now filled with water up to their knees. When the dory rolled over yet again, the two men swam for it and were able to slosh gasping up onto the beach. The pair walked four miles before the Coast Guard spotted them and took them aboard a rescue boat, seventeen hours after they had gone into the water. The dory was found in the surf not far from where the two men had abandoned it, but the body of William Wells was never recovered.

Wells's death spurred the Columbia Bar pilots to find a better way, and they did in 1967, with the arrival of the new pilot boat *Peacock*. The vessel had been custom-built for the Columbia River Bar Pilots in Bremen, Germany, based on the rescue boats the West Germans used in the North Sea. Ninety feet long, with an eighteen-foot beam, and powered by a pair of Caterpillar diesel engines that could provide a top speed of twenty-six miles per hour, the *Peacock* was a giant leap beyond any boat ever seen on the Columbia Bar. Not only was she truly self-righting, virtually unsinkable even in the worst weather, but the *Peacock*'s design eliminated nearly all of the dangers of being put aboard or taken off ships. In her aft section, the vessel carried a motorized twenty-three-foot "daughter boat" that could be boarded out of the stern then put into the water on a hinge that was used to bring the boat in when it "plowed" into the rear of the boat upon its return. The *Peacock* was so buoyant that pilots could surf the biggest swells in it. More than four thousand bar crossings without a single serious incident were made with the new pilot boat in its first year of service.

Even if the *Peacock* made them safer, many of the pilots expressed mixed feelings about the vessel. Days spent on the windowless new pilot boat felt like "living on a submarine," as one pilot put it. It was stark and cramped inside. There was nothing to look at but the instruments and each other, and no deck to fish from during downtime, like the *Columbia* provided. Within a matter of months, all of them had agreed that the *Peacock* should be the "winter boat" and that the *Columbia* should remain the bar pilots' "summer boat."

Even when they were using the *Peacock*, though, pilots continued to risk their lives by working the Columbia Bar. That was driven home in the harshest way possible in the spring of 1973, when Captain Edgar Quinn, whose survival of the capsized dory had been so celebrated eleven years earlier, was swept away by a wave as he boarded the *Maritime Queen*. Quinn was rescued by a Coast Guard helicopter but had been in the water so long that he died of hypothermia-induced heart failure at the hospital.

Even when the *Peacock*'s daughter boat was being used, pilots continued to get into it from the deck of a ship by rappelling on a rope slung from the rail. In February of 1994, Captain Michael Dillon was hanging from the rope with his feet braced against the side of a car transporter, waiting for a swell to carry the daughter boat close enough to jump in. He had found what he thought was the right moment, and let go of the rope, only to watch the daughter boat suddenly lurch away on a back current. He fell into eighteen-foot swells, where the crew of the ship lost sight of him in seconds, even using their spotlights. "I was amazed at how quickly I drifted away from them," Dillon would say later. He was two miles south of the South Jetty within twenty minutes of going into the water. He saw the Coast Guard helicopter coming toward him, Dillon remembered, but felt certain the crew would miss him in the dark of almost midnight. He went onto his back so that the reflectors on his float coat would be most visible, and shined his flashlight at the chopper, Dillon said, but was nevertheless amazed when the helicopter hovered, then dropped a rescue swimmer with two harnesses.

Putting pilots aboard ships with a helicopter began in the late 1990s and soon became standard procedure. Pilots still had to get off the boat by descending down the side of a ship on a Jacob's ladder or by rappelling on a rope, however. In January of 2006, Captain Kevin Murray had been trying to step off the ladder hanging from the rail of a 558-foot log carrier called *Dry Beam* into the *Chinook*, the boat that had replaced the *Peacock*, when exactly the same thing that had happened to Michael Dillon happened to him. In twenty-foot seas and wind gusting to fifty miles per hour, the pilot boat had bounced away just as Murray tried stepping onto it, and he tumbled into the water. Three days later, his body washed up on the beach seventy-five miles north of the Columbia's mouth.

NO BAR PILOT HAS DIED on the job since Kevin Murray, but that's no indication that the danger of the work has been seriously reduced. Pilots still climb up and down the sides of ships on rope ladders. More often, yes, they are dropped aboard or taken off by helicopter, but frequently they swing at the end of their tether in squalls filled with forty- or fifty-mile-per-hour winds. Dan Jordan, a bar pilot in his late fifties, described to me walking out onto a log raft in rough seas to be taken off by a helicopter, and it sounded like a very long few minutes indeed.

The pilots are highly regulated freebooters. They aren't paid salaries but instead divide the fees they collect from the thousands of ships they take across the Columbia Bar each year. It's work my father would have been suited for, a job that requires a sense of command supported by layers of technical calculation, involving underfield clearances and ranges of maneuverability that vary enormously from ship to ship. While the Coast Guard can close the bar to tugboats and fishing boats and other smaller craft, only the pilots choose whether it's safe for large ships to cross. What to do, for example, with a bulk carrier that is designed to haul huge quantities of wheat or corn as inexpensively as possible, and far too underpowered to push through big waves, on a day when the breakers are twenty-five feet high and the wind is gusting to sixty miles per hour, is a decision with enormous consequences, and pilots make calls of that magnitude regularly.

Even after pilots are hired, they spend years training and studying before they're allowed to take a ship across the bar on their own. The degree of specific knowledge required of them seems endless. I obtained a copy of a recent "Bar Pilot Exam," which consisted of forty-seven questions. A perfect answer to each of them is required for a passing grade. Here's one question: "You are inbound with vessel drawing 28 feet, it is low water, and between #11 Buoy and Fort Stevens Dock. An inbound vessel crowds you over to the southward. What mark would you use to know you were still in good water and would not ground your ship?" Answer: "Use as a range, the back red light of the Flavel Range on the red flashing light of Fort Stevens Dock open to East, to carry 29 feet of water. Open this range slightly to eastward, and carry 30 feet."

And yet it's the ability to deal with what can't be learned that pilots admire most. Back in 2005 a pilot guiding a six-hundred-foot bulk carrier inbound across the bar found himself headed for a collision with a sport fishing boat that would have certainly killed those aboard the smaller vessel. The pilot blasted the ship's horn repeatedly and veered as close to the shore as he dared, but the fishing boat kept moving in the same direction. The boat's owner, as Dan Jordan explained it to me, "had gotten his license by taking an auxiliary Coast Guard class where he was told to always stay to the right. So he kept going right, even when it put him directly in the path of the ship." Finally, the pilot had to make a potentially disastrous decision to ground the big ship. Luckily, the hull remained intact, and the ship was able to float free at the next high tide, "but it could have gone a lot worse," as Jordan put it.

Dan showed me a photograph taken from the bar pilot's helicopter of a big container ship passing between literally hundreds of fishing boats and other small craft on a summer day, the lane for passage so narrow that it left no margin for error. "You can't turn a ship that size, and you can't steer it around anything," he said. "There's nothing to do but set a course, sound the horn, and hope those boats stay out of the way. Even though it's beautiful out, those are some of my least favorite days. Because you have to depend on other people."

When Jordan talked about what he thought might be the most important part of the job, it brought my father to mind again, wondering how he would have handled it. "The moment you come aboard, you have to settle everyone down," he said. "These sailors might have been at sea for months, and now the first time they're seeing land it's on the Columbia Bar. They don't know the channels, and they don't know the currents. Maybe it's foggy and windy and rough, and you can see the disorientation in their eyes. They might make a mistake. So they look to you for a sense of calm and certainty, and you better project it from the moment you set foot on the deck."

My father would have been able to project the confidence required, I felt certain, but I wasn't sure about the calm. He was impatient with people. While Dan was speaking, I flashed back on one of my last outings with my dad. He and I had taken my son and one of my nephews out fishing on Lake Billy Chinook in Central Oregon. The boys were six and seven at the time, as I recall. At one point my nephew became startled and confused by a jerk on the line and dropped his pole into the water. My father snatched it up quickly and as he did slapped the back of Shane's hand hard when the boy reached to grab hold of it. Shane was so shamed and scared that he began to "blubber," as my dad called it. I caught my father's eyes with mine and stared into them. He saw my disapproval and sadness and flinched from them. A moment later he began trying to show Shane how to hold his pole and how to give a little line and then reel in. It was as if he thought the instruction he offered could cancel the hurt he'd caused. And when Shane's only response was a quivering chin and a blank stare at the surface of the water, my dad turned his attention to my son, telling him what a good job he was doing with his pole, trying to make it right with his other grandson. It had nothing to do with him favoring one boy over the other. It was simply that he was leaving Shane to figure it out on his own. I knew all too well what that was like.

CHAPTER TEN

OUR FIRST INDICATION that the forecasts we had relied upon were not holding up came as a pleasant surprise. The low clouds that were supposed to press a wan sky down on the bar until nightfall had dissolved into baby blue by noon, and half an hour past that all we could see above was the sun blazing down upon us. I was grateful that back at the boat launch Ray had suggested the precaution of putting on sunblock.

The wind had risen a little, and at first I thought the increased turbulence in the river was because of that. I heard the bar before I felt it. A few minutes at most after I thought I'd detected a roar in the distance, it filled my ears. The wave heights ahead of us began doubling and then redoubling. All at once, those "foaming surges," as Alexander Ross had described them, surrounded us on every side. Some part of me was thinking, *We can't be there already*, when a wave that came down on us across the port side of the bow filled my mouth with salt water, as if to make sure I understood that we had reached the point where the ocean met the river and subsumed it.

I had no thought of how far this abruptly altered reality we were in extended. There was no sense of something up ahead, just this pandemonium of waves that seemed impossibly close together, as if piled one atop the other, tossing the boat like a kite in blustery wind. Beneath us was utter convulsion; I imagined this was how it would feel to be on the water above the epicenter of an earthquake.

Ray and I were both pumping our legs furiously, all we knew to do against the push of the incoming tide and a world infinitely more powerful than we were. The wave in front of us was above our heads. I couldn't imagine how we were going to get over the top of it, and I knew there was more of the same on the other side. I was stricken for a moment when we tipped right and I saw the starboard ama completely underwater, with the left ama raised to the height of our heads. Water was splashing in over the gunwale across my right shoulder when another wave raised the bow of the trimaran to a point where Ray and I were both leaning forward to avoid being flung back across the stern. Falling out of the boat here did not seem survivable. I sucked in each breath with the clear physical knowledge of how deeply, how desperately I wanted to live.

We went over one large swell, into its trough, and then up the face of another, just holding on at that point. The sail swung from one side to the other, the line raking the top of my head. I saw Ray pulling on the rope with both hands, shoulders turned hard to port. Holding the rudder steady took every bit of the strength in my right hand, wrist, and arm, even as I sensed that it didn't matter much.

For a long ninety seconds or so it felt as if we were skidding sideways, not headed forward, with the starboard ama still in the water, until we were pushed somehow onto the top of a breaker that seemed to hold us there, pedaling in place, suspended at the highest point of the bar. This was the "standing wave" at the outer edge of the Columbia's mouth that I had read about, a kind of frenzied equilibrium in which the opposing forces of current and tide struggled to resolve the tensions between them. It came from deep beneath the surface, I knew, and yet here it was, pushing us as far on top of the water as we could be.

I took one quick look down into the trough below, and in an instant I knew what this was all about, what I had been looking for out here on the bar in a kayak, or clinging to a rock wall a hundred feet above ground without a rope, or taking a blind curve on a dirt road in a war zone.

It was a sense of release I sought, of being set loose from a worry that had been at the core of me for as long as I could remember, a worry that my father had put in place many years earlier, a worry that I carried with me constantly, that I clung to even as it clung to me, even all these years later, long after my dad was dead and gone, an existential worry. And just now my soul was free of it and him and everything.

THE STANDING WAVE FELL AWAY finally, dropping the trimaran onto a transitional teeter-totter of rolling breakers. It felt for a time as if we were stranded in a back-and-forth that was like the sea being sloshed in a giant bowl, and then without any perceivable transition we were out of that bowl and in the ocean for real.

It was instinct for me, but perhaps experience for Ray, that compelled us to pedal straight into the waves for a couple of hundred yards, until we were well clear of the bar, out of the breakers and into the swells. Only then did we turn our boat north and see, off to the right, the waves splashing across Peacock Spit, with Cape Disappointment looming above.

I was struck by the belated realization that people on a vessel coming in across the bar had a very different experience than those, like us, crossing out did. Coming in must give people a sense of arrival, of achieving safe harbor, I imagined. There would be a sigh of relief followed by an easy feeling of accomplishment. This discernment of the obvious came to me in the experience of exactly the opposite, my overdue discovery that there was no *completion* in crossing the Columbia Bar outward, no ending of any kind, because when the bar spat one clear on the west side of it, where one found oneself was in the Pacific Ocean.

And this wasn't the ocean that Kenny and I had gazed out upon from the beach in Seaview that morning. The swells here were twice the size of those, three and four feet high, with random six-footers coming at us when waves combined, or "stacked," as surfers put it. And they appeared to be stacking regularly.

Kenny would claim later that he had seen the wave train coming in hours earlier than had been forecast, had seen it, he said, before we even reached the bar. I use the word "claim" not because I doubt Kenny, but because I don't remember him mentioning this until later, shortly before the unexpected breakers nearly killed Ray and me.

Even though our planned course was to turn north up the coast, Ray and I had to be careful immediately not to let the waves, the big ones anyway, hit the trimaran flush on the side, because those six-footers were clearly capable of flipping us.

Ray asked then if I saw Kenny anywhere, behind us maybe. I turned to look over one shoulder, then the other, and saw nothing but ocean. Only at Ray's urging did I pivot in my seat and climb reluctantly on hands and knees atop the gear we had lashed to the back of the boat, holding on with both hands. After at least a minute of scanning the horizon I finally saw the speck of a giant man in the distance, coming our way beneath a taut sail.

Ray and I turned the trimaran back in that direction, making a large sweeping circle for the ten minutes or so it took Kenny to catch up with us. He arrived beside us out of breath, but smiling. I thought he looked a bit shaken beneath his grin, even slightly ashen, though all he expressed was some slight chagrin about having fallen so far behind Ray and me. The two of us pedaling together had been more than he could keep up with, Kenny admitted, then added in a more somber tone that he had been pushed far inside on the North Channel when he'd tried to come away from the jetty during the bar crossing, and it had been an "all-out effort" to work his way clear and emerge into the ocean.

The waves were bigger than we'd seen that morning, Kenny acknowledged, but I don't recall him seeming overly concerned about it. At his suggestion, we dug celebratory beers out of our coolers and drank them as we drifted in the sea, rocking back and forth and gazing up at Cape Disappointment. When one of the stacked waves came, we turned and surfed it toward land. The way the trimarans twisted as they rode over the bigger swells probably should have tripped some sort of alarm, but I can't remember even thinking much about it.

The shore there was barricaded by big rocks, thirty and forty feet above the waterline, that had sheared off of the cape eons ago to form a solid wall stretching north all the way from Peacock Spit. They'd been named "The Elephant Rocks" by some anonymous nineteenth-century sailor who looked at them and saw the backs of pachyderms. The only opening in the Elephant Rocks was a crevice so narrow that not even a trimaran could have squeezed through.

I wondered if that might be the entrance to Dead Man Cove, but Ray insisted that no, Dead Man Cove was the broader opening we floated past a few hundred yards north of there. I wondered if Ray was wrong and if that was really the way into another fabled defile, Beard's Hollow.

I'd looked down on an inlet I'd been wrongly told was Beard's Hollow from far above at the edge of the trail to the North Head Lighthouse two weeks earlier, and thought it was one of the most extraordinarily lovely spots I'd ever seen. The northwest end of Cape Disappointment plunged down into the sea at a steep angle there, behind the wall of rocks that showed from sea. Moss and ferns clung to the cape's lower half, with dozens of small coast pines sprouting out of the basalt, curved but vertical, their glistening greenery making a marvelous contrast to the wisps of fog that floated among them. Below was a small but spectacularly beautiful beach that made me ache to be on it. The feeling was deep and strangely poignant. Down there, I felt, it might be possible to arrive finally at the bottom of everything.

Both Beard's Hollow and Dead Man Cove had been named for seamen whose corpses had been pulled from the water there. This dated back to January of 1853, when the barquentine *Vandalia* set sail from San Francisco bound for Portland with somewhere between nine and twelve persons aboard; no one knows the number with certainty. What happened to the *Vandalia* is one of the Columbia Bar's many mysteries. It was last seen on January 9 by the crew of a passing ship, the *Grecian*, who described observing the *Vandalia* waiting to enter the river's mouth, struggling a bit, perhaps, but holding her own. A week later, the *Vandalia* was found upside down on what would become Benson Beach,* the long and narrow strip of sand that stretches from the edge of the North Jetty to the base of the North Head Lighthouse.

---

* The beach is named for the shipwreck there of the previously mentioned steamer *Admiral Benson* in 1930.

When word of the wreck reached Ilwaco, a group of men raced to the scene, where they confronted members of the Clatsop tribe who were attempting to plunder the wreck and, the Ilwaco men believed, the remains of the dead. Only the bodies of four of those who had been aboard the Vandalia were ever recovered. One was that of Captain E. N. Beard, whose corpse had been found floating in the eerily isolated loch that was named for him. The body of a fourteen-year-old boy who had been aboard the ship was nearby. Two other corpses were found in the exquisite bight south of Beard's Hollow that became known as Dead Man Cove. The history is a bit vague, but it was my impression that the name Dead Man Cove attached over time, as the bodies of drowned sailors, pushed in by the tide, were regularly found there, and in Beard's Hollow, over the next few decades. Other than Captain Beard's, the names of the dead whose remains were recovered all have been forgotten, as have those whose corpses were never found.

As we finished one beer and opened another, Ray suggested that we might pedal the trimarans through the opening in the rocks and explore for Dead Man Cove. Kenny shook his head: "Not me. You guys want to try going in there, okay. But I wouldn't advise it." The opening was so narrow that the chances of a trimaran being tossed against the rocks was high, Kenny said; we might get in there on jet skis, another time, without him.

I was growing impatient and slightly nauseous, just floating up one side of the waves and down the other. I wanted to get moving, be headed somewhere. "Let's keep going," I told Ray and Kenny, "head up the coast to Seaview and make our landing."

I feel some shame now about being oblivious at the time to a calamity from thirty years earlier that had begun almost exactly where our trimarans were drifting, one that made greater implication of some dark purpose connecting the misfortunes spread across the storyline of the Columbia Bar than any other I know of.

SATURDAY, JANUARY 12, 1991, was the thirtieth anniversary of the "Triumph/Mermaid Incident," as it was described in that morning's *Daily Astorian*. A public memorial and reunion was to be held that afternoon, one attended by most of the survivors, as well as assorted civilian officials and Coast Guard brass. YOU HAVE TO GO OUT, read the heading at the top of the program that had been prepared for the event, and on the plaque that would be presented "in honor of those who answered the call with the supreme sacrifice." Below, on both the program and the plaque, were the names of each of the Coast Guard vessels that had been involved in the rescue operation initiated by the *Mermaid*'s distress call. At the bottom was: "Presented by the family of Darrell J. Murray CHBOSN USCG Ret, with the kindred family who shared this unique experience."

Darrell Murray had struggled more—or at least more publicly—with the aftermath of the *Triumph/Mermaid* disaster than any of the other survivors. While Murray was able to recover in a couple of months from the only significant physical injury he suffered in the sinking of his boat, a fracture dislocation of his right shoulder, the man's mental wounds had proven far more difficult to heal. In 1967, six years after the deaths of the seven men who haunted him, Murray sought psychiatric treatment at the Naval Hospital in Bremerton, Washington. There, he was diagnosed with a depression of some sort, offered counseling and a short course of medication, then sent on his way. He didn't get better.

In June of 1979, now retired from the Coast Guard, Murray sought treatment for a condition he believed met the criteria of a new diagnosis that had surfaced in the treatment of Vietnam War veterans, post-traumatic stress disorder. His decision and the distress that motivated it would become a personal crusade that went on for years. The psychiatrist who treated him at the Veterans Hospital in Sheridan, Wyoming, the state where Murray was now living, had, after ruling out bipolar disorder, described the man as increasingly debilitated by a "chronic depressive process," with anxiety as a major feature. Eventually, his doctor at the Sheridan hospital added a diagnosis of PTSD, entitling Murray to both regular treatment and some increased retirement pay.

The VA's Medical and Regional Office Center at Fort Harrison, Montana, however, did not concur. For one thing, the factotum who wrote the VA's report noted, both sick-call records and the chart of the reenlistment examination Murray had taken on February 16, 1961, only a little more than a month after the "purported" deaths of those aboard the *Triumph* and the *Mermaid*, were "negative for complaints or injuries allegedly suffered" by him that suggested post-traumatic stress disorder. More significant, though, was that no verification of the incident Murray "described" in which supposedly "seven persons and four boats were lost" had been provided or could be found. Therefore, "in the absence of service records showing the veteran as involved in the incident described, the grant of service connection for PTSD was, at best, premature," the VA ruled.

Murray was placed in this particularly bizarre catch-22 because the federal government was refusing to release any records it might possess that related to the *Triumph/Mermaid* calamity on the grounds that they contained confidential information about other veterans. The Freedom of Information Act application Murray filed and eventually prevailed with was what unearthed the Coast Guard investigative report that became the main basis for what I would write forty years later about what had happened to those involved in the wrecks of the *Triumph* and the *Mermaid*.

During the years after his visit to the hospital in Sheridan, Murray began reaching out regularly to the others who had survived from the four boats that went down on the Columbia River Bar in January of 1961, enlisting them in his efforts not only to validate his own suffering but to demand some sort of recognition and memorial for those who had died that day.

Honoring both Murray's longstanding efforts and his recent death had been a considerable part of what impelled the thirtieth anniversary reunion in Astoria on January 12, 1991. The speeches were short, but most of the men who had lived through the events described were there to hear them. Prior to the reunion, it had been planned to note that this day was not only the thirtieth anniversary of the *Triumph/Mermaid* tragedy but also the fifty-fifth anniversary of the sinking of the SS *Iowa* on the Columbia Bar, "a remarkable coincidence," as a publicity release issued during preparations for the reunion and memorial had described it.

Mention of that coincidence was never made during the event itself, however, because the audience and most of Astoria was still in shock from the news that on the previous day, the Coast Guard's attempt to rescue the crew aboard the fishing boat *F/V Sea King* from just outside the Columbia Bar had failed spectacularly, resulting in the loss of three lives, one of them belonging to the man who would become, arguably, the most honored hero in the history of the USCG.

The *Sea King* was a seventy-six-foot stern trawler (a boat designed to pull nets behind it) with a crew of four aboard when it departed Astoria late in the afternoon on January 9, 1991, planning to fish for three days off the coasts of Oregon and Washington. The voyage was both successful and uneventful until the *Sea King* made its return approach to Astoria during the early-morning hours of January 11.

At around 5:00 a.m., the *Sea King* skipper, Darrin Nichols, realized the vessel's steering was malfunctioning. He believed the problem was caused by ice that had shifted and might have reduced the viscosity of the fluid in the hydraulic line, Nichols said later. But when the ice was moved, the problem with the steering persisted. At six, the captain sent a crewman to inspect the lazarette, the small hold aft of the cockpit where stores were held. The lazarette was filled with seawater, the crewman reported back, probably because its starboard hatch cover hadn't been secured; he had taken care of that. Nichols sent his two other crewmen to open the lazarette's drainage valve, so that the water would seep into the engine room, where pumps could send it back out into the ocean.

By 8:00 a.m., though, it had become clear that the engine-room pumps could not keep up with the flooding. A crewman was sent to the fish hold to see if he could close the lazarette drain valve, but there was so much debris—fish, bin boards, and chunks of ice—in the hold that the captain feared the crewman would be injured and ordered him out. The engine room continued to fill with water. What would come out later was that the owner of the *Sea King* had removed a watertight wall between the trawler's engine room and its fish-holding compartment. Without that protection and the buoyancy it provided, the *Sea King* had been in trouble from the moment it began taking on water.

It was 8:39 a.m. when the *Sea King* skipper sent a distress signal to the Coast Guard's Cape Disappointment Station, reporting that it was four nautical miles north of the Columbia River Bar (almost exactly where Ray and Kenny and I had sailed toward Seaview after crossing the bar), taking on water and in danger of sinking. By what seemed at first a fortunate coincidence, all four of the forty-four-foot boats assigned to the National Motor Lifeboat Rescue School at Cape D were engaged in training exercises only a little more than five miles away from where the *Sea King* had sent its distress signal. One after the other, the four rescue boats headed toward the trawler. By the time the first motor lifeboat, CG-44381, reached the *Sea King*, the trawler's decks were awash.

At 8:44 a.m., the Coast Guard Search and Rescue Coordinator at Group Seattle was notified of the operation and assigned the commanding officer of Group Astoria to take charge. This would become important later when the long and agonizing assignment of blame began.

The Group Astoria commander dispatched a helicopter to assist at the scene. The chopper reached the *Sea King* at 9:02 a.m., shortly before the motor lifeboats began to arrive. At 9:10 a.m., the helicopter lowered four gasoline-powered "dewatering pumps" to the deck of the trawler. When the *Sea King*'s crew reported that they were having trouble getting the pumps started in the trawler's flooded engine room, the chopper lowered an Aviation Survivalman (ASM) to assist them. The helicopter then left for Air Station Astoria to get more pumps, leaving just the four motor lifeboats and the ASM at the scene.

The ASM soon reported that he could not get the pumps running, either. The motor lifeboat coxswain, who was now the on-scene commander of the operation, reported to Station Cape Disappointment that the *Sea King* could not be towed across the bar as long as its engine room remained flooded. The duty officer at Cape D advised that the weather forecasts were becoming concerning, with predicted winds approaching seventy miles per hour and seas above sixteen feet. He recommended that the *Sea King* be brought in across the bar now, while it was still possible. The commanding officer at Cape Disappointment called the motor lifeboat a short time later, at 9:51 a.m., said that waves on the Columbia Bar were now between four and six feet high, with an occasional eight-footer, and he too recommended that the *Sea King* be brought in across the bar before sea conditions worsened.

At 10:03 a.m., though, the *Sea King*'s captain reported that a clogged fuel oil filter had shut down his main engine, and that as a result he no longer had either power or steering. At the same time, the ASM sent word that he was still having trouble getting the pumps to take suction. By 10:08 a.m., the Group Astoria commander ordered the helicopter to pick up two machinery technicians at Station Cape Disappointment and take them to the *Sea King* to assist the ASM already aboard. At the same time, the largest and best Coast Guard boat on the Columbia Bar, the fifty-two-footer built to replace the one John Lee Culp had gone down in thirty years earlier, was dispatched to take the *Sea King* in tow. The fifty-two-footer was named *Triumph II*.

The helicopter arrived back at the rescue scene before the *Triumph II* made it there. After the two men who were to help the ASM with the pumps were lowered to the trawler's deck, the decision was made to lift all "unnecessary" *Sea King* crew members to the helicopter and carry them to the safety of Station Cape Disappointment. The first of the two crewmen chosen by the captain was hoisted to the copter without incident, but while the second man was being lifted, the rescue basket became entangled in the trawler's rigging, causing the hoisting cable to part and the basket containing the crewman to drop fifteen feet onto the after main deck. He was seriously injured, though how seriously was difficult to say, because the man was wearing an immersion suit and the Coast Guardsmen on board worried that trying to remove the suit might cause further injury.

Moments later, Charles Sexton, a Coast Guard petty officer who was also an emergency medical technician, volunteered to transfer by helicopter from his motor lifeboat with a basket litter. On board the *Sea King*, Sexton performed a quick examination, then informed the flight surgeon at Group Astoria that the injured man was conscious, alert, and complaining of radiating pain in his left arm, down his back, and through his hips. Out of concern he might have suffered a spinal injury, Sexton had the injured crewman strapped to the litter, covered with a sleeping bag, and placed on top of the main fish hold.

By then the *Sea King* was dead in the water, and its captain was reporting that he doubted the main engine could be restarted. The *Triumph II* arrived twelve minutes later and prepared to take the trawler in tow. In the thrashing seas, it took until 11:31 a.m. to fit the towing bridle through both the *Sea King*'s port and starboard chocks, then begin pulling the trawler toward the bar.

The good news was that the water had finally been pumped out of the engine room. The bad news was that none of the Coast Guardsmen on the scene, nor any of their commanders at Group Astoria or Station Cape Disappointment, was aware that the flooding had started in the lazarette, and that this compartment was still full of water.

In the absence of the helicopter, the coxswain of motor lifeboat CG-44381 had again been assigned the role of on-scene commander. To prepare for the tow of the *Sea King* across the bar, the coxswain took what appeared to be an excellent series of precautions. First, he ordered one motor lifeboat to stand by at the western edge of the bar near Buoy No. 7. Second, he instructed the *Triumph II* and the *Sea King* to proceed on the "red side" of the bar, where the even-numbered buoys were, so as to stay as far away as possible from Peacock Spit. Third, he outlined the procedures that should be followed by those aboard the *Sea King* if the *Triumph II*'s towline parted or if the trawler needed to be quickly abandoned. The coxswain then positioned his own vessel and the two remaining motor lifeboats around the *Sea King* to retrieve anyone aboard the trawler who went into the water.

The underlying problem, though, was that the *Triumph II* and the *Sea King* could make little headway once the tow began. The trawler, thirty-two feet longer and nearly twice as heavy as the boat pulling it, was weltering in the heavy seas. The commander at Station Cape Disappointment suggested altering course to port by 120 degrees, and this did increase the speed of the tow, but it also multiplied the rolling and pitching of the *Sea King*.

The two mechanical technicians aboard the trawler were able to get its main engine restarted at five minutes past noon, just as the trawler passed over what was known as the "ten-fathom curve" at the outer edge of the bar and headed for the shallower water of the river entrance. The swells, though, were steepening. The motor lifeboat stationed near Buoy No. 7 reported to Cape Disappointment that conditions on the bar were steadily deteriorating. A series of radio reports from the *Sea King* indicated that the pitching and rolling of the trawler had increased dramatically and that waves were breaking over its starboard bulwark. The injured crewman was moaning in agony each time the boat pitched, and the engine room was again flooding, which had caused the dewatering pumps to once more lose their prime.

At 12:09 p.m., shortly after the *Triumph II* reported being rocked by breakers more than twelve feet high, the coxswain who had become on-scene commander informed Cape Disappointment that he doubted the *Sea King* could be saved. The coxswain and the commander at Cape D agreed that either the trawler should be evacuated or the tow moved offshore until conditions improved.

The coxswain of the *Triumph II*, however, said he did not believe the *Sea King* could be evacuated in seas that were getting heavier by the minute. The coxswain serving as on-scene commander reported that his boat had been knocked over to between 90 and 120 degrees by a pair of large sea breaks. "I was very concerned about [the *Sea King*]," he would explain later. "I knew it had low freeboard. We had seven people on there. I decided it was time to get people off."

It was not until 12:13 p.m. that the Coast Guardsmen aboard the *Sea King* even began to suspect that the essential problem was the removal of the wall between the fish hold and the engine room. The captain had not told them, but one of the mechanical technicians had overheard a crewman saying that the water in the engine room was coming from the fish hold.

At 12:19, the coxswain of the *Triumph II* reported that his boat had nearly been sent "airborne" by a towering breaker, and that he was reducing speed and moving away from the bar to prevent the capsizing of his own vessel. Shortly after this abortion of the first attempt to bring the *Sea King* in across the bar, the coxswains of the four motor lifeboats on the scene, the commander at Cape Disappointment, and the chief at Air Station Astoria began a series of radio and telephone conversations about whether the trawler should be abandoned. All agreed with the coxswain of the *Triumph II* that the prospects for saving the *Sea King* were bleak and that it was time to prepare for the evacuation of those aboard the trawler. The helicopter, which had left the scene to refuel, was ordered back.

Finally, the operations duty officer at Air Station Astoria got the commanding officer of Group Astoria on the telephone and briefed him. The conversation was recorded and would become primary evidence of fatal misjudgment when the case was reviewed. Near the end of the conversation, the commanding officer at Group Astoria wondered if the Coast Guard cutter *Iris* might be brought to the scene to assist with any evacuation. Did he know the current location of the *Iris*, the commanding officer asked. He did not, the duty officer at Air Station Astoria answered.

"If we can move the *Iris* out there, let's, you know," the commanding officer said then. "I don't, I don't disagree with the decision to evacuate, but if we can possibly save the vessel, we should try." The duty officer agreed, and said he would get the *Iris* underway to the scene as rapidly as possible.

While those two men were speaking, the helicopter arrived back at the scene, where the pilot was instructed to evaluate whether the injured crewmember should be medevaced to the hospital, and whether the others on board the *Sea King* could be evacuated by either a boat-to-boat or boat-to-water transfer. It was then that those on board the *Sea King* discovered the injured crewman's basket litter was not fitted with hoisting straps. With his own basket still torn up by the earlier mishap, the helicopter pilot decided that any evacuation should be postponed.

By 12:49 p.m., the *Iris* was en route to the *Sea King* rescue operation, but it would need nearly two hours to arrive. The helicopter hovering over the trawler was ordered back to Air Station Astoria to refuel and to pick up a basket litter fitted with hoisting straps. The Cape Disappointment commander ordered the *Triumph II* to pull the *Sea King* to a buoy outside the bar and await the arrival of the *Iris*. Three of the motor lifeboats at the scene were recalled to Cape Disappointment.

The helicopter returned to the rescue scene at 1:34 p.m. The pilot, though, decided within a minute or two that the weather and the sea, the arrangement of the *Sea King's* standing rigging, and the trawler's yawing, pitching, and rolling made trying to hoist the injured crewman too dangerous unless his situation became life-threatening.

The commanders monitoring the situation from land were still considering whether to try a second tow of the *Sea King*. The coxswain of the motor lifeboat remaining at the scene reported that he was encountering twelve-foot breakers and did not think a tow was advisable.

The *Iris* arrived at 2:46 p.m., and its commanding officer immediately took charge of the operation. He ordered that the *Triumph II* make a second attempt to tow the *Sea King* across the bar, flanked by the *Iris* and a motor lifeboat that had just arrived on the scene. The four vessels headed in formation toward the mouth of the Columbia at almost exactly 2:30 p.m. As they set out, the skipper of the *Iris* and the helicopter pilot discussed plans for "extracting people from the water" should the *Sea King* have to be quickly abandoned. It was agreed that the motor lifeboat would perform the rescues while the helicopter spotted, and that the *Iris* might launch its daughter boat, the *Iris II*.

Conditions on the bar were only getting nastier. The coxswain of the motor lifeboat reported encountering eighteen-foot seas west of Buoy No. 7 and fifteen-foot seas in the middle of the main ship-ping channel. The tow seemed to be working, though, maintaining a speed of about seven miles per hour, and the *Triumph II* was lining up on entrance to the river.

At 3:12 p.m., the *Sea King* reported that the injured crewman had been moved into the deckhouse, because seas breaking over the trawler's port quarter had been soaking the man and they feared he might become hypothermic. The only place to put the injured crew-man's litter, though, was on a table in the deckhouse, where it had to be held by men on both sides. One was Charles Sexton, who had refused an opportunity to be hoisted off the *Sea King* by helicopter, telling the pilot that he could not leave the injured man without a medically trained attendant.

At 3:21 p.m., the *Sea King's* main engine again shut down. The engine would remain inoperative for only three minutes, but that was long enough for the *Triumph II* to lose both its course and its forward momentum. Within moments it was being driven toward the dangerously shallow water near Peacock Spit known as the Middle Ground. The *Sea King's* engine was running again by 3:25 p.m., and with its help the *Triumph II* attempted a course correction, but the tow was still being pushed toward Peacock Spit.

At 3:33, the *Sea King* reported that its main deck was again awash because of a wave that had just broken over its stern. They were increasing speed, the trawler's captain reported, in an attempt to hasten the drainage of seawater through the freeing ports. The *Triumph II* replied by increasing its speed also. At 3:34, the tow was within a quarter mile of the Middle Ground, and the motor lifeboat stationed about 150 yards off the trawler's port quarter reported that the *Sea King* seemed to be riding lower in the water.

The skipper of the *Iris*, though, thought things still looked good. The *Sea King* "was reacting very nicely," he explained later, "riding very well, as a matter of fact. I would say that she was rolling and pitching less than my ship was. I remember being very pleased at seeing how she was riding."

At 3:39 p.m., the tow entered the Middle Ground. A Coast Guardsman aboard the motor lifeboat was shooting video footage of the tow that showed both the *Sea King* and the *Triumph II* being struck by huge waves, created by the leverage of breakers in shallow water. One minute later, the *Sea King* rolled to port, and its bulwark went into the sea. Water began flowing through the watertight doors of the deckhouse, trapping the injured man and the two attending him inside. Moments later the captain radioed that his vessel was about to go over and that all aboard were abandoning ship. The *Sea King*'s helmsman, the ASM who had come aboard first, and Charles Sexton all tried to free the injured crewman from his litter and find a way to pull him outside. The ship was rolling over rapidly now, though, and sank beneath the waves, disappearing from view, within fifteen seconds.

Of the four men in the deckhouse, only the ASM would survive.

Even the "post-accident" rescue and recovery efforts were something of a fiasco. Shortly after being launched with a crew of two, the *Iris II*'s twin outboard engines failed, one after the other. It was then that the two men aboard discovered that the walkie-talkies on the boat were inoperative.

The motor lifeboat still on the scene picked up five of the seven men who had been aboard the *Sea King*, among them the injured crewman. Missing were Petty Officer Sexton and the *Sea King*'s helmsman.

Group Astoria recommended that the injured crewman be medevaced to Air Station Astoria. The lifeboat's coxswain expressed concern about the man's declining condition, and the *Iris* skipper ordered that the injured man be flown directly to Station Cape Disappointment, where he was taken by ambulance to Columbia Memorial Hospital. There, he was pronounced dead by drowning.

Charles Sexton was fished out of the water by the crew of the motor lifeboat minutes later and flown to Air Station Astoria, where he was also taken by ambulance to Columbia Memorial and pronounced dead on arrival, also by drowning.

The search for the helmsman went on until the following morning, but his body was never found.

I first learned of the *Sea King* sinking when I was in Tom Molloy's office, saw a photograph of Charles Sexton prominently displayed, and asked about him. After briefly telling me the story of Sexton's heroism, Tom led me into the lobby of his office building, where a statue of Sexton stands just inside the doors. I understood that Sexton, by his own decision, had gone onto the *Sea King* and stayed there for six hours, tending to the injured crewman as the trawler was pulled onto the Columbia Bar. Of course he had become an exemplar of valor to those who performed rescues on the bar.

Soon after, I discovered that the Coast Guard had gone far beyond the statue in honoring Sexton for his sacrifice, awarding him its highest medal and securing a presidential citation. The first barracks that new Coast Guard recruits live in at the Coast Guard Training Center in Cape May, New Jersey, was renamed "Sexton Hall" in his honor. To top it off, the Coast Guard named one of its eight Sentinel-class cutters the *Charles Sexton*.

When I tried to look into the story of the *Sea King*, I was struck by how little information was available. There had been almost no news coverage. I could find neither investigative reports nor boards of inquiry records, just a single medal citation from the Coast Guard and an accompanying press release. The handful of web articles by local amateur historians were brief and made up mostly of what was in the medal citation.

I could have simply taken that readily available information, limited my study of the *Sea King* disaster in the same way, and included it in this book in some summary manner, and I rather wish I had. But on one of my visits to the Maritime Museum's library, I came across a September 16, 1992, Associated Press article that had been published in the *Seattle Times* under the headline COAST GUARD BLAMED— PANEL RULES IN FATAL OREGON SINKING.

A panel formed by the National Transportation Safety Board had voted unanimously, 4–0, to hold that the Coast Guard's "botched rescue attempt" was partly responsible for the deaths of the three men who'd drowned in the *Sea King* wreck, the article stated. The panel distributed blame between the trawler's owner, captain, and crew, and put some as well on government inspectors who had failed to note the removal of the wall between the fish hold and the engine room that was the major contributor to flooding in the *Sea King*. The panel accused the trawler's captain of having failed to inform the Coast Guard from the beginning that the lazarette was full of water.

At the same time, the Coast Guard was faulted on many fronts, most especially for the decisions by the commanding officer at Group Astoria and the captain of the *Iris* to attempt a second tow across the bar without first having removed those on board the *Sea King*. "It seems to me the primary consideration was rescuing and towing the ship, not rescuing lives," one panel member stated.

The Associated Press article also reported that the families of two of the crew of the *Sea King* had filed a $6 million lawsuit against both the boat's owner and the Coast Guard. My attempt to see where that had gone led to a dead end: the case had been settled out of court, and the records sealed.

Eighteen Coasties in addition to Charles Sexton received commendations for their roles in the attempted rescue of the *Sea King*. Something about that troubled me. It wasn't that I suspected a cover-up, exactly, but rather an obscuring of failures. Even allowing that thought was uncomfortable. I was a fan of the Coast Guard, as admirable a group of uniformed men and women as I've met outside the New York Fire Department.

The Coasties saved lives every year in the county where I lived, and where they lived also. They were good neighbors I encountered in stores and on sidewalks. I instinctively saw things from their point of view. The primary faults for the disaster that day back in 1991 lay with the owner of the *Sea King* and its captain. And then there had been weather worsening unexpectedly, multiple equipment failures, a series of unfortunate events; the only thing predictable about the Columbia Bar was its unpredictability.

The Coast Guard out there that day had been trying to save the *Sea King* and rescue the four men aboard it. But then that was the problem: saving lives should have been the prevailing consideration during the rescue operation, not protecting private property with public resources. Much as I wanted to disregard the NTSB ruling and the lawsuit filings, I couldn't. It would not be fair to the relatives of the men who died that day, some of them no doubt still alive.

So I had to look for what I could find, and though it was frustrating, I felt a certain relief as well that nothing was available. Other than the NTSB's findings and the statements of the members of its panel, all records, including the Coast Guard's own investigation, were unavailable. Then, unfortunately, I came across an obscure Coast Guard pamphlet titled "Team Coordination Training Exercises & Case Studies: Boats, Cutters and ATON,"* dated August 1998. The last half of the pamphlet was made up of twenty-two case studies. The first among these was captioned "F/V Sea King Capsizing." The events of that day were laid out in sequential detail, and reading through them it was clear that the decision by the operation's senior commander, the head of Group Astoria, to try the second tow of the *Sea King*, a decision concurred in by the leader of Air Group Astoria and repeated by the skipper of the cutter *Iris*, and not objected to by any of the others in leadership positions that day, had been a disastrously bad one. After looking through the rest of the case studies, I found that every one ended with a section titled "Lessons Learned." Only the study of the *Sea King* did not include such a section. Even acknowledging that lessons had been learned would have been, for the Coast Guard, a betrayal of officers who were doing the best they could with what they knew. I understood, I just couldn't go along.

I regret that I reached out to Tom Molloy with my questions about the *Sea King*. This was before I had found the training pamphlet, but after I had read about the NTSB ruling and lawsuit filing. I was asking Tom to speak on behalf of the Coast Guard, which was stupid

---

* Aids to Navigation (ATON) include buoys, beacons, and lighthouses.

and unfair, and he never replied. Then I read the training pamphlet, and because I knew the story, I felt I had to tell it.

I certainly didn't want to diminish the heroism of Charles Sexton and the others who risked their lives that day to save the *Sea King* and those aboard it. Though I'd never belonged, I felt loyalty to the Coast Guard. But I felt greater loyalty to the truth, even if the truth, as in this instance, was as pitiless as the Columbia Bar.

CHAPTER ELEVEN

BEYOND THE RAMPART OF ROCKS and the view of Cape Disappointment, it was all sandy beach stretching miles up the Long Beach Peninsula to Willapa Bay. Washington's ocean beaches are in general nowhere near as beautiful as Oregon's, not only lacking the drama of the oceanfront down south, but with shorelines that tend toward gravelly gray rather than sandy light brown. The Long Beach Peninsula's beaches are the best Washington has, and we were enjoying our cruise north with their relative safety in sight off the starboard side. We had stopped pedaling and were using only sail.

The swells were growing steadily larger, though, and all three of us were eying them with mounting concern. This is the first I recall of Kenny's saying that he'd seen the wave train arriving hours earlier than expected. "I could feel it coming out of the south just as we went past Clatsop Spit," he told me when I asked him about it later. "I was sort of trying to pretend it wasn't happening, but I knew it was. That's why it got so bumpy right as we crossed the bar."

Ray was goading him a little, especially when some six-footers rolled up on us: "This is what you call a flat ocean, eh, Kenny?"

Wave predictions were usually quite reliable, Kenny insisted, in his own defense. "It was forecast to drop to as low as a half meter, then come back up tomorrow," he said.

"Well, it's come back up today," Ray replied, with a derisive snicker. It was a friendly game of mockery and one-upmanship that he and Kenny played constantly.

I still wasn't worried. The beach was right there. I could have slipped off the trimaran and swum to the sand pretty easily, I reckoned. Kenny, though, told me later that he *had* been worried, and was getting more worried with every passing minute. "I was watching up the coast, and I saw the waves were coming in sets of seven to nine," he said. "There was usually only one big wave in each set, though, so I figured we were probably okay." Bear in mind, Kenny said, "when you're out on the ocean looking at waves, they're harder to judge. Surfers like to study the waves for half an hour on shore before they go out, because it's way more difficult when you're on the ocean."

In fact, the surfers already were out in force on the beach at Seaview, drawn by word that some very rideable waves were coming. As we approached, we saw them pointing at us, several shaking their heads. I assumed it was because we were in their way. The families and couples on the beach were watching us too, using their palms like visors against the afternoon sun that was now over our right shoulders.

Our appearance must have been dramatic, coming in off the sea in such unusual craft. We stopped and sat just outside where the waves were breaking, considering the situation. A beach landing clearly was going to be more exciting than we'd planned.

I can't remember whether it was Ray or Kenny who first brought up the possibility that we could turn around, sail back the other way up the coast, recross the bar, and land at the very same dock where we'd launched a few hours earlier. They threw it back and forth for a few minutes, Kenny clearly a little more inclined to turn around than Ray was, although "I really did want to get off the ocean," Kenny told me later. "And the beach was right there."

I must admit that I weighed in on the side of just going ahead with the beach landing. I knew how silly it would sound to point out that I'd already gone to the trouble of dropping my car at Seaview, so I gave my other bad reason, this being that the beach landing was what we'd planned and we'd all feel regret later if we didn't follow through.

In the end it was Ray's call. "Let's do this," he said.

Kenny told us to go ahead, he'd see what happened. The big man did offer a piece of prudent advice, though, which was to try to pick the smallest wave we could, ride it in as far as possible, then try to catch another small wave to the beach.

As Ray handed me the paddle I was supposed to steady us with, he grinned at me and said, "Seems like a big wave will carry us a lot closer to shore, doesn't it?"

I may have grinned back. A flaw we shared was the tendency to weigh all options carefully, then decide that "On the other hand, fuck it" worked too. It's what happens to boys for whom taking action has been the only real alternative to despair.

A six-foot-plus wave came early in the next set, and Ray and I pedaled atop it. Any notion that we could surf a breaker that size in a vessel as ungainly as the trimaran vanished almost instantly. We were swung like a tilt-a-whirl car on the crest of the wave, then plunged down sideways when it began to break. My back paddling did little or nothing to correct us, and I was looking down at Ray as we inverted to well past forty-five degrees.

RANDALL SULLIVAN

What we didn't know, and Kenny didn't either, was that the beach at Seaview was a maze of small sandbars, creating amazingly random depths. Whether the shoal we slammed into with the back of the portside ama saved us is questionable, but this collision did happen right at what felt like the tipping point, and just at the instant I thought we were going over we bounced backward briefly, then the wave whirled us again. I was on the low side for a fraction of a second, until the wave spun us even more violently, putting Ray on the bottom again.

Time *did* slow in what I imagined might be our last seconds of life. I was looking straight down at Ray, observing the expression of helpless terror on his face as the trimaran was flung toward vertical again. This time it *really* felt like we were going over, and from my position on top of the wave it occurred to me that I probably had at least a chance to leap clear, assuming I possessed even a vestige of the agility that had been the main basis of any athletic talent I'd had when I was younger. If the flipping boat caught me before I was clear, though . . . Well, that would be bad.

But Ray's position was truly desperate: if the boat flipped, he would go over backward, headfirst into the sand, with the boat right on top of him. A broken neck seemed all but certain.

Again the back of the portside ama struck a sandbar, but this time it dug in as if to vault us further toward the tipping point. We were turning over for sure, I knew, when it finally occurred to me to pull my feet out of the pedal straps and plant them on what had previously been the bottom of the boat. I felt the trimaran shudder as it lifted me to a point where I was directly above Ray, and then, astoundingly, the aka that braced the portside ama snapped, and the sudden give that produced created some sort of counter to our forward momentum and the main hull of the boat came back down just a little

208

as the wave spilled us out into a cavity between two sandbars, maybe thirty feet from the waterline.

I remember seeing the ama floating loose in the water for a second, and then, I'm not sure how, I was out of the broken trimaran and pulling it up onto the beach with the rope at the bow of the boat. Ray climbed out of the boat a few seconds later and helped me drag it all the way up onto the dry sand. I was only vaguely aware of all the people standing and staring at us, but then I heard some of them begin to applaud. Ray grabbed me by both shoulders, his face inches from mine, pale eyes wide, taking short, rapid breaths. "Do you . . ." he got out, then choked up. "Do you know . . ." he managed on his second attempt, but this time hyperventilation stopped his voice. He squeezed my shoulders, looked down at the sand for an instant, then again stared directly into my eyes: ". . . how close we just came to dying." His voice was somewhere between a gasp and a croak.

"I do know, Ray. I do," I told him. I patted his arm. "Breathe slow, brother."

A brief expression of suspicion passed over his face. "Why are you smiling?" he asked.

"Am I?" As a matter of fact, I was. "I'm just happy that we made it," I told him.

Ray nodded, but without conviction, as if he doubted it was that simple.

I held his gaze another moment, then turned finally to face all the people on the beach who were still gaping at us. The spectacle we'd created only really registered with me then. Stunned expressions were everywhere. Some of the surfers tried to scorn us, I think, but even they were so overwhelmed by what they'd just witnessed that they looked more dazed than disdainful. A lot of the other people were smiling, some appreciatively, like that was the best entertainment they'd enjoyed in a long time.

I was still too happy to be alive to feel embarrassed, so I smiled back. My phone burred. I pulled it out of the waterproof lanyard case I carried it in and saw that Kenny had sent me a text from out there on the sea. "Shoot a video of me coming in," it read.

I tried, but after about seven or eight minutes of keeping my phone aimed at Kenny as he paddled in place, letting waves pass under him, I got tired of it and ended the video. He later sent a long and detailed text to his brother (a waterman extraordinaire himself) explaining what was going on. Out of respect for his accomplishment, of which Kenny was justifiably proud, here's the whole thing:

After watching their ama rise overhead twice, I hung outside for 10 minutes timing waves, practicing backstrokes, and getting jacked. The beat was classic 7 or 9 waves on about 8 seconds. 3 to 5 bigs and about 30 seconds of flats in between. I chased after a fourth, backed off a steep 5 by jamming paddle straight down on port and leveraging it off the aka to stop a hard right broach and somehow came out of the white water pointed straight at the beach. Max pedal on the Mirage drive and kayak paddle to get through the impact zone. Not fast enough and wave 6 spun me hard, so jam full vertical paddle against starboard aka and feather to stop the oversteer. Bounced an ama on the high tide bar and spun sideways in a foot of water. Got out of the boat before the next wave and pushed it ahead through 3 feet to dry sand.

I did get the last minute or so on video, and kept the camera on Kenny as he stepped up onto the beach looking thoroughly exhilarated. "Wow," he said. "That was absolutely the scariest thing I've done in years."

His success seemed to have an inexplicably deflating effect on the onlookers, who by now were mostly turning away to their own business. The surfers were getting ready to go into the water, and a couple did as I congratulated Kenny, and Kenny taunted Ray. "After I watched you guys crash—and you *did* crash," Kenny told Ray, "I decided to take the good advice I offered you."

Ray was still so shaken that he couldn't manage a retort. We helped each other peel off the top halves of our drysuits, then tied the arms around our waists before Kenny took a celebratory selfie of the three of us standing on the beach. I knew Ray was beginning to recover when we looked at the photo on Kenny's phone and he accused me of standing on higher ground so that I looked taller than him, when he was actually an inch taller than me. I found that hysterical, considering that in the photo he and I, each over six feet tall, looked like midgets next to Kenny.

The three of us agreed that Kenny would stay with the boats while I drove Ray back to Cape Disappointment Park to get his van and trailer. All during the drive, Ray kept apologizing for having nearly killed me. I told him I had gone along with the decision to make the beach landing—if it could be called that—the way we did, so it was on us both. He nevertheless repeated his apology at least a couple more times before suddenly observing, almost angrily, "You're happy, aren't you? We didn't come close enough to dying on the bar, so you needed more drama. Isn't that right?"

Instead of answering, I attempted to divert Ray by offering him some amusement at my own expense, telling him a story from back in October of 1985. I was driving a sports car on Sunset Boulevard with two writer friends, my Los Angeles running partner James Dallesandro in the front passenger seat and my oldest New York pal, Michael Daly, stretched out on the tiny backseat. We were somewhere between the Palisades and Westwood and I was negotiating the curves the same insane way I always did back then, using both of the two eastbound lanes as I swerved in and out of traffic to sustain a steady sixty miles per hour in a forty-mile-per-hour speed zone. James turned to Michael and told him, "I hate to be in the car when he's at the wheel. For him, driving is a test of manhood."

Michael needed only a beat to reply, "For him, *everything* is a test of manhood."

I'd laughed pretty hard at myself back then, and did again now thirty-five years later. Ray laughed too. "You still drive like that," he said.

"No, I don't," I told him. "I've been slowing down ever since my kids were born, and I'm barely above the speed limit most of the time these days."

Ray thought for a few seconds. "You *were* glad we almost got killed," he said. "Don't tell me you weren't."

"Yes, I suppose I was glad we *almost* got killed, Ray. But I was just as terrified as you while the whole thing was happening."

"*Why* were you glad, you motherfucker?"

"Hard to say." I thought for a moment, then shook my head apologetically. "I think only coming close to being killed could make me feel like I'd really done something," I answered finally.

"In other words, it was good material. Is that right? You crazy bastard!"

I shrugged. "Don't take it personally," I said.

"I'm taking it *very* personally."

"Hey, the whole beach landing thing was your idea. I just went along," I reminded him.

"I'm not even sure now it *was* my idea."

"Well, if that helps you feel less guilty, okay."

I must admit I took some pleasure a week or so later when Ray confided he had gone to see his old friend Malcom Black, a grizzled waterman that he and Kenny both revered, and Malcom threw him off his boat for having put my life at such risk. In my defense, it was only a small and brief pleasure that I felt. Though after that, if I'm honest, I did join in the consensus verdict that the entire near-death disaster had been Ray's fault. I knew that, although he would never admit it, my friend relished his reputation for recklessness.

In a way, he proved it by apologizing several more times for nearly getting me killed before I dropped him off at his van in Cape Disappointment Park.

The perfect ending to the day came when Ray drove onto the beach at Seaview, where Kenny and I had been standing and talking for at least twenty minutes. By then Kenny had devised the perfect course for Ray to steer his trailer into position to make loading the boats as easy as possible. Like a member of the ground crew at an airport, I guided Ray along the route Kenny had laid out. And of course Ray got stuck in the sand. It provided an ideal opportunity for Ray to deride Kenny and for Kenny to show how little it bothered him.

"I think two guys can move this thing," Kenny told me.

I looked at how deep the wheels were in the sand, but figured, *Why not try?* We unhooked the trailer, then heaved into the rear of the van on each side, Kenny going high and me low. And with Ray revving the engine, the van did begin to inch forward.

"Give it more," Kenny yelled at me. I thought I was actually making the van move more than he was, so I backed off for a second, as if to reposition myself, and the van's wheels spun in the sand. I looked at Kenny, who said, "Okay, okay," then dug my feet in again and pushed with all my might. The van was out of the sand and on the gravel a few moments later.

More people on the beach put up a cheer for us, one that combined mockery and admiration in just about equal proportions. To me, the sound was pleasing.

On their way back to Portland, Ray and Kenny stopped off at my beach house so we could hose the saltwater off the boats and the trailer and the van.

When my wife came outside to congratulate us for surviving, Ray began to again apologize profusely for the beach landing, and for nearly getting us both killed. After only a minute or so, put off by Ray's intensity and recognizing that the three of us were still in our own little world, Delores went back inside. Seconds after she disappeared from sight, Ray told me, "Dee always has to be the babe. She *is* a babe. But she always *has to be* the babe."

If Ray was down to scoring obvious points, I figured he was set to go. We hugged before he went. "I'm really glad we did this," he said.

"I'm glad, too," I told him. "Thanks."

He stood and looked into my eyes for a few moments, as if there was so much more to say, then climbed into the van and drove away.

RAY AND I DID HAVE a deeper relationship after. A good deal of that was a result of our bar crossing. More significant, though, I think, was what we had shared about our experiences as boys while preparing for the voyage. Ray had told me a lot previously, but I probed for more during those weeks and months. Usually, I'd lead with "I recall you telling me" about this or that event. He would often express surprise I remembered as much as I did, then describe what had happened in much greater detail. It was a tremendous relief to be able to talk about his childhood trauma with someone who wasn't too disturbed to hear him out, or so intent upon a therapeutic resolution that the conversation became reductive, someone who just listened, and then maybe offered up some part of his own similar suffering.

One thing I noticed was that in recounting the abuses we'd endured at the hands of our fathers, Ray and I were both quite protective of our mothers. Seeing this in him made me see it in myself. I noticed that Ray literally flinched when I asked about the effect of a mother who was consumed by her career. He talked about being proud of her for overcoming all the obstacles a woman of her generation faced, and the advantages her local celebrity as a TV news anchor had provided to him in Quincy after he moved there for his senior year of high school. And he seemed genuinely regretful about how harshly he'd judged her when he was younger because of her lack of aptitude for being a wife or mother. "She always made supper," Ray pointed out. But even while they were eating there would be a pair of televisions on, tuned to the local and national news broadcasts on the two network affiliates in the Quincy market. "Both with the sound on," Ray remembered. "She'd mute one when she didn't want to hear that part, but she'd watch both, and before she'd go to bed she'd watch the news again."

In his mom's house, Ray was Ricky. Frederick was his middle name, drawn from his mother's side of the family. Speaking the names "Ray" or "Raymond" was not allowed. "I can remember being split between 'Ray' and 'Ricky' from the beginning," he explained, "and it extended to cards, letters, presents, everything. In school, however, Mom let me stay as Raymond. It was confusing as hell for my friends."

"Had to be pretty confusing for you as well," I ventured.

"Everyone in Dad's world called us Big Ray and Little Ray," he replied. "So I can see why Mom agonized over this."

"You're very understanding of her," I said.

"I didn't use to be," Ray said. "I carried a stupid grudge against her for years."

I asked about his younger brother, who I knew had committed suicide several years earlier. I had met Jim once, a sad and disoriented drug addict, as I remembered him. "I'm not sure why he was so lost," Ray said. "He was left on his own a lot. He had elderly grandparents, nobody gave him much attention. The thing he had going for him in my eyes was that he was basically a no-problem child. He would come home and watch TV."

I felt a comment about his mother was implicit in what Ray had just said, but I wasn't sure he heard it and so didn't push further.

I was just getting close to Ray when his mom killed herself, back in 1992, five years after his father drank himself to death at the age of fifty-nine. Maggie Thomas was a lifelong smoker and very ill with lung cancer at sixty-two, when she made herself a Manhattan, carried it out into her garage, closed the doors, turned on the car engine, and went to sleep forever.

It was fascinating and a little unnerving to see how five years later Ray had leveraged her death in the lawsuit against Philip

Morris. He used vengeance as fuel, but at the same time proceeded like the coldest-blooded assassin ever. As many as ten other lawyers were on the case, but Ray and another lawyer, Bill Gaylord, were the ones who had tried it in court, winning a verdict worth 100 million dollars. Philip Morris's stock value dropped by two billion dollars in a day. Ray had asked me to be there for his closing argument. He made it very simply, placing a photograph of the dead man whose wife was his client on an easel in front of the jury, then telling them that he knew they'd already listened to hours of expert testimony and read mountains of documents, and that now he wanted them to just look at this man for a moment and think about his absence from the world.

Afterward I waited to squeeze his elbow, and when I did Ray choked up and said he'd been thinking not about the man in the photograph but about his mom the whole time. I've never known anyone who has combined ferocity and tenderness more uniquely than Ray.

He understands deeply the effect his father had on him, but he's willfully blind, it often seems to me, about how his mother has shaped him. I've seen it from the first in his relationship with Grace, who has cycled between pulling him close and pushing him away the entire time they've been together. After he's sent away, Ray retreats into a wounded and lonely place that he deals with by keeping busy with his many acquaintances and activities, then runs back to her when she beckons him that the exile is over. "You don't understand it, but it's very exciting to me," he's explained more than once, usually adding something along the lines of "You could never handle a woman like Grace."

He can diagnose my own mother issues to his full satisfaction, of course. "Your mom was a babe, and you've always had to be with babes yourself. You've gone from one babe to another. The only thing they've had in common is that they were beautiful."

"It's not quite that simple," was my response. "Keep in mind that my mom was Sully's babe."

"And?"

"And that's the rest of it."

"Your mom revered you."

"Revered? I think that's a bit much."

"No, she revered you."

"I wasn't aware of it."

I thought about the several intimate conversations my mom and I had in the last year of her life, and how she'd tried to free me from what she described as being "tormented over your father." She'd said a lot of negative things about him, nothing I hadn't heard before, and that never made me feel better. But seeing and hearing her try to understand how I was trying to process the pain from way back when with her before she was gone was tremendously touching.

On her deathbed, I was holding her hand, and I told her that Dad had been taking dancing lessons and was waiting to show her what he'd learned. That brought a smile. She loved him, and wanted me to forgive her for it. I did more than that; I gave them my heartfelt blessing, and it freed me as much as anything I've ever done, including crossing the Columbia River Bar.

CHAPTER TWELVE

ON THE MORNING OF JANUARY 15, 2022, six months less a day after Ray and I and Kenny had crossed the Columbia Bar, the US government issued a tsunami warning for the Pacific coast. An undersea volcano had erupted near the island kingdom of Tonga and was sending huge waves in all directions. "Stay away from port harbors and low-lying beaches!" the National Tsunami Warning Center advised.

Ray and I had been planning all week for a Saturday hike from the North Head Lighthouse across the spine of Cape Disappointment, looking for a way to Dead Man Cove. We decided not to cancel but weren't entirely incautious. We would time it, we agreed, so that if we were able to get to the cove and its little beach, it would be at right around 2:00 p.m., when the tsunami warning was to expire.

We felt similarly compelled to search out that place of haunted legend. Stories of the spirits of the dead in frightful aspect were chilling yet titillating, and connected—in my mind, at least—to the fact that the name Dead Man Cove seemed to have been achieved by a process of accretion, as the corpses of drowned men were found there over the decades following the wreck of the *Vandalia*. I'd seen one of the few photographs of the cove extant, and told Ray it appeared to be an extraordinarily lovely spot, with a tiny beach and a small island where a single tree grew. I wondered if that beach was the one I'd looked down upon from near the lighthouse. Ray wanted to see the place too, and feel it.

We knew already that the Coast Guard, which owned the land there, had closed the trail to Dead Man Cove because it was steep, narrow, and slippery and they had tired of difficult rescue operations caused by people who got hurt, some seriously, trying to reach the fabled spot. Arrests and fines were promised for anyone who went past the trailhead barrier. Ray got the idea that we might find a back entrance off another trail that ran to the base of Cape Disappointment along its southeast facet. On Google Maps we could see that part of this trail ran very near the cliffs above Dead Man Cove.

I knew it was a long shot, but a hike with Ray in search of Dead Man Cove would be an opportunity to discuss another ghost who had been on both our minds.

Doug Swanson was a former classmate of Ray's at Lewis & Clark Law School, and the two had been partners in the firm Swanson, Thomas and Coon for almost a quarter century. I truly met him only once, when he and Ray and I had lunch together in the summer of 2004. I found Doug charming and entirely likeable. He was fifty-one at the time, but youthful enthusiasm is what I remember best about the man. He seemed to be grinning during the entire meal as he peppered me with questions about my job at *Rolling Stone* magazine and how I combined that with raising children as a single father. He wanted me to get more connected to Portland, instead of just living there while I worked out of New York and Los Angeles. Afterward Ray said something about Doug seeing himself as this street-smart city boy, when he was in fact the son of a University of Chicago computer science professor who had lived comfortably all his life. Doug's main jobs at Swanson, Thomas and Coon were finding clients and calculating damages, as I understood it. He was the firm's front man, while Jim Coon did most of the legal research and case preparation. Ray found and interviewed witnesses and represented the clients in court.

When Doug went missing about three months after that lunch, I saw things I had vaguely recognized about Ray thrown into vivid relief. His response had been a mobilization that was as near to total as I'd ever observed in anyone.

Doug had last been seen on the evening of October 19, 2004, when he'd attended a parent-teacher conference with his wife for their twelve-year-old son at the Sunnyside Environmental Middle School. The parents had arrived in separate cars, and afterward Doug told his wife he needed to put in a few hours of work at the office. When it was past midnight and she hadn't heard from Doug, she called Ray and Jim, and from them learned that her husband hadn't been at the office. Several of the people who worked at the firm went over to Doug's house to sit with his wife and family. On the drive over, Ray had proposed various plausible explanations to himself, but none of them matched up with the Doug everyone knew. "So I walked in trying to organize a posse or search party and could see immediately that they were not interested in that kind of energy," Ray recalled. While the others chose to keep vigil and no more, Ray began to copy photos of Doug to make "Missing" posters, then drew up a list of places he might have been seen that evening, and had visited every one of them by the following morning.

When Doug didn't show at the office the next day for a 9:00 a.m. meeting that he himself had arranged, everyone feared the worst. Ray, who had not slept at all the night before, told me he wasn't aware how distraught he was until he walked out the front door of the building with a pile of papers in a backpack and they spilled out all over the sidewalk because he had forgotten to close the zipper.

Ray was absolutely relentless for the next couple of days. We spoke once, very briefly, because he couldn't give up the search for more than a few seconds. The shaky yet murderous intensity in his voice concerned me, but I knew Ray had to do what Ray had to do.

He searched Doug's office from one end to the other that day, looking for clues, then got on Doug's office computer and searched that, too. He compiled a list of "possible clues" and began to follow them up immediately, not stopping to eat, and had to be reminded even to take a drink of water. He believed he had developed a couple of "leads," Ray told me when I talked to him a second time, again for only seconds. He was following up on those when he learned that Doug's Subaru had been pulled over in Northeast Portland with a young man and woman in the front seats and no sign of Doug.

For the next twenty-four hours, Ray waited along with everyone else to learn what had happened. It was even more shocking and terrible than the worst that any of them had imagined. The horror of it was magnified for Ray, I believe, by the sense of betrayal he felt. Unknown to anyone close to him, Doug had been living a double life for months, arranging rendezvous with various young prostitutes he met on an Internet chat line. "We all believed he was still the great family man among us, so devoted to his wife and child," Ray remembered. "I mean, there wasn't even a hint about any of this."

Doug's demise had been as sad as it was sordid. On the night of October 19, after leaving the parent-teacher conference at his son's school, he had arranged a meeting with a young prostitute named Lydia Way at an apartment in a spotty Southeast Portland neighborhood.

Within seconds after Way opened the door and let him in, Doug was confronted by a frenzied meth freak named Stuwart Lueb, who was pointing a pistol at him. What particularly upset Ray was that the pistol had been a pellet gun and that Doug hadn't fought for his life in the few moments when he'd had a chance to do so. "Doug was very anti-gun, so I guess I can understand how he wouldn't have known it was a pellet pistol," Ray said. "But how he could have been so passive is really hard for me to accept. 'Charge the gun, run from the knife,' that's the rule." Ray seemed to feel responsible that he hadn't taught Doug this basic law of survival.

What Lueb, with Way's help, had done next was put a rubber-ball gag in Doug's mouth and plastic handcuffs on his wrists, then pistol-whip him while demanding PIN numbers for the bank and credit cards he found in Doug's wallet. "Doug had really bad asthma, so he was probably struggling to breathe right from the start," Ray said. That struggle no doubt became more desperate after Lueb and Way stuffed him onto the floor between the front and back seats of the Subaru, still bound and gagged.

When a pair of Portland police officers spotted Doug's Subaru in Northeast Portland on the evening of October 21 and pulled the car over, Lueb was at the wheel, with Way in the passenger seat. Also in the car were a plastic bag filled with crystal methamphetamine, a glass pipe, and a leather-bound planner with $200 in cash and torn scraps of paper where Doug's name and information on his various bank accounts had been written.

The district attorney who handled the case had known Doug and considered him a friend. He spent all of that night sitting up with Lueb, eventually offering a deal that took the death penalty off the table and promised a life sentence that didn't eliminate the possibility of future parole. What he got in exchange was the location where Doug's body had been left, along with details of the crime and its aftermath.

Lueb and Way had driven around for most of the night Doug disappeared, with him still in the back of the car, begging for his life each time the ball gag was taken out, and giving up further information about his finances in order to try to stay alive. A fellow meth head named Mark Lee Hudgens had joined them at some point, and was in the car also when they arrived at an Office Depot, where Doug's credit card paid for the check-writing software that Hudgens would use to produce eighteen checks drawn on Doug's personal and business bank accounts.

When exactly Doug died from suffocation Lueb claimed not to know. All he could or would tell the prosecutor was that he had put a black plastic garbage bag over Doug's head and tied his body to a tree in the Mount Hood National Forest. During his statement, Lueb tried to convince himself, and the prosecutor, that Doug might not be as dead as he had seemed to be. This delusional belief that he could possibly escape a murder charge was part of what the prosecutor used on Lueb to get the location of Doug's body, which was recovered on the morning of October 22, just as the first news reports about the "Portland attorney's disappearance" were coming out.

The way Ray dealt with Doug's death was incomprehensible to every other one of their friends and associates. The first thing Ray felt it necessary to do was obtain the location where Doug's body had been found and drive there. It had been far from easy, but Ray managed to convince the police to let him visit the scene after the medical examiners and photographers had completed their work. "I went over to the place, got down on my knees, and ran my hands through the dirt and leaves where his body outline was marked," Ray told me. "This was the first time I calmed down enough to weep for him."

The other people at the office didn't want to even hear about it. Ray wasn't done, though. He obtained a list of all the places Doug had been driven with the ball gag in his mouth before he was tied to that tree in the national forest, and he drove himself to every one. I remember him telling me about being at the Portland Zoo, where Lueb and Way had driven Doug while they smoked crystal meth and decided what to do with him.

Even more unfathomable to the others who were mourning Doug was how Ray behaved at the funeral home. "Somehow it seemed important to see him and what they had done to him," Ray explained. The mortician told Ray the body hadn't been prepared for visitors yet and was startled when Ray replied that that was the way he wanted it. His greatest interest, Ray remembered, was in determining whether Doug had any defensive wounds. "I was able to look him over and see for myself," said Ray, who was terribly disappointed—actually angry, as I recall it—that there were no wounds suggesting Doug had fought back.

Doug's brother and their law partner, Jim, were with Ray at the mortuary, and both "were disturbed by my behavior," he remembered. "But it seemed so clear to me that that was what I needed to do."

The entire experience became one more time when Ray realized he was responding to trauma in a very different way from others. "But I just gave myself leave to do what I thought was important," he explained, and accepting the necessity of that became an acceptance of himself, of who and what he was, and of what he knew that many others did not.

"It was sorrowful not to be able to join the gathering of friends and family at his house," Ray told me, "but isolation in my reaction was familiar to me, and I understood it."

I understood it, also. The night after our January 15 hike at Cape Disappointment I watched *Ray Donavan: The Movie*. The television show had been one of the few I felt compelled to see from beginning to end, and the movie was a fitting coda. The most compelling part of *Ray Donavan* had always been its exploration of the toll repressed trauma takes on individuals and families. The movie addressed this subject more directly than the show ever had. "He taught you how to forget," daughter Bridget tells her father, Ray Donavan, at one point, speaking of Ray's own father, Mickey Donavan. Forgetting the terrible things that had been done to him and that he had done to others was what had protected Ray Donavan at the same time as it had warped him. Mickey had done worse and thought about it even less. He was a man who knew how to let it go and move on, no matter how grievous it might be. Later, in what sets up the climactic scene, Ray Donavan talks to his on-and-off psychoanalyst, played by Alan Alda, who tries to help him explain why he is what he is. Trauma kills memory, and by killing memory, it kills us, the Alda character explains.

The exchange made an enormous impact on me, but there was something I only thought to say about it to my own Ray a couple of weeks later. "We are heroes of remembering," I told him.

He smiled sheepishly yet also with tentative appreciation.

"Heroes," I repeated. "Because we refused to forget. We chose, both of us, to remember every blow we took, every humiliation we suffered, every loss that left us feeling empty or abandoned. And nearly all of the same we inflicted on others. Somehow we knew, you and I, even as boys, that we'd better not forget. We knew we'd lose ourselves if we did. We may have had to do stupid, impetuous, dangerous things to jog our memories, but we did them, because to us the pain and the risk were worth it."

Ray was tearing up, and my voice was trembling, but we held one another's gaze. "We face it," Ray said, and that made me laugh. I was thinking of the text he'd sent me on my seventieth birthday, a text that was so Ray, and so what made him my dear friend.

"Barely 70," it read, "not 70 in spirit, a lively 70, does not seem his age of 70, a powerfully built 70. Give me a break, 70."

"That's right, Ray," I said. "We face it."

WE COULD FIND NO WAY to Dead Man Cove. No alternate route ever branched from the trail we were on. At one point the meandering path led along the top of a cliff on the seaward side of the cape. We hoped there might be a view of the cove from above, but a precipitous mossy slope ended in a deadfall to the rocks below, and we could see nothing through the cloud of fog that rose from below. When I ventured a few steps out onto the slope holding a branch of salal, I felt the wet earth give slightly under my feet and scrambled back up to the trail, where I stood panting with my hands on my knees for a few moments. Before continuing on, Ray and I made jokes about one of us vanishing without a trace on the way to Dead Man Cove. It took me longer than it should have to catch my breath.

Maybe a mile in, Ray told me that the trail we were on was used to condition the special operations forces that trained at nearby Camp Rilea. I had no problem believing it. The trail was astonishingly rugged, a twisting series of steep ups and downs on slippery clay, bulging everywhere with the thick roots of giant spruce trees. I had no sense at all of where it ended and wondered if I could manage the full out and back. The special forces were likely wearing fully loaded packs when they made this hike, I pointed out to Ray at one point, trying to manufacture some resolve. I didn't bother to mention that those guys were probably all in their twenties. The two of us had an unspoken rule that age was never to be used as an excuse, so I was surprised when he told me at a point further on, "You know, we probably won't be able to do this in five years." Somberness weighed on me for a time after he spoke those words. Ray was in extraordinarily good shape for someone his age, and if he doubted he would be able to do this in five years then it was a cinch I wouldn't. We walked on in silent contemplation of how truly short our time was.

Another story about my father came to mind, and I told Ray how when my dad was in his late seventies he had been contacted by the attorney representing a chemical company that had long ago manufactured the solvent used to clean the inside of the fuel holds of merchant ships. Every sailor who had been sent down to scrub those holds with that solvent had died young from a couple of the same cancers, and their families had filed a class action suit. He was the only one still alive, and the company wanted to offer him as a kind of exhibit in their defense case.

"He didn't help them out, did he?" Ray asked.

"He talked to them," I said. "But as far as I know he never testified for them."

"Good."

"My dad was industrial strength," I said. "Really, it's pretty impressive that he lived to be eighty after smoking four packs of cigarettes a day for forty-five years and drinking heavily most of that time. And then he died in the middle of telling my mother a dirty joke."

"You've got the same genes."

I smiled ruefully. "That's not as much of a comfort as you might imagine," I told Ray.

After about two miles of hiking, I sensed open space through the trees ahead, and sure enough, ten minutes later we emerged into a clearing next to Baker Bay, where we learned from a small monument installed there that we were standing on the spot where the members of the Lewis and Clark Expedition had first seen the Pacific Ocean. Meriwether Lewis had stayed behind at what the expedition called Station Camp on that day, November 18, 1805, when Captain William Clark led a party of eleven other men, including the legendary French-Canadian explorer Toussaint Charbonneau and the black slave York, on a twelve-mile hike around Cape Disappointment to this rise of ground now called McKenzie Head. Exhausted, the group had decided to camp for the night right there.

"Men appear much-Satisfied with their trip beholding the high waves dashing against the rocks & this emence ocian," Clark had written in his journal.

For someone like me, who had grown up next to the Pacific Ocean, it was simply not possible to imagine seeing it for the first time at thirty-five, Clark's age when he made that entry. Then again, it was even more impossible to imagine being thirty-five in a time when that was the average life expectancy.

And yet one had to try to imagine, or else Clark's words lacked all meaning. We were all stuck at a place in time, except in our imaginations, and the older I got the more essential that understanding became. I could remember being a boy, but I could only imagine my dad as a boy. His own father had beaten him with plow handles and horse bridles. At twelve, thirteen, fourteen, he'd spent his summers laboring alongside his father on neighboring farms to make the money needed to first obtain and then keep the land they worked mostly before sunrise and after sunset, putting in sixteen-hour days seven days a week, with no idea that there was such thing as vacation. Just months before he went into the Maritime Service, my grandfather saved the farm by winning a bet that my father could drag three hundred pounds of baled cotton behind him while in harness.

Being used that way had embittered him until he'd broken free by going to sea. But even then he had felt bound to his parents, had sent a piece of every paycheck to help them support his younger siblings.

It was a sense of duty and the sacrifice that had brought him to that small town on the Oregon coast, where he gave up going to sea and began working on the docks, and it had to be accounted for in any summation of his life. My investment in the sense of duty and the sacrifice in the stories of those who had died on the Columbia Bar were a portion of that accounting, and what they made me feel was in my path toward reconciliation.

The last time I saw my father, almost at the end of his life, I sat next to his hospital bed and recalled the good times we'd had, nearly all of them involving something the two of us had done together, with no one else around: the hunting, fishing, and camping expeditions. He was always better with me when it was just the two of us. He had been deeply disappointed, I knew, when I gave up hunting right after shooting my first deer.

A considerable part of me, I admit, wanted him to acknowledge the terrible things he'd done to me when I was a child, and to apologize for them, and that same part was crushed when he didn't. But I kept silent about wanting that, because what was the point of doing otherwise, with him on his deathbed?

RAY AND I WERE MAKING the return trip on the trail to the North Head Lighthouse when I found myself wanting to say something to counter the heavy air around us, something impassioned on behalf of us two and our generation of men.

Look at us, I said to Ray. We experienced the worst of what had become in the parlance of political correctness "toxic masculinity," but we had refused to renounce masculinity itself and both believed deeply in something we called "manhood." "Be a man" was an injunction that he and I both still used and that continued to carry heft for us, even if the forces of whatever was being called progress these days weighed against it. Like a lot of men from our generation, we'd done our best to build an enduring bridge between the troubled past and the uncertain future. The greatest thing we'd done, I believed, was break a cycle of physical abuse that had been handed down not just over the decades before us, but across millennia. We hadn't beaten our sons, unlike our fathers, our grandfathers, our great-grandfathers, and ancestors who likely went back centuries. All the weight of that brutal history had fallen on us and we'd shouldered it. We had committed ourselves to rejecting the worst while embracing the best of what we inherited from our fathers, and our fathers' fathers. And what that had produced was a paradigm shift that was in its own way unparalleled. Hundreds of thousands, maybe millions, of our sons would never know the anxiety and shame that living in fear of a father's violence engenders in a boy.

Ray and I each understood that we hadn't been great husbands, but at the same time we both believed—I'd say, knew—we'd been excellent fathers, to our sons and to our daughters. Our sons we'd fostered, but never coddled. Of course we'd passed on some measure of our own damage; the most painful part of being a parent is learning that to do otherwise is not humanly possible.

I recently told my son a story about something that happened at my twenty-year high school reunion: I was headed down a narrow hallway at the Multnomah Athletic Club when out of the door to the bathroom I was headed for stepped a guy who had bullied me mercilessly in junior high. Without so much as thinking, I began to walk straight at Chris, staring into his eyes. He was not even remotely a match for me at that point in our lives, and yielded ground immediately, but I kept coming at him, forcing him to edge closer and closer to the wall on his side, until at the end he could only get past by literally squirming along the wall with an abject expression on his face.

"That must have felt good," Gabriel ventured.

"Good?" I repeated. "Hell, no! It made me feel terrible."

"How, exactly?"

I realized I had an opportunity to compensate for some of my mistakes as a father, like making the weekend I spent in the Los Angeles County Jail sound more like a colorful escapade than the forty-eight hours of living hell that it actually was.

I thought, then said, "I felt ashamed, for myself and for Chris. I was thirty-eight years old at the time, not some teenager. Twenty years later, I still feel ashamed. But now I'm proud of being ashamed."

"Proud of being ashamed," Gabriel repeated. He laughed and gave me a hug. "I'm glad you told me, Dad."

All three of the sons Ray and I had raised, his two and my one, were notable among their friends for what even those Gen Yers and Gen Zers called "manliness," and this included traits that were perhaps more negative than positive. Their edges were a little sharper than those of their peers.

When we clashed during his teen years, my son regularly accused me of favoring his twin sister, of "protecting your little girl" in ways I wouldn't have thought to protect him. My defense was always some version of "boys and girls are different" and so are the relationships sons and daughters have with their father. I don't think differently now, really, and I'm prepared to go to my grave behind that binary belief. Unlike my own father, though, I don't feel the need to be rigid about it. When my son and daughter enjoyed wearing each other's clothes around the house at twelve or thirteen, other than a sardonic comment about how good Gabriel looked in a dress, I let them enjoy it.

At times my wife has accused me of being a chauvinist, and my retort has always been that the most feminist thing anyone can do is raise a great daughter, and she has to concede the point, because she herself thinks my daughter Grace is one of the finest young women she's met, a blend of kindness and strength that is rarely seen, and among the bravest people either of us has ever known.

Ray is proud of his daughter also, and close to her. Three weeks after we crossed the bar, Ray suggested to Meredith an epic road trip in the last week before she began her first year of medical school. What Ray wanted was to retrace his childhood, from South Bend to Michigan's Upper Peninsula to Quincy, a three-thousand-mile round trip that he proposed to make with Meredith by trading off behind the wheel while the other slept. It was an offer I doubted I could have gotten either of my kids to accept, but Meredith took it. What surprised Ray, though not entirely, was that she didn't want to know at all about the harsh details of his upbringing.

I'd asked about the shooting incident that had damaged his hearing, and Ray had answered by talking his way into the Laurium mansion, then taking a photo of the bullet holes that were still there on the edges of a V in a strip of hardwood wainscoting. "Five tight ones" was the caption he put on the email he sent the photo in, and I had to admit, crazy as Ray's father may have been, he was a damn good shot.

Ray hadn't been able to persuade Meredith to go inside the Laurium house with him and take a look, he told me after their return. "She didn't want to see the bullet holes," he explained. "The violent things that happened, it upsets her, for me, that I went through that. She doesn't like to hear about it."

His sons were the same way, Ray told me. "When you and I talk about the terrible things that happened to us, it's a kind of exorcism. But to my kids—our kids—it's threatening."

I nodded. "With my kids, I think part of the threat is the feeling that they're connected in some way to this stuff, through DNA or dharma or whatever it is," I said. "The sins of the father's father, and his father, and so on, the fear that this shit is passed down through invisible circuits."

Ray nodded.

"Maybe part of our job is making sure they don't know about it," I suggested.

"You might be right."

"I might be wrong, too. Keeping it from happening to them, for certain; keeping them from knowing about it, I'm not so sure."

"Is there a part that wants them to feel sorry for you?" he asked.

"I try not to give that part too much attention."

Ray thought about it. "They don't need to know," he said.

I thought too. "Agreed," I said finally.

"But then there's the book you're writing," Ray said.

"They'll probably never read it," I replied, and we both thought that was terribly funny. We couldn't stop laughing for quite a while.

BACK AT THE LIGHTHOUSE, Ray and I gave up on so much as gaining sight of Dead Man Cove, absent a willingness to either climb over or sneak around the Coast Guard barricade at the head of the trail there. Ray, I think, would have considered either option, but I didn't want to risk getting on the bad side of the Coasties.

We decided then that at least we would take a look at Beard's Hollow, after checking to make sure the trail there was open.

It was a short drive to the wooden bridge that started the way to Beard's Hollow. But we were bewildered by the broad asphalt path that lay at the bridge's end. We had walked just a short distance on the paved ground when I told Ray, "This doesn't feel right."

No, it didn't, he agreed. We walked a bit further, noticing that the path we were on had been built across a gully with sandy cliffs rising on both sides, filled with large rocks and strewn with a jumble of rotting logs that looked as if they had been heaved up by a tidal wave. The map on Ray's phone said we were at Beard's Hollow, but the ocean was hundreds of feet away, hidden behind a broad dune. We knew it was there only because we heard it.

The two of us wandered about with a sense of disorientation until we found a small marker stating that we were standing where the ocean had been two hundred years earlier. It made no sense until I realized that the jetties had done this, funneling the silt out of the Columbia's North Channel into this long and narrow defile until it was filled up at its entrance and became a shore that held the sea back. Beard's Hollow was no more, not as a part of the Pacific Ocean, anyway. This spot where the bodies of Captain Beard and that young cabin boy and uncounted others had been found floating in a pool of seawater during the nineteenth century was a dry gulch now.

I find it difficult to explain why this so astounded and disturbed me, other than that it was as if history had been erased, even if I understood rationally that only a natural feature was gone.

An emotion akin to despair washed over me, and for a moment Ray and I were two specks on an enormous orbiting rock surrounded by a universe so vast and indifferent that it reduced us to atoms at the brink of fissure. Then, like an ocean wave, the feeling passed, and when it had we stood with our feet planted on the solid ground in the cold fog, with the ocean roaring from behind a bank of sand, and belonged right where we were.

No matter whether Beard's Hollow existed or did not, what Ray and I had done and what we had built between us while doing it endured.

Ray gave me a curious smile, and I clapped him on the shoulder. Brotherly love, I had decided, while not as passionate or as deep as the love I've felt for women and children, is far more inclusive. I felt it in that moment, felt that Ray and I were accompanied by a host of men that stretched farther than I could see, their ranks filled with our other brothers: those men who had held on as well as they could to the rigging of the *Rosecrans* in a slaughtering sea, watching one another be stripped away then sucked into its depths; the Coast Guardsmen who had clung in the towering sea and stinging chill to the propeller of a capsized rescue boat, and the ones who'd been driven to the bottom aboard the *Triumph* and the *Mermaid*; Edgar Yates going down with his ship as a skipper who had "misjudged and failed"; Charles Sexton drowning with the injured man he refused to leave; the eight men dead after Captain Thorn sent them across the bar from the *Tonquin* in small boats; and all the rest who had struggled or suffered or died, here at the mouth of the Columbia River. They were innumerable but not nameless, and those closest to us in the spectral gathering were the ghosts of our fathers, and of the boys Ray and I had once been.

All together now, brothers, I sang silently, *all together now, those who are gone, and we who shall soon be.* All of us have lived through it. And even if we are dead, that is still true.

SOURCES

Books

No work was more fundamental for me than Willard Bascom's 1964 masterpiece *Waves and Beaches* (Anchor Books), republished in 2020, with additional text and illustrations by Kim McCoy, whose work is wonderful in its own right. There is no better book about the relationship between seas and coasts.

The opening section of this book was informed by Lisa Penner's *Salmon Fever: River's End Tragedies on the Lower Columbia River in the 1870s, 1880s, and 1890s* (Amato 2006) and especially by the outstanding work *The Chinook Indians: Traders of the Lower Columbia River* (University of Oklahoma Press 1988), authored by Dr. Robert Ruby and John A. Brown.

James A. Gibbs's book *Pacific Graveyard* (Binfords & Mort), published first in 1950, then in a revised edition in 1964, is, among other things, a catalogue (and I use the word respectfully) of every major shipwreck on the Columbia Bar, many described in some detail, others neatly summarized. Gibbs's book is also a good basic history of the early exploration of the bar and of the construction of the South and North Jetties.

I was led by Gibbs to other works that were most helpful, including and especially William D. Lyman's 1909 classic *The Columbia River: Its Myths, Its Scenery, Its Commerce* (G. P. Putnam), which includes the Clatsop story of Konapee, the Iron-Maker, which Lyman got directly from the remnant of the Clatsop tribe.

The Konapee story was first put into print in Gabriel Franchere's journal *Narrative of a Voyage to the Northwest Coast of America*, published first in French by the Montreal publisher C. B. Pasteur, then in English in 1854 by the New York publisher Redfield. In his journal, Franchere describes his 1811 meeting with an old white man living with a tribe in the Cascade Mountains who said he was the son of one of four Spaniards wrecked on Clatsop Spit more than eighty years earlier.

Franchere's journal, along with the one written by Alexander Ross (*Adventures of the First Settlers on the Oregon or Columbia River, Being a Narrative of the Expedition Fitted Out by John Jacob Astor*, first published in London in 1849 by Smith, Elder) were primary sources for Peter Stark's outstanding *Astoria: Astor and Jefferson's Lost Pacific Empire*, a rousing retelling of the stories of both the seagoing and overland expeditions that Astor sent to the mouth of the Columbia River in 1811.

Don Marshall's *Oregon Shipwrecks*, published by Binford & Mort in 1984, is in many respects an update of Gibbs's book, and also a work of great value to me.

Also excellent is *Shipwrecks of the Pacific Northwest*, an anthology edited by Jennifer Kozik of the Maritime Archeological Society that was published by Globe Pequot of Guilford, Connecticut, in 2020.

Though Calvin Trillin's article "The Magnficent Flavels" was first published in the *New Yorker*, I read it again in the anthology *Astorians: Eccentric and Extraordinary* (East Oregon Publishing 2010, edited by Karen Kirtley), where it is followed by a number of entertaining short histories, written by an assortment of local writers, about characters who are mostly invisible yet entirely present in my own work.

In the telling of the stories of the *Triumph/Mermaid* catastrophe and of the wreck of the *Sea King*, I was aided by a pair of books published by the US Naval Institute, the 1967 volume *Guardians of the Sea: A History of the US Coast Guard, 1915 to Present*, by Robert E. Johnson; and the 2005 work *Rescued by the Coast Guard*, by Dennis Noble.

Other Sources

I've written in the body of the book, but it bears repeating, that I got indispensable aid and advice from the Columbia River Maritime Museum, especially from its deputy director Bruce Jones. I owe special thanks to Marcy Dunning, who runs the museum's Ted M. Natt Maritime Library. Also, "The Columbia River Jetties," an article written by Gary Kobes and published in the spring 2021 edition of the museum's quarterly journal *The Quarterdeck*, filled in a good many blank spots for me. I perhaps owe deepest thanks of all to Larry Gilmore, former curator of the Columbia River Maritime Museum, whose lecture "Captain George Flavel (1823–1893)," delivered at the Flavel House on February 6, 1986, is by far the best source on the life and times of Captain Flavel. Thanks to the museum's library for having preserved the text of that lecture. I am also grateful for the paper Gilmore prepared for the museum in 1989 under the title "Columbia Bar Pilots: A Chronological History."

While the shipwreck display in the Maritime Museum was what first got me thinking about the intersection of history and geography on the Columbia Bar, it does not compare with the interactive map of the shipwrecks on the bar and up and down the coasts of Oregon and southern Washington created by Eric Schrepel for the Northwest Power and Conservation Council. This stunningly detailed map allows one to very nearly pinpoint each shipwreck and at the same time to place it in its historical context. I went back to it again and again while working on this book. Also excellent is the shipwreck map focused solely on the bar that was created by *Oregonian* photographer Mark Graves and *Oregonian* reporter Jamie Hale, based on the Gibbs book.

Equally helpful, especially for the opening section of this book, was the map of the Columbia Basin created by the Washington DC organization American Rivers. The history of the Columbia published by the Northwest Power and Conservation Council provided not only quick and easy access, but surprisingly detailed descriptions. The history of the river in the Oregon Encyclopedia is superb also.

I offer an appreciative nod to the amateur but hardly amateurish historian Finn J. D. John, whose website Offbeat Oregon History is a treasure trove that includes expansive and highly readable 2012 articles on the 1880 fishing fleet disaster ("In 1880s, Salmon Were the Real 'Most Dangerous Catch'") and the wrecks of the *Triumph* ("Coast Guard Catastrophe Sprang from Bad Boat Design") and *Mermaid* ("Coast Guard's Worst Columbia Disaster Started as Routine Rescue").

Newspaper archives provided great background on the fishing fleet disaster, in particular the *Oregonian* articles of May 5–6, 1880;

the *Astorian* coverage of May 6–10 and May 30, 1880; and the *San Francisco Chronicle*'s September 4, 1880, article.

I'm especially indebted to the *Chinook Observer*'s March 29, 2018, article "'This Nest of Dangers': How Legends Come to Be."

I had already written the section on the wreck of the *Rosecrans* when I read the *Astorian*'s November 20, 2021, article (by Mallory Gruben) about the study of the *Rosecrans* by the Clatsop County Genealogical Society's Mel Bashore, "Local Historian Examines the Mystery of a 1913 Shipwreck," and learned much I did not know about Captain Lucien Field Johnson.

The archived *Oregonian* articles kept in the Maritime Museum's library were the basis of much that I wrote about the sinking of the *Iowa* and its aftermath. Especially helpful was the long January 5, 1961, article headlined "Peacock Spit Earns Grim Cognomen . . . 'Graveyard of the Pacific.'"

Local historian Nancy Lloyd's December 20, 2018, article for the *Chinook Observer*, "The Triumph-Mermaid Disaster," was excellent, and I was assisted also by the *Observer*'s uncredited article of March 31, 2019, "Sole Survivor of Triumph Disaster Honored by Coast Guard."

Other articles that supported the story of the *Triumph/Mermaid* tragedy included a fine one Michael Paul wrote for the *Quarterdeck* (16, no. 3); John Thompson's January 3, 1977, article about Darryl Murray for the *Daily Astorian*, "Survivor Tells of '61 Bar Disaster"; and several other articles published without bylines in the *Astorian*: "Coast Guard Holds Inquiry to Learn Details of Disaster; Five Men Are Still Missing" (January 20, 1961); "Coast Guard Honors Those Lost in 1961 Tragedy" (January 14, 2014); and "Triumph-Mermaid Drive Ends, Surviving Children Get Funds" (March 3, 1961).

My main source on the *Triumph/Mermaid* disaster was, as stated, "US Coast Guard Investigation Report No. 12,413, Involving the Loss of the CG-52301 (Triumph)," dated June 6, 1961.

Here are some other documents that fleshed out the story of that rescue gone wrong: the "Office Memorandum" signed by J. A. Kerrins, Chief, Office of Operations, US Coast Guard, on June 6, 1961; the letter sent from Admiral A. C. Richmond to "Mrs. John Culp" dated May 10, 1961; the Coast Guard memorandum headed "Recommendation for awards; justification of" dated May 17, 1961; the Coast Guard's Office of Public Affairs May 19, 1961, press release titled "John Culp"; the Veterans Administration memorandum headed "Post Traumatic Stress Disorder Claim by Darrell J. Murray" dated December 6, 1982; the letter written by Kathryn Murray (widow of Darrell Murray) to the commander of the 13th Coast Guard District in Seattle, Washington, on January 15, 1990; and the press release titled "First Reunion on 30th Anniversary Triumph-Mermaid Incident, 12 January 1961–12 January 1991, Astoria, Oregon."

The chapter on the Columbia River Bar Pilots post–Captain Flavel includes information gleaned from the *Sunday Oregonian*'s September 30, 1962, article "Pair Survive in Wind Whipped Sea" and the *Daily Astorian*'s December 6, 2018, article "Death Sparks Maritime Lawsuit." That chapter was also supported by a pair of documentaries produced by television stations in Portland—the one Ed Jahn did for Oregon Public Broadcasting (*Columbia River Bar Pilots*) that aired on October 20, 2016, and the one Pat Dooris did for KGW-TV (*Those Who Serve*) that aired on August 2, 2019.

I was informed also by the oral history former bar pilot Ted Mather did for the Clatsop County Historical Society on January 25, 2002.

Very little has ever been written about the wreck of the *Vandalia* aside from the books by Gibbs and Marshall, so I particularly appreciated the piece "Vandalia Is Lost" that Elleda Wilson wrote for her "In One Ear" column in the January 16, 2020, edition of the *Astorian*.

As stated, I learned that there was controversy surrounding the *Sea King* sinking from a September 16, 1992, Associated Press article by Scott Sonner. This propelled me to locate my main source for that part of the book, the US Coast Guard pamphlet (No. G65302) titled "Team Coordination Training Exercises & Case Studies: Boats, Cutters and ATON."

Most of what I wrote about Doug Swanson's death came, obviously, from conversations with Ray Thomas, but I did refer to the Associated Press articles of October 22 and 25, 2004, that went out under the headlines POLICE ARE LOOKING FOR MISSING PORTLAND ATTORNEY and TWO HELD IN DEATH OF PORTLAND ATTORNEY. I was helped most, though, by the Angela Valdez article that was published in the November 1, 2005, edition of *Willamette Week* under the headline METH, SEX AND MURDER.